ALTERNATIVE PERSPECTIVES IN THIRD-WORLD DEVELOPMENT

Also by Masudul Alam Choudhury

COMPARATIVE DEVELOPMENT STUDIES: In Search of the World View

THE EPISTEMOLOGICAL FOUNDATIONS OF ISLAMIC ECONOMIC, SOCIAL AND SCIENTIFIC ORDER, 6 vols

THE FOUNDATIONS OF ISLAMIC POLITICAL ECONOMY
(*with Uzir Abdul Malik*)

Alternative Perspectives in Third-World Development

The Case of Malaysia

Edited by

Masudul Alam Choudhury
Professor of Economics
University College of Cape Breton
Sydney, Nova Scotia, Canada

Uzir Abdul Malik
Associate Professor
Department of Agricultural and Resource Economics
Universiti Kebangsaan Malaysia
Selangor, Malaysia

and

Mohammad Anuar Adnan
Associate Professor
Department of Economic Development and Planning
Universiti Kebangsaan Malaysia
Selangor, Malaysia

Foreword by Y. B. Dató Mustapha Mohamed
Minister for Entrepeneur Development
Government of Malaysia

palgrave

Published by
PALGRAVE
Houndmills, Basingstoke, Hampshire RG21 6XS and
175 Fifth Avenue, New York, N. Y. 10010
Companies and representatives throughout the world

PALGRAVE is the new global academic imprint of St. Martin's Press LLC Scholarly and Reference Division and Palgrave Publishers Ltd (formerly Macmillan Press Ltd).

ISBN 0–333–64026–8

This book is printed on paper suitable for recycling and made from fully managed and sustained forest sources.

A catalogue record for this book is available from the British Library.

Transferred to digital printing 2001

This book is dedicated to the
Twenty-Fifth Anniversary of
Universiti Kebangsaan Malaysia in 1995

Contents

List of Tables

List of Figures

Acknowledgements

As editors of this book, we wish to thank the following institutions and sources of assistance, which have been instrumental in the successful completion of this edited work of contributed chapters. Our thanks are due to the Faculty of Economics, Universiti Kebangsaan Malaysia, for inviting Professor Masudul Alam Choudhury as Visiting Professor during the period April–September 1994, during which time this project was initiated. We thank the University College of Cape Breton for awarding a grant for the production of various aspects of this project.

Our thanks are due also to the various contributors to this book, who expediently met their deadlines. In all of these, the cooperation of the Dean's Office at the faculty of Economics, Universiti Kebangsaan Malaysia, is much appreciated.

Our thanks go too to Mr T.M. Farmiloe, Editorial Director of the Macmillan Press, London, who was able in conjunction with his aides and the Macmillan associate, St Martin's Press, New York, to offer us a contract promptly. This helped us to initiate our work in good time.

Finally, it is our pleasure to render this work in commemoration of the Twenty-Fifth Anniversary (1995) of Universiti Kebangsaan Malaysia.

MASUDUL A. CHOUDHURY
UZIR ABDUL MALIK
MOHAMMAD ANUAR ADNAN

Foreword

The era in world history emerging after the Cold War is strewn with many an interesting question of human volition. Such questions are bound to influence profoundly the global scene for a final determination. On the one hand, the dismantling of communist and socialist doctrines and the lost fervour for Marxism have come to mark the end of an old way of thinking of political economy and the epistemology of social theory. The demise of these schools of thought and the rise of global capitalism in the guise of what has come to be flagged as New World Order and Globalisation are equally entrenched in age-old Eurocentricity. As during the old mercantilist age followed by its cultural, economic and political dominance of occidental power during the eighteenth century and subsequently, so also today during the enactment of the globalisation process the world is seen to come to an age under the old epistemology of the socioeconomic process.

Thus at the end of the twentieth century and the coming of the twenty-first, great social, economic and political problems loom large. The Western model of development, organisation and culture has failed to solve these age-old problems. All this happened even as Western societies prospered in their own closed domains, while the developing countries sank deeply into abject financial indebtedness and in their inability to function on their own.

Even as this Eurocentric might rages on in modern history, today the Asian economies have suddenly come to pose an alternative that is formidably different in its social, economic and cultural colours from the stereotype of the Western model. The epistemological question embedded in all these points to a distinctly indigenous approach to a fresh understanding and solution. Malaysia today is a grand example on the economic and moral front. It is a model very different posed by variants of the Harrod–Domar model. It is similarly different from the lacklustre conception of development as a change dominated by the production and use of capital. Malaysia presents a socioeconomic model that bravely embraces the modern age with its technological fullness with the strength of its own moral conviction.

The happy blending of the material with the moral values in the pursuit of the future, defining new socioeconomic goals and carving out a world of plenty and caring is indeed the alternative perspective of Third-World development. It is the central focus of this rich collection of articles written by eminent scholars and ably brought to fruition by the editors.

The central focus of this work is indeed to discover, define and apply or prescribe the new perspective of socio-economic development in the Third World within the framework of a methodological approach toward simultaneously realising ethical and material values. Markets, privatisation, globalisation, institutional change, international trade and economic integration, agricultural and grassroots development, and the Islamic worldview, are seen by the authors of this book in their endogenous aspects within the context of Malaysia, and of Malaysia *vis-à-vis* the world.

The book comes at a time when new epistemological questions are displacing the old and now defunct approaches to growth and development, wherein moral values have always been left out or neutralised by the crave for material gain alone. Mammoth consequences are found to prevail in the case of environmental depravation and loss of human sustainability. Instead, the approaches prescribed in this book point to a methodological reorientation in areas such as resource allocation, market pricing, organisational structure, trade and economic integration, sectoral rearrangement and grassroots developmental focus, all that can engender a socio-economic future that presents development as a complementary process for realising the moral and the material without substituting one for the other.

Y.B. DATO' MUSTAPA MOHAMED
Minister of Entrepreneur Development
Government of Malaysia

Notes on the Contributors

Mohammad Anuar Adnan is Associate Professor in the Department of Economic Development and Planning and Deputy Dean of Academic Affairs at the Faculty of Economics, Universiti Kebangsaan Malaysia (National University of Malaysia), Bangi, Selangor, Malaysia.

Supian Ali is Associate Professor in the Department of Economic Analysis and Public Policy at the Faculty of Economics, Universiti Kebangsaan Malaysia.

Haji Mohammad Alias is Associate Professor in the Department of Economic Statistics and Dean of the Faculty of Economics, Universiti Kebangsaan Malaysia.

Masudul A. Choudhury is Professor of Economics at the School of Business, University College of Cape Breton, Sydney, Nova Scotia, Canada, and Director of the Centre of Humanomics at the same university.

B.N. Ghosh is Professor in the Department of Economics, School of Social Sciences, Universiti Sains Malaysia (Science University of Malaysia), Penang, Malaysia.

Abdul-Ghafar Ismail is Lecturer in the Department of Economic Analysis and Public Policy at the Faculty of Economics, Universiti Kebangsaan Malaysia.

Uzir Abdul Malik is Associate Professor in the Department of Agricultural and Resource Economics at the Faculty of Economics, Universiti Kebangsaan Malaysia.

Mohammad Haflah Piei is Associate Professor in the Department of Economic Development and Planning and Deputy Dean of Student Affairs, Faculty of Economics, Universiti Kebangsaan Malaysia.

H. Osman-Rani is Professor of Economics in the Department of Economic Analysis and Public Policy, Faculty of Economics, Universiti Kebangsaan Malaysia.

M. Zainuddin Saleh is Associate Professor in the Department of Economic Development and Planning at the Faculty of Economics, Universiti Kebangsaan Malaysia.

Chamhuri Siwar is Professor in the Department of Agricultural and Resource Economics, Universiti Kebangsaan Malaysia.

1 Introduction

Masudul A. Choudhury, Uzir Abdul Malik and Mohammad Anuar Adnan

Traditional views on economic growth and development, and the differences between these concepts in terms of their measurements and structural questions, are well known from the literature. The conflict between the paradigms of growth and development can be traditionally studied as one between economic efficiency, stability and sustained economic performance, on the side of economic growth; and distribution, political and ethical forces in market transformation, self-reliance, employment generation and more currently, sustainability, on the side of development. Yet a central issue has remained unaddressed regarding both these ends, namely, the ethical issue of economic transformation using the nature of markets, its interface with polity, the global economy and the policy prescriptions to support the momentum of such change.

In a globalised economy of today, the concept of globalisation has increasingly come to mean collective adoption of a standard model of a liberal concept of economic change. The missing question of sustainability, which Heilbroner incites – 'Is there hope for man?' – needs to be seriously addressed (Heilbroner, 1991, pp. 11).

The views on alternative perspectives of Third-World development presented in this book are not intended to create a dismal picture of a future world under capitalist market transformation, as the Marxist paradigm once did against capitalism. Rather, it is to chart the blueprint of mankind's sustainable future critically by viewing the structure of economic growth, so that Heibroner's question can be answered in the affirmative.

The ethics of development is, then, the inherent value component of structural change that is invoked in this book. Yet the process leading towards understanding the concept of an ethics-centered development paradigm evolves by a critical examination of the traditional views on economic growth and development. Such an approach is adopted in this book deliberately in order to unfold the ethical paradigm in the face of the traditional concepts (Goulet, 1994).

The South-East Asian economies, in which Malaysia is now exemplary regarding performance in economic growth, and social and political achievements, present a clear vision of the future. This goal is known in

Malaysia as Vision 2020. With this happy prospect in the Third World's modern socio-economic realities, the following question naturally looms: what kind of growth and development models are to be ameliorated for the present and future in order to attain congenial structural transformation – not simply the measurement of levels of economic growth and quantitative development?

We have come to know from the literature about Eurocentric models of growth, development, political change, social theory and scientific paradigms (Mehmet, 1993). In each of these areas, the Eurocentric model has entrenched itself in an epistemological premise that dwells on certain intrinsic values of the Occident. These emanate from values of neo-liberalism that are made to sustain a methodologically individualistic outlook, alienating competing groups. The picture of methodological individualism is not found to change even when a futuristic knowledge-based information model is construed for capitalistic transformation (Drucker, 1993). The concept of self-interest, although not a derogatory one when seen as a natural invocation of human nature, is not necessarily of the Hobbesian type or of the atomistic type as pronounced by Smithian *laissez-faire*. It is not like the carnal type of self-interest based on Benthamite positivism. It does not share in the essence of social Darwinism. Earlier still Cartesian philosophy of the social and natural sciences also shared in this view of methodological individualism and logical positivism. Self-interest, if it is to have an acceptable connotation of its own, must mean an evolution through collective interest, wherein individual interests are best served and in turn find the meaning to contribute to the well-being of each and everyone. Does this seem Utopian? Yes, in the Eurocentric model of capitalistic and neo-liberal hegemony. But it is not so when cooperative models of society and economy are made to replace methodological individualism. We look at a few examples in this regard and formalise theories of just such a medium of economic development in this book.

On the other hand, the metaphysical views of the sciences, and the moral philosophies of Kant, Hume, Wittgenstein, Spinoza and Berkley as some of the idealists, in spite of their moral leanings, could not relieve the power-centric approach of occidental culture of its intrinsic dualism and pluralistic reductionist approach to moral and material well-being (Russell, 1990). The two competing facets of the total moral–material reality remain perpetually entrenched in the Eurocentric model of growth, development and change (Mittleman, 1988).

The economic order is consistently seen in the Western approach to economic theory and organisation to pass through three phases. It shifts from the primitive stage to the agricultural stage. It then shifts to the industrial stage, moving thereafter to the modern stage. Finally, economy and society evolve in this way to the post-modern stage. The occidental world is always seen to converge on its capitalistic or market transformation in this way. Fukuyama (1992) calls this convergent pattern of society the last hold-out of mankind – the end of history. Hegel (1956) saw it as the convergence of society towards Germanic civilisation.

Thus there must be a sense of caution in such a stereotyped, power-driven, hegemonic, Eurocentric model of economic growth and development (Mazrui, 1993; Choudhury, 1994). Such models and prescriptions must therefore be critically examined, while alternative perspectives of Third-World development are provided at this juncture of the dawning of new life in the developing world. The critique of Eurocentricity must not be viewed as an emotional revolt against its disparagement of developing countries, which have now entered the globalisation scene in the form of multinationals, development organisations and collective world-views under convergent schemes of powerful nations.

Beyond purely emotional feeling and the rhetoric that rages around it is the more solemn need to prescribe, establish and apply alternative perspectives of development. Such an experience is indeed a learning process, which, far from the emotions that fired the now defunct concepts of Marxism–Leninism, the new international economic order, the new world order and OPEC, is an interactive knowledge-forming world-view between the hitherto conflicting camps. The end goal is to restore harmony through discourse and collective goodwill. The Eurocentric model of globalisation is to be rejected only on two conditions. These are, first, to formulate the interactive world-view of development within the ethical paradigm, as opposed to the individuating alienation of the Eurocentric model; second, to establish and apply this paradigm in the actual *process* of structural change by the collective self-reliance of nation states and integrating blocs (South Commission, 1990). The end result, then, is the restructuring or launching of objective globalisation in these alternative perspectives of Third-World development (Mehmet, 1996).

In all these directions of a newly envisioned future, Malaysia presents a dynamic example of modernism with a difference. In the chapters presented in this book, the following case studies of Malaysian experience in economic growth and socio-economic development are presented as alternative views in the following areas: Malaysian microeconomics and macroeconomics issues, the political economy of development, the ethical viewpoint of growth and development, alternative prescriptions and policies revolving around agricultural–industrial shifts, poverty alleviation and human development, privatisation, international trade, institutional change, polity–market interface and grassroots development.

The alternative perspectives of Third-World development emanating from the Malaysian experience are then seen to be precisely this: there is a substantive meaning and process in the endogenising of ethical values in development by means of a full gamut of economic, social, political and institutional processes. The meaning and its viability of the ethical paradigm of development is examined from the point of view of an alternative model to Eurocentricity. That is the model of interactive and complementary linkages amongst inputs and outputs in this *process*. By thus rejecting the groundwork of the Eurocentric view of development and adopting the interlinked or complementary world-view, some chapters of this book have gone into the replacing of the much adhered to neo-classical marginal substitution principle of textbook theory and structural adjustment models of the World Bank and her associated organisations, both nationally and internationally.

In Chapter 2, Professor Osman-Rani delineates the general trends in Malaysia's microeconomic and macroeconomic indicators over the period 1960–93, and sounds a cautious note on the pattern of change that Malaysia should adopt towards Vision 2020. The argument is made to rest on a need for increased domestic investments and relatively less dependence upon foreign direct investments; a better linkage between the agricultural and manufacturing sector respecting productivity growth and sharing of resources, incomes and wealth. Professor Osman-Rani's contribution, as a survey of the Malaysian economy, puts the issues in their proper perspectives to open up the dialogue in the subsequent chapters that take up many of the issues addressed in Chapter 2.

In Chapter 3, Dr M. Zainudin Saleh continues the Malaysian economic survey of Chapter 2 in greater detail. Many interesting macroeconomic analyses, policies, programmes and subsequent transformations of the Malaysian economy over the last two decades are examined. The interesting point brought out in this chapter is the highlighting of the need for intersectorial linkages, particularly between the agricultural and manufacturing sectors. One also finds in this topic the reality of high debt-driven economic transformation that follows a definite focus on industrialisation. On the other hand, industrialisation may not lead to the much needed realisation of its impact on the growth of small and medium-sized industries. Thus, proper policy measures and monitoring of the economy are needed. The adverse increase in foreign debts and deficits in Malaysia during the period of industrialisation led to a diminution of domestic saving. The saving gap was then made up by the large flow of foreign direct investments. Dr Saleh undertakes an interesting and fairly detailed examination of Malaysia's balance of payments structure in this regard. He points out that although foreign direct investments were needed to alleviate Malaysia's foreign deficit and debt problems during her period of industrialisation, the cause and effect of sectorial interlinkages would be to look towards Malaysia's own capacity to develop projects and finance them. The future trend in saving and investment is shown to be increasingly driven through an internal mobilisation of resources and a declining dependence on foreign direct investments and industrial component imports.

In Chapter 4, Supian Ali and Dr M. Anuar Adnan point out some of the economic miracles of Malaysia in particular, and of the adjoining South-East Asian economics in general. The authors argue that these successes were made possible by an indigenous approach to economic policing and market transformation process. They point out that such transformations are found not to be premised in neo-classical models of development. The authors also argue that to address macroeconomic policies, microeconomic questions need to be addressed as well. Although government presence is still very strong in these countries, the Malaysian economy has benefited from government patronage. In the face of rapid privatisation now being consciously pursued in Malaysia, it is deemed necessary to find a balance between government and an indigenous approach to market transformation, wherein growth, development and equitable distribution can be harmoniously shared. The authors point out in this regard that the *process* of development in Malaysia reflects the ethical approach towards self-actualisation of the citizens in social and ethical values as growth proceeds. In this perspective, a focus on human resource development is placed foremost.

In Chapter 5, Dr Uzir Abdul Malik elaborates on the important policy and programme of privatisation in Malaysia. Dr Malik thus further expands discussion of the programme of privatisation from where it was left in Chapters 2–4. The market transformation process for economic growth as well as the distribution of equity shareholding by target groups called Bumiputeras in the Malaysian economy, and the growth of all sizes of businesses and enterprises, is shown to be hinged on this important programme of privatisation. Privatisation is also seen here to be a programme that increasingly relieves the government of public spending and brings into the picture greater responsibility for the spending role of the private sector. Thus both efficiency and equity, along with innovative ways of diversifying the economy in cost-effective ways, are shown here to be provided by the programme of privatisation. Dr Malik points out that the proper programming of privatisation is very important for Malaysia's socio-economic growth and restructuring, because Malaysia presents the most prominent model of a deliberate undertaking by a national government among the developing countries. Besides, the process that has thus been opened up in the privatisation programme is an irreversible one.

In Chapter 6, Dr Abdul-Ghafar Ismail provides a brief note on the role of monetary policy in Malaysia's development programme. Money is seen to be equated here with a unit of mobilisation of financial resources through the capital market. The chapter points out that in the face of the policy of Bank Negara Malaysia to liberalise interest rates interbanks, no active monetary policy on interest rate fixation is pursued. The exchange rate thus remains in a perfect float, unless occasional intervention is necessary. One such intervention proved to be a fiasco in 1994. Apart from these occasional monetary interventions, interbank liberalisation of interest rates has caused Malaysian interest rates on average to remain low in the long run. On the other hand, shares have performed fairly well in the Kuala Lumpur Stock Exchange. Besides this, there is a spur of Islamic financial instruments across most banks in Malaysia today. These instruments have created a massive turnover of savings and shareholding in interest-free transactions. The Malaysian capital market is thus shown to be utilising the ethical instrument of non-interest or low-interest financing as the alternative to active monetary policing of interest rates by Bank Negara.

In Chapter 7, Dr M. Haflah Piei elaborates on a macroeconomic area that is of crucial importance to Malaysia's development and her global relations. This is international trade. Dr Piei takes this issue beyond the level discussed in the earlier chapters. The interesting point to note in this chapter is the alternative in terms of the several regional integration diversities in South-East Asia that he proposes to counteract the Eurocentric advance of the United States of America under the guise of the Asian-Pacific Economic Cooperation (APEC) hegemony. The author sees US intervention in APEC as an extension of the North American Free Trade Agreement to all the Americas and onward expansion to the South-East Asia region. The motivation underlying this is seen to be what the author calls 'aggressive unilateralism' of the US in matching conditionalities with GATT, MFN and the World Trade Organisation over South-East Asia and thus with the global economy. Dr Piei points out that there are enough lessons of caution and strategy to be adopted by Malaysia through the Asian Free Trade Agreement, the subregional trade triangles and the East Asian Economic Caucus. Such strategies must look at masterminding alternative patterns of safeguards and strategies for growth and sustainability in a globalising world of the future, which could otherwise be overshadowed by the Eurocentric model of trade and production-sharing hegemony led by the 'aggressive unilateralism' of the United States of America and an increasingly inward and protective economic grouping of the European Community.

Chapters 2–7 treat issues of economic development in Malaysia as is currently perceived and realised. There are undercurrents and references to alternative perspectives in the following areas: intersectorial linkages; future evolution into more domestic demand for investment and less reliance on imported components and foreign direct investments; use of various policies and programmes to realise equity with growth; proper attention to be given to agriculture along with industrial diversification; and the need for polity–market interface in such transformation processes. The theme of alternative perspectives of Third-World development is taken up with the case study of Malaysia, by critically examining the current process of Malaysian growth and development within a global perspective. By not taking up an ideological stand on behalf of any particular economic theory in depth, these chapters remain both a positivistic approach to economic change and a delineation of the existing state of the pursuit of economic growth and development in Malaysia.

In Chapters 8–12, the positive picture and delineation of the state of the art in Malaysian development experience is extended to the normative perspective as well. Here development problems are invoked in the light of alternative paradigms in critical perspectives. Thus, Malaysian experience in growth and development is subjected to a policy-theoretic critical examination. The following issues discussed and formalised in these chapters are the following: the political economy of growth and development in contrasting paradigms; grassroots and microenterprise development as an alternative model of global transformation; polity-market interface in social market transformation; ethical values of development; poverty alleviation as a primal target of human development. Thus Chapters 8–12 carry the normative–positive methodology of critical examination of Malaysia's development experience beyond the positive approach presented in Chapters 2–7.

In Chapter 8, Professor B.N. Ghosh presents a discussion on the political economy of development in Malaysia that goes to show that Malaysian development owes much to the complementarity of linkages among the following groups: the capitalist class, the working class and the political elites. The emerging Malaysian model is inherently of the capitalist type as productivity change creating sectorial shifts is seen to be reflected in the occupational shift in the economy. The result is still the usual transition through substitution, from an agricultural base to an industrial base and finally over the years, to a service base of the economy. Such a pattern of evolution is the picture presented by the historical record of Western economies as they took to a certain pattern of technological change that caused economic shifts while adopting skill-intensive, labour-saving, capital-deepening and controlled population growth. The balance of political and economic power needed to sustain such a tempo of growth rested on the power of mercantilism that was played out both on the high seas and through financial institutions that control production, world resource sharing and resource mobilisation. The latter days' rise of information economy along with the human resource development that goes with it, is a means of intensifying the neo-mercantilist power of Western economies. Multinationals escaping the harsh restraints of tough environmental laws in industrialised nations, and foreign direct investments looking for fast returns, aim at export-oriented industries at the cost of sectorial shifts in developing countries. The Malaysian economy provides these prospects to the foreign multinationals. Professor Ghosh's conclusion on the kind of capitalist model with a human face adopted in Malaysia in view of her agricultural–industrial shift explains the nature of the social, political and economic interlinkages that the three agents he mentions can bring about to induce participatory changes.

In Chapter 9, Professor M.A. Choudhury presents an overview of a comparative theory of economic growth in neo-classical, Keynesian and Islamic socio-economic perspectives. In this way, he tries to show that the most crucial focus of economic growth as a developmental process is to bring about sustainability that would be embedded in the socio-economic order. This invokes an all new approach to theorising and policy analysis which cuts across sectors, markets, goods, skills and countries. Such a universal orientation of interlinkages and diversification of economic activities invokes the principle of unification as a premised in *Shari'ah*. This essentially is the foundation of the interactive–integrative process of continuity and causation that generates growth, distribution, stability and well-being in the Islamic political economy simultaneously. This differentiates it from all other systems where neo-classical economics is embedded in its principle of marginalist substitution. The Keynesian system is shown to be ethically neutral as no decision-makers exist within it. In the final analysis, Professor Choudhury contends that only the Islamic system can provide definite and stable consequences in regards to matters relating to fiscal and monetary policies and their relations with real markets.

In Chapter 10, Dr Haji Mohammad Alias and Professor Masudul A. Choudhury argue that in the face of a distinct shift of agricultural activity towards manufacturing in Malaysia, the model of structural change being adopted follows the neo-classical one premised in its marginalist substitution principle. The message of Chapters 8 and 9 is thus carried over to the present chapter. This perspective of development is procrastinated to be disadvantageous for Malaysia, which, it is argued, should aim at developing overall productivity and not simply productivity in the manufacturing sector under the force of a capital-widening expansion. The alternative prescription of complementarity among alternatives in the industrialisation process is shown to require a great degree of collaboration between the private and public sectors to streamline such a menu. Although the Malaysian Government has spelled out several well-meaning policies for the realisation of economic efficiency along with distributive equity, and for due attention to be paid to the agricultural sector, the distributive element is still not found to be effective, as the target groups of Bumiputeras, who live off agricultural lands, are yet to be fully ameliorated in terms of productivity, economic ownership, and hence entitlement.

In Chapter 11, Professor Chamhuri Siwar writes on the important topic of poverty alleviation by addressing the human development criterion of structural change. In this he recognises the need for integrated rural development both through government policy interventions and market transformation. Consequently, by this interface the ethical question of appropriate perspectives on market transformation is highlighted. Examples of such an interface are shown to be the successes attained by Malaysia's New Economic Policy, which has now been transcended by the New Development Plan. Although the human development index as a well-being index invoked by the author is similar to the HDI constructed by UNDP, yet the issues respecting Malaysia's successful experience in poverty alleviation is taken up in its own distinctive right. Integrated rural development, within which the poverty alleviation well-being index is considered, is shown to invoke both a grassroots development orientation and a focus on agricultural development in the midst of Malaysia's outlook on industrialisation. The grassroots focus is shown to be taken up by the case of Malaysia's rural development project called *Amanah Ikhtiar*. The issues dealt with here are indeed matters revolving around due recognition of proper sectorial, polity-market and communitarian linkages. These define the theme of an alternative perspective of Third-World development, here exemplified by the case of Malaysia.

In Chapter 12, Professor M.A. Choudhury discusses the increasingly distressing situation of the poor, especially in the developing countries. They seem to be alienated in the development process of the global socio-economic evolution. In this context the function of the grassroots as defined by Professor Choudhury is very important in enhancing the collective well-being and this is largely achieved through the process of promoting entitlement, empowerment, distributive equity and economic efficiency among the grassroots. Foreign trade activities as well as policies carried by international development organisations have the effects of marginalising the poor, especially those in the agricultural sector. This also includes the structural adjustment model of privatisation, which has been actively encouraged by such organisations. The microenterprises as part of the grassroots also remain marginalised as a result of sheer market transformation, privatisation and globalisation of the national economies. Being a multiracial nation, the Malaysian government is very concerned with the well-being of the poor, especially when it is concentrated among the indigenous Bumiputeras. But participation of the grassroots in socio-economic activities is still quite limited to bring about sustainable development. Such a development could only take place when it involves the simultaneous attainment of entitlement, enpowerment, distribution and economic growth as a result of complementary nature of organisational relation, socio-economic goals and variables of the grassroots.

Chapter 13 is a conclusion on the paradigm of alternative perspectives of Third-World development centred around the concept of a caring society. The Malaysian New Development Plan and her National Declaration (*Rukunegara*) are today emphasising the concept of a caring society as Malaysia advances to her Vision 2020. This chapter points out how the socio-economic developmental world view can be based on the social criterion of well-being. The latter in turn was developed by using the Principle of Universal Complementarity in Chapters 9–12.

References

Choudhury, M.A. (1994) 'A Critique of Modernist Synthesis in Islamic Thought: Special Reference to Political Economy', *American Journal of Islamic Social Sciences*, 11(4), pp. 475–503.

Drucker, P.F. (1993) *Post-Capitalist Society* (New York: HarperCollins).

Fukuyama, F. (1992) *The End of History and the Last Man* (Don Mills, Ontario: The Free Press).

Goulet, D. (1994). 'Material and Moral Incentives as Economic Policy Instruments', *Humanomics*, 10(1), pp. 5–24.

Hegel, G.W.F. (1956) *The Philosophy of History*, trans. J. Sibree (New York: Dover Publications).

Heilbroner, R.L. (1991) *An Inquiry into the Human Prospect* (New York: W.W. Norton).

Mazrui, A. (1993) 'Islam and the End of History', *American Journal of Islamic Social Sciences*, 10(4), pp. 512–35.

Mehmet, O. (1990) 'Alternative Concepts of Development: A Critique of Eurocentric Theorizing', *Humanomics*, 6(3), pp. 55–67.

Mehmet, O. (1996) 'On Globalization and Capitalization', in M.A. Choudhury (ed.), *Topics on Globalization and Structural Change: Special Issue of Managerial Finance*, 22(5).

Mittleman, J.H. (1988) 'Sources of Received Ideas About the Third World', in *Out from Underdevelopment* (London: Macmillan), pp. 27–86.

Russell, B. (1990) *A History of Western Philosophy*, repr. (London: Unwin).

South Commission (1990) *The Challenge to the South* (Oxford: Oxford University Press).

2 Malaysia's Economic Performance: An Overview

H. Osman-Rani

INTRODUCTION

In 1993, Malaysia's GDP was estimated to be around RM163 billion or approximately US$65 billion. In terms of GNP per capita Malaysia already surpassed US$3000 by 1993. This puts Malaysia among the more successful developing economies, and by the World Bank standards, Malaysia is already into the upper-middle-income group of countries and has joined a newly industrialising economy status (World Bank, 1993). The size of its GDP is about the same as countries like Greece, Ireland and New Zealand and larger than the more populated countries like the Philippines, Egypt, Pakistan and Colombia.

Despite recessions, its GDP per capita growth during 1980–91 was close to 3 per cent, much higher than the world average. Income distribution and the poverty rate have also been improving. In 1993, the incidence of poverty was 13.5 per cent as compared to over 40 per cent in 1976. Yet, the rate of inflation has been kept reasonably low. The annual change in the consumer price index has averaged around 4.0 per cent in recent years.

Malaysia's labour force participation rate in 1993 was 66.8 per cent (87.0 per cent for male and 46.1 per cent for the female labour force). It is now enjoying full employment. Its unemployment rate was 3 per cent and is expected to reduce further. There were 7.4 million Malaysian workers out of a 7.6 million labour force and 19 million population in that year. In addition, there were about one million foreign workers in the country (*Far Eastern Economic Review*, 29 December 1994–5 January 1995). Significant employment creation in recent years has been in manufacturing, services and construction. The tight labour market situation has pushed Malaysia into adopting policies which encourage skilled- and technology-intensive production processes and high value-added goods, thus giving rise to higher wages and labour productivity.

There is a mixture of reasons for the economic success. The important ones are the high level of domestic financial savings which sustained the high investment levels, rapid growth of output in the manufacturing sector, promotion of exports and liberal trade policy, encouragement of foreign investment, and a combination of fundamental and interventionist policies. Fundamentals include such traditional government commitment towards providing basic physical and human infrastructure, securing financial institutions, as well as ensuring political, economic and social stability. Interventions include a mandatory savings mechanism, privatisation of government organisations, fiscal discipline, an explicit wealth-sharing programme, public and private sector cooperation, and providing the long-term guidance and vision. However, the changes have not always been smooth. There were problems to be tackled and adjustments to be made along the way. We shall discuss the major factors mentioned above in the following sections. We begin by examining the changing economic structure, followed by the potentially strong domestic sector with special focus on savings and investment, the vibrant external sector and the role of foreign investment, and finally the state–market relationship.

THE CHANGING STRUCTURE OF THE ECONOMY

In the 1960s, Malaysia's real Gross Domestic Product (GDP) grew at an average of 6.5 per cent per annum. Nearly 40 per cent of this growth was attributed to the industrial sector (broadly defined to include mining, manufacturing, construction, utilities and transportation) or 17 per cent to the manufacturing sector alone. In the 1970s, Malaysia managed to grow faster at 7.8 per cent per annum, of which nearly half was contributed by the industrial sector, including 25 per cent by manufacturing. The GDP growth declined somewhat to 6.2 per cent per annum during the 1980s, mainly because of the world economic recession and price downfall of Malaysia's major export commodities as well as the domestic structural problems during the period, but the contribution of the industrial sector continued to rise. Immediately after the short recession in 1985–6, the real GDP (in 1978 constant prices) grew at an average of over 8 per cent per annum during the 1986–93 period. By 1993, the GDP share of the industrial sector already exceeded 50 per cent, while that of manufacturing reached 30 per cent. The share of the agriculture sector (agriculture, livestock, forestry and fishing) dipped below 16 per cent and that of services levelled around one-third.

Figure 2.1 shows the remarkable structural changes taking place in the Malaysian economy since 1960. The industrial sector gained nearly 30 per centage points in its share of GDP during the period 1960–93, mainly at the expense of agricultural sector. In the 1960s, the agricultural sector pro-

Figure 2.1 Sectorial share of GDP, 1960–93.

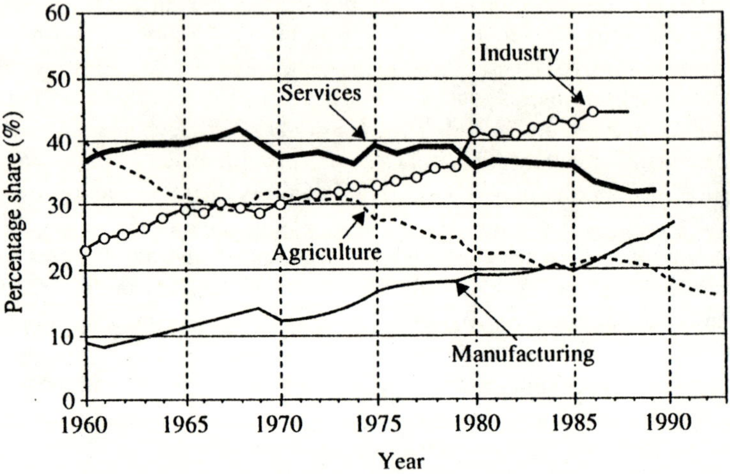

Source: Government of Malaysia: *Treasury Economic Report* data (Kuala Lumpur) (various issues).

vided the backbone of Malaysian exports and the economy, and this in turn generated the high level of domestic savings that eventually contributed to the rising level of investments. It strengthened the development of the physical and social infrastructure which then provided the basis for the growth of the industrial sector (Sheng, 1984; Tan Tat Wai, 1984). The share of the industrial sector overtook that of agriculture in around 1970 and overtook the share of services a decade later. Manufacturing, as a subcomponent of the industrial sector, has changed more drastically than other sectors. Its share of GDP more than tripled from less than 10 per cent in the first half of the 1960s to about 30 per cent in 1993, while its contribution to the industrial sector increased from around one-third to about three-fifths.

The size of the manufacturing sector started to overtake the agricultural sector by the mid-1980s. By then, the process of transition from agriculture to industry can be regarded as complete, and the economy is presently moving through the second transitional period from an industry-based towards a service-based economy. This transition has been accompanied by stable demographic transition (stable population growth of about 2.5 per cent per annum) and a satisfactory distributive pattern (achieving a low level of poverty and income disparity). Studies on income distribution tend to show that since 1970 growth in Malaysia was accompanied by improving income distribution, resulting from a rising share of wages in family income and a more even distribution of wages, with the broad expansion of education and improvement in literacy (Shari and Zin, 1990; Krongkaew, 1994). This second transitional period is expected to occupy the 1990s and beyond before Malaysia becomes a full-fledged developed economy and the service sector becomes more prominent than the industrial sector. During the next one or two decades from now, the Malaysian economy is expected to be preoccupied with rapid industrialisation and greater linkages with other sectors, including the external sector. While Malaysia is to participate in the globalisation process, it is at the same time pushing for greater expansion of the domestic market. In doing so, Malaysia hopes to be able to elevate the economy to a fully developed status by the year 2020.

THE DOMESTIC SECTOR

In line with the country's growth performance, Malaysia's domestic absorption which measures the domestic purchasing power has also been increasing at a rapid pace. During the slackening period of 1980–5, the total domestic spending increased at a rate of 4.2 per cent per annum, but during the five years after the 1985–6 recession, it was nearly 12 per cent per annum. By 1993, the total purchasing power or the potential domestic market was approximately RM100 billion in 1978 prices or RM160 billion in current prices.

However, the domestic absorption includes both spending on domestic output as well as on foreign imports. Therefore, if we deduct imports from absorption, the remainder is spending on locally produced goods and services. Malaysia's domestic expenditure on imported goods and services has been increasing at a substantial rate in recent years, from RM 33.7 billion or 61 per cent of GNP in 1981 to RM131.1 billion or 85 per cent in 1993. In 1981, expenditure on imports accounted for only 50 per cent of total domestic spending, but by 1993 it exceeded 85 per cent. In other words, the purchases of domestically produced goods and services by domestic residents have become relatively insignificant. This is partly because Malaysia's production has been relying more and more on its foreign markets and partly on the need for imported intermediate and investment goods for its productive activities.

Inspite of these trends, the domestic private consumption expenditure which accounts for about half of the total domestic demand, has been increasing from an average of 3.7 per cent annually (in real terms) during the first half of 1980s to an average of 9 per cent during the 1986–93 period. The growth of public consumption expenditure is expected to be slower following the policy to reduce the role of government in economic development. Nevertheless, it would still complement the private consumption expenditure. Private investment too has been increasing much faster than public investment after the 1985–6 recession, and through privatisation and deregulation this trend is expected to continue into the future.

While Malaysia is opening its doors to foreign competition and preparing to compete for a greater share of the global markets, it is also aware of the competitiveness and risks involved in international trade. Past experiences demonstrate that although export-oriented trade policies can enhance economic growth, they become effective only when external demand conditions are favourable (Osman-Rani and Piei, 1990). Foreign markets are subjected to the cyclical nature of the global economy and the successive long phases of rapid expansion and slow growth that have characterised international business. In addition, the threat on the world trading system in terms of rival economic blocks, new protectionism and the eventual elimination of the Generalised System of Preference status that Malaysia currently enjoys, for example, is still looming large. As a hedge against such risks and uncertainty, Malaysia cannot afford to neglect its domestic policies and prospects of its domestic markets, with the view to eliminating some impediments to its industrial development and international trade performance, and widening the domestic markets.

In this respect, there is room for selective import-substitution strategies which could supplement the export-oriented strategies. The manufacturing sector in particular is also going for long-term investment in import-substitution of intermediate and investment goods. The recent slowdown or irregularity in foreign direct investment and the present low ratio of domestic to foreign investment (40 to 60) also conjure the fact that Malaysia has to push for domestic investment through an increase in local investment. Consequently, the Malaysian Government launched the Domestic Investment Initiative (DII) programme in 1993 with the aim of encouraging greater domestic investment. Under the DII, six strategies have been identified: (i) increasing the domestic value added; (ii) strengthening and improving accessibility to the local capital markets; (iii) developing Malaysian multinational anchor companies; (iv) strengthening SMI development; (v) strengthening the institutional support; and (vi) developing infrastructure for domestic use through special industrial estates, and provision of common user services such as testing and designing (MITI, 1994).

Since the total expenditure on imports is very substantial compared with that on locally produced goods, potentials in the production to replace these imports are tremendous. This is especially so for the dynamic manufacturing sector which is still very narrow-based and therefore needs greater diversification, not only to spur growth but also to insulate if from adverse fluctuations to which the nation is prone.

According to a study by Bank Negara (1992), on average about two-thirds of the total cost of manufacturing companies was incurred on the purchase of raw materials, only one-half of which were produced locally. Among the industry groups which use a relatively high proportion of raw materials are wood and wood products, non-metallic mineral products, rubber products, machinery and electrical appliances, basic metal and metal products, and food, beverages and tobacco. In these industries, linkages between producers and suppliers of materials, where the SMIs can play their role effectively, are important means to generate greater local markets. However, industry groups which still have a high import content necessary for their intermediate inputs are the electronics industry, paper and paper products, transport equipment, and textile and wearing apparel. There is certainly a need for a higher usage in domestic components in these industries. In this respect, the motor vehicle industry is expected to be a catalyst for generating production of parts and components by domestic producers, but its effectiveness will be realised as the motor industry gradually shifts from the traditional assembling of completely knocked down (CKD) to the manufacture of parts, components and whole vehicles for wider international markets.

Of course, Malaysia has to produce not only the goods and services that the Malaysian consumers want, but also what the producers want, namely, capital goods and the technology and the services of skilled manpower. In other words, Malaysia needs the capital goods and the technology structure that is dependent on local capabilities, a well-trained human capital base, a thriving private domestic enterprise with the SMIs becoming the backbone of the country's industrialisation. This in itself is expected to open up opportunities for domestic investment in capital goods, physical as well as human. Malaysia is importing more than RM50 billion of capital goods, mainly in the form of plant and machinery, transport equipment and metal products. It is in this area of production that import-substitution strategy is expected to be enforced aggressively in coming years.

Import trends also indicate that there are ample investment opportunities in the production of consumer goods for the domestic market, but consumer goods of high quality. That includes, for example, fast food, fashionable clothing and footwear, sporting goods, toys, and wide-ranging consumer durables such as furniture, electrical goods, computer software, children's books and car accessories. Malaysia's imports of consumer goods increased fourfold within the last decade. Its total imports are now about RM20 billion and still increasing.

With Malaysian society growing in size and becoming more educated, knowledgeable and affluent, and enjoying higher standards of living, we expect changes to take place not only in terms of the quantity and variety of goods and services demanded but also in terms of quality. The pressure to improve on quality comes both from the demanding buyers and the more open competition from abroad. The bottom line is the ability to invest, to compete and to remain competitive. But investment needs financial support to start with.

SAVINGS AND INVESTMENT

A high rate of savings is necessary to spur growth since the latter depends not only on a high rate of investment but even more so on the efficient use of investment capital. In Malaysia, savings have been an important source of financing domestic investment. If national savings fall short of investment, then capital has to be supplemented from abroad and/or from the reserves in order to fill the gap. In the Malaysian case, the rate of gross domestic savings has been relatively high and increasing.[1] In the 1960s, it was around 22 per cent and by 1986–90 it surpassed 35 per cent. Malaysia's savings rate is certainly one of the highest in Asia (Chandavarkar, 1993). However, Malaysia's large external debt has brought about a lower national savings rate, thus reducing the resource gap. Nevertheless, the substantial capital inflow, mainly consisting of government borrowing and foreign direct investment, has often helped the economy to finance much of the investment outlays in the country without recourse to foreign exchange reserves. Therefore, Malaysia has never really experienced a long period of large deficits in its balance of payments to an extent that they were not sustainable (Lin See Yan, 1992). Perhaps the only period when Malaysia felt the scary deficit in the balance of payments was in the first half of the 1980s, when the average deficit was 8.5 per cent of GNP and the highest being 14 per cent in 1982. Private savings declined significantly to an average level lower than the 1960–5 period. During this period, the government needed the big push in public investment which reached almost as high as private investment. Consequently, the nation's external debt also increased to over RM40 billion by 1985 (with debt-service ratio of nearly 16 per cent) as compared to RM10 billion in 1980 (with the debt-service ratio of 4 per cent). However, with a deliberate and fast structural adjustment, both the public investment and external payment deficits were immediately improved. During the period 1986–90, Malaysia experienced a resource surplus of 1.9 per cent of GNP. By 1990, the debt-service ratio was also down to 7.7 per cent. However, with rising investment requirements and increasing consumption expenditure, a savings–investment gap emerged again in the early 1990s. The deficits were largely contributed by the private sector which experienced much higher investment as a per centage of GNP, due particularly to the aggressive privatisation drive since the end of the 1980s.

By and large, Malaysia's high savings rate was attributed to several factors. They include the importance of commodities (especially petroleum, oil palm and rubber), prudent public sector expenditure, and household saving, including the compulsory contribution by the majority of the workforce to the Employees' Provident Fund (Merican, 1992).

High private savings have been largely contributed by the household sector, and can generally be attributed more to the strong growth performance than to the 'forced saving' schemes (Kharas, 1991; Lin See Yan, 1992). Indeed, the household sector has been a consistent net lender to both the corporate and public sectors. On the other hand, the corporate sector has been a consistent net user of savings to finance its investment needs. Apart from the private and public savings, another major source of funds is the long-term capital from abroad. External borrowing became less important since 1983 and it is expected to reduce further with the decline in the value of ringgit *vis-à-vis* the yen and the dollar, particularly the former.

An important feature of public financing in Malaysia is that the government often finances its expenditure and overall deficits from non-inflationary sources, such as the social security, provident, pension and insurance funds. The government resorted to foreign borrowing only as a residual financing in which about 60 per cent are from external market loans and the remainder from external project loans (Salleh and Osman-Rani, 1991).[2] In 1993, the Federal Government external debt accounted for about RM19.4 billion or 12.5 per cent of GNP as compared to its peak of RM25.4 billion in 1991 (20.7 per cent). In 1980, Malaysia's external debt was only RM4.9 billion or less than 10 per cent of GNP. The ratio of markets to project loans was almost reversed. The success in maintaining growth and stabilising the resource gap reflects prudent macroeconomic management and the market-oriented and open economy approach.

THE EXTERNAL SECTOR

Being one of the most open economies in the world, Malaysia's growth has much to do with its trade performance and its outward-looking development strategy. In 1993, exports and imports accounted for about 170 per cent of GNP and its export–GNP ratio was 86 per cent. This pattern has not changed much since Independence in 1957. What has changed is the trade structure which follows accordingly the overall economic structure. The transition from the agro-based to the industry-based economy has brought with it changes in the composition of its exports and imports.

Until 1970, Malaysia's exports were still dominated by two major commodities, namely rubber and tin. These two commodities contributed over 50 per cent of total exports in 1970. The manufactured share in total exports was less than 12 per cent. Through the export diversification strategy, the share of rubber and tin in total exports declined to about 35 per cent and manufactured exports increased to 22 per cent in 1975. By 1985, the biggest export was manufacturing (32.8 per cent), then petroleum (22.9 per cent), and palm oil (10.4 per cent), while the rest contributed less than 10 per cent each. Since then, the manufactured exports have been increasing very fast following the aggressive export-oriented industrial policy push. By 1993, exports of manufactured goods was 70 per cent of the total. The second biggest export was petroleum, which accounted for only 6.6 per cent, and third palm oil – 4.8 per cent.

Rapid structural changes also occurred within manufactured production and exports. In 1980, nearly half (or 48 per cent) of total manufactured exports consisted of electrical and electronic products and machinery, 13 per cent textiles, apparel and footwear, and 8 per cent food, beverages and tobacco. These are basically labour-intensive products. By 1993, manufactured exports have become more concentrated. The percentages are, respectively, 61, 6 and 3.

Similarly, import composition has also changed in line with domestic demand and supply. Import-substitution industrialisation during the 1960s has brought about a decline in the share of consumer goods in total imports, but an increase in the shares of investment and intermediate goods. For example, in 1961, the proportion of consumer goods in total exports was 46.7 per cent, compared with 17.1 per cent for investment goods and 28.4 per cent for intermediate goods. In 1970, the proportions were 28.5, 25.2 and 35.3 per cent, respectively. This trend continues following the export-orientation strategy since 1968. By 1992, the proportions were 16.2, 42.2

and 41.6, respectively. Imports of investment goods have been largely a function of foreign direct investment flows (Ariff, 1994).

Malaysia's major export markets have traditionally been the developed countries, namely the United States, Japan and Europe. But at later stages, market penetration ratios show that Malaysian manufacturers have also made significant gains in Australia, the Asian NIEs and ASEAN (ibid.). Malaysia's exports are very much affected by factors like low tariffs structure (Ariff, 1975; Lee, 1986; Chen, 1991), export incentives (under Investment Incentives Act 1968 and later replaced by the Promotion of Investments Act 1986), physical infrastructure (particularly the Free Trade Zones and Licensed Manufacturing Warehouses) and the exchange rates. Free Trade Zones especially were crucial in the export of manufactured goods although their relative importance has been declining. In 1980, about 70 per cent of manufactured exports originated in the export processing zones, mainly from foreign firms. But by 1989, as the economy developed, the proportion of exports from the zones declined to 40 per cent (World Bank, 1993). Under the Promotion of Investment Act 1986, tax incentives for exports were increased and imports liberalised. As a result, the average effective protection to industry declined from 31 per cent in 1979–80 to 17 per cent in 1987 (Edwards, 1990). With respect to the exchange rate, the overvaluation of the ringgit or a shock in the effective exchange rate can have detrimental effects on Malaysia's trade balance as experienced in the first half of the 1980s (Ariff and Semudram, 1987; Gan, 1989). However, Malaysia has often been successful in maintaining stable exchange rates through its adjustable or managed floating rate regime.

In its attempt to promote exports, Malaysia has to face protectionist forces in the export markets of the developed economies, especially for its commodities, and competition from the newly industrialising countries as well as from developing countries with cheap labour and cheap resources (like Indonesia, Thailand and the Philippines). At present, Malaysia still enjoys the Generalised System of Preferences accorded her by advanced countries which have enabled her to have preferential access to their markets.[3] However, with the rapid growth Malaysia is experiencing, the GSP status is not expected to remain for long. The narrow export base can create further fluctuations in the economic stability. However, in the past, Malaysia has been able to safeguard its stability fairly well despite its openness, partly due to its built-in stabilisers, such as high marginal propensities to save and to import, and prudent macroeconomic initiatives.

FOREIGN INVESTMENTS

Fundamental to the growth of exports and the Malaysian economy in general is the role played by foreign direct investment (FDI). The contribution of FDI can be seen not only in terms of production and exports but also in terms of structural changes taking place in the economy, that is, transforming the economy from being agriculture based to an industry based. In the process, it provides the needed capital, technology, marketing channels and management. At the same time, the characteristics of FDI have undergone major changes over the years. In general, the FDI is certainly much bigger than the foreign portfolio investment.

Until the 1960s, foreign investment was predominant in agriculture, mining and trade. Since the 1970s, it has become more prominent in manufacturing. In total, the foreign share of equity in the corporate sector has declined gradually from 61.7 per cent in 1971 to 25.4 per cent in 1990, but increased again to 32.4 per cent in 1992 (Malaysia, 1993), mainly due to the liberal policy of the government towards foreign equity participation and attractive economic performance. One estimate shows that FDI contributed annually around 8 per cent of gross domestic capital formation in Malaysia in the 1980s and this figure has risen to around 20 per cent by early 1990s. In terms of foreign equity share in manufacturing, it was estimated to be around 40 per cent in 1985, 58.6 per cent in 1988, 73.8 per cent in 1989 and 64.4 per cent in 1990 (Atan, 1994).

It is through the DFI-led industrialisation that the Malaysian economy has become increasingly integrated with the global economy, particularly with the United States, Japan and Europe. These countries have traditionally been major sources of foreign investment in this country. Other countries also have substantial shares, especially recently. These include Singapore, Taiwan, Hong Kong and Australia.

The main impetus for the expansion of the manufacturing sector came from foreign firms that began expanding their operations to benefit from the import-substitution strategy under the Pioneer Industries Ordinance 1958 (PIO). They continued to dominate the large manufacturing activities in the country even after PIO was replaced by an export-biased Investment Incentives Act of 1968 (IIA), and the latter again was replaced by a more liberal Promotion of Investments Act 1986 (PIA). Many of the incentives and facilities, like pioneer status, investment tax allowance and Free Trade Zones (FTZs), were taken advantage of by foreign investors, apart from the political and economic stability of the country. Foreign investments have contributed a significant proportion of fixed assets, output and employment, which together with superior technology and market outlets have propelled manufacturing growth of the country. Foreign firms too have contributed and offer great potential for Malaysia's development in terms of technology transfer, skill training or upgrading and R & D activities (Ali, 1994). Foreign capital generally showed higher productivity and efficiency, and provided higher labour productivity, but low linkages with other sectors. Among the reasons for the low linkages are the export-orientation of the firms in FTZs and a heavy dependence on import capital and intermediate goods, the inability of local firms to supply inputs to and process outputs from foreign firms, and the lack of dynamic efforts by the government to integrate the export sectors (Rasiah, 1992; Ghazali, 1994).

Despite the negative effects, Malaysia has still a lot to gain from foreign investments. And through experience and proper planning and management, together with the upgrading of local skills, knowledge and technological capabilities, this gain can be maximised. The Action Plan for Industrial Technology Development, introduced in 1990 by the Malaysian Government, proposes to provide an environment that allows indigenous technological capabilities to be further developed in support of industrialisation. However, the planning and management require not only strong government involvement and commitment but also an effective role of the market in stimulating economic growth. While foreign capital has driven change, much change has generally been unstable and unsecured. The switch to domestic policy orientation is inevitable in the long run if Malaysian economy is to be fully industrialised.

STATE–MARKET MIX

The government has always played an active role in Malaysian economic development. However, its role has been changing over time. In the 1950s and 1960s, the government played a limited interventionist role. But with the launching of the New Economic Policy (NEP) in 1971, the role changed significantly. There was a direct government participation in the management of the economy in order to reduce poverty and to restructure the society in favour of the Bumiputeras (mainly the indigenous Malays). But from the early 1980s onwards, with the significant decline in world economic growth, the failures of many state enterprises and burdened by a fast growing public debt, the government shifted towards more flexible administrative guidance. Instead, the private sector was encouraged to play a more active role in the running of the economy, aided by the 'privatisation' and 'Malaysia Inc.' concepts.

Despite the shift in the role of the government as against the market and the private sector, the public sector continues to be an important provider of employment and income, a producer of goods and services, an investor of capital and a manager of the economy. In order to finance its activities, the revenues and expenditures of the public sector have also increased dramatically to a point which is now equivalent to more than one-quarter of GDP in terms of revenue and one-third in terms of expenditure. Despite the privatisation policy and the industry-led growth since early 1980s, Malaysia still has one of the largest public sectors among countries at a comparable level of economic development, and much higher than the average advanced countries (Osman-Rani and Saleh, 1994). Over the period 1966–92, public expenditure increased by nearly 13 per cent per annum. The high growth was mainly due to high expenditure on public enterprises.

The rising level of public expenditure imposed considerable constraints on public sector financing. The Federal Government's current balance has always been in surplus, but due to the heavy development expenditure, the overall balance has almost always been in deficit. At its peaks, for instance, the government was accounting for half the total investment in the country; and as a result the budget deficit sky-rocketed and, as noted earlier, external debt reached a danger level with servicing exceeding 20 per cent of gross exports, the World Bank limit of prudence. The continuing public sector deficit implied significant competition with the private sector for funds. Thus, although Malaysia's level of gross national savings was high, a big proportion of the savings was used to finance the overall government deficit, thus leaving less of a share for the private sector. But through privatisation and prudent management of the economy, the state's external debt-service ratio managed to fall to below 2 per cent and the budget turned surplus during the first half of the 1990s.

As an employer, the public sector employment increased from 398 000 (or 11.9 per cent of total employment) in 1970 to 757 000 in 1981 (reaching a peak of 50 per cent of total employment) and to 859 000 (12.2 per cent) in 1992. During the whole period 1970–92, government employment increased at an average annual rate of 3.9 per cent as compared to 3.5 per cent for total employment. However, the rate of growth of government employment started to decline after 1983, that is, when the privatisation programme was implemented and the government decided to take steps to check the employment growth in the public sector. To date, over 10 per cent of employees have already been taken off the state payroll (Jayasankaran, 1995). In general, the growth of public sector employment is directly related to the growth of the wage bill of the sector. The wage bill as a per centage of GNP increased continuously from 6.5 per cent in 1971 to 13.9 per cent in 1992.

After the mid-1980s, the private sector became the engine of growth, while the public sector continued to play a supportive and complementary role to ensure that the basic infrastructure and other amenities were sufficiently provided to encourage private sector development. Government intervention tends to be confined to reducing or eliminating market distortions. It ensures smooth functioning of the market forces as well as fair market prices. At the same time, the government would continue to reform the tax structure to increase Malaysia's competitiveness and to ensure high savings for investment needs, environmental protection and human resource development. The privatisation programme was strengthened by the introduction of the Privatisation Master Plan in 1991. The plan involves the transfer of management responsibility, assets or the right to use assets, and personnel to the private sector. Methods of privatisation implemented include the sale of equity or assets, the lease of assets, management contract and build-operator-transfer and build-operator methods. In general, a study shows that the privatisation projects have led to gains in social welfare (Bank Negara Malaysia, 1992). While under the NEP (New Economic Policy), the state was given the responsibility to uplift the economic status of the Bumiputeras *vis-à-vis* the non-Bumiputeras, and under the National Development Policy (NDP) which replaced the NEP after 1990 privatisation became the main tool to attain NEP objectives.

To ensure closer cooperation between the government and the private sector, the Malaysia Incorporated policy has been actively pursued. The government is taking various measures to be private-sector friendly. They include the formation of the Malaysian Business Council as a national umbrella body for consultation between the public and the private sector, annual dialogues to review the progress achieved and to plan for the future, and provision of incentives to the private sector to encourage human resource development and R&D. In short, like many other market-driven economy, the balancing role of the government will continue to be an important factor in the Malaysian socio-economic discourse.

TOWARDS THE FUTURE

When the Prime Minister of Malaysia, Dr. Mahathir Mohammad, announced in February 1991 the plan for 'Vision 2020 : the way forward', the long-term mission immediately attracted a great deal of interest, and the response from the people towards attaining the objectives outlined has been encouraging. The vision provides broad policy directions in order to achieve a developed economy status by the year 2020. It calls for all-round and well-balanced development in terms of national unity, economic development, social justice, policy stability, system of government, quality of life, ethical and moral values, national pride and confidence.

However, having a plan and a dream is one thing, the implementation is another. It is in the implementation that the real issues and challenges will be found.

Among the challenges facing Malaysia for its future success are the promotion of scientific and technological awareness, increasing the number of engineers, technicians and scientists, development of human resources, strengthening the public and private sector cooperation, creating a strong and viable Bumiputera commercial and industrial base in line with the other ethnic groups, broadening and deepening the industrial sector to spearhead the economy, and facing the dynamic global competition coupled with environmental constraints imposed by the developed economies. The domestic policy is expected to be the main determinant of the future growth and stability.

With Vision 2020, the Malaysian economy and society is envisaged to have achieved the following within a generation: global-oriented industrial economy, technology structure that is dependent on local capabilities, a well-developed human capital base, a thriving private enterprise, a united nation with ethnic equality, a society that is mature, literate, caring, democratic, confident, and just, and a people committed to human freedom and environmental care. To achieve such a massive transformation is certainly a gigantic task. It needs concerted efforts by all Malaysians to strive for the common goals, constant monitoring of policy implementation and achievements, and above all to know how to share the products of change.

Notes

1. Malaysia's gross domestic savings are higher than the national savings because of the country's dependence on foreign investment which creates a large amount of net foreign payments abroad.
2. The biggest contributors of market loans are from the United States and Japan, while project loans come mainly from Japan and the World Bank.
3. In 1993, for example, Malaysia's GSP exports totalled RM18.2 billion, with the European Union accounting for 52.7 per cent (MITI, 1994). The major products for GSP exports in 1993 were electrical and electronic products

(31.8 per cent), machinery and transport equipment (12.7 per cent), textiles, clothing and plastic products (10.0 per cent), rubber goods (6.7 per cent) and wood manufactures (5.5 per cent).

References

Ali, Anuwar (1994) 'Technology Transfer', in Jomo, K.S. (ed.), *Malaysia's Economy in the Nineties* (Kuala Lumpur: Pelanduk Publications).

Ariff, Mohamed (1975) 'Protection for Manufactures in Peninsular Malaysia', *Hitotsubashi Journal of Economics*, 15 (2).

Ariff, Mohamed (1994) 'External Trade', in Jomo K.S. (ed.), *Malaysia's Economy in the Nineties* (Kuala Lumpur: Pelanduk Publications).

Ariff, Mohamed and Semudram, M. (1987) 'Trade and Financing Strategies: A Case Study of Malaysia', Working Paper No. 21 (London: Overseas Development Institute).

Atan, Ghazali (1994) 'Foreign Investment', in Jomo, K.S. (ed.), *Malaysia's Economy in the Nineties* (Kuala Lumpur: Pelanduk Publications).

Bank Negara Malaysia (1991) *Bank Negara Annual Report 1991.*

Bank Negara Malaysia (1992) *Bank Negara Annual Report 1992.*

Chandavarkar, Anand (1993) 'Saving Behaviour in the Asian-Pacific Region', *Asia-Pacific Economic Literature*, May, 7 (1).

Chen, Y. L. (1991) 'Kos Perlindungan: Satu Kajian Kes Perusahaan Perkilangan di Malaysia pada tahun 1987', M.Sc. Thesis, Universiti Sains Malaysia, Penang.

Edwards, Chris B. (1990) 'Protection and Policy in the Malaysian Manufacturing Sector', Policy Assessment of the Malaysian Industrial Policy Study (MIPS) and the Malaysian Industrial Master Plan (IMP) (Vienna: UNIDO).

Gan, W. B. (1989) 'The Ringgit Exchange Rate and the Malaysian Economy', in Lim Kok Cheong and Abidin, Mahani Zainal (eds), *Strategy for Growth: Towards a More Competitive Economy* (Kuala Lumpur: Persatuan Ekonomi Malaysia).

Government of Malaysia (1993) *Mid-Term Review of Sixth Malaysia Plan, 1991–1995* (Kuala Lumpur: Percetakan Nasional Malaysia Berhad).

Jayasankaran, S. (1995) 'Privatization Pioneer', *Far Eastern Economic Review* (FEER) 19 January.

Kharas, Homi (1991) 'Malaysian Saving in the 1990s: Problems and Prospects', in Lee Kiong Hock and Nagaraj, Shyamala (eds), *The Malaysian Economy Beyond 1990: International and Domestic Perspectives* (Kuala Lumpur: Persatuan Ekonomi Malaysia).

Krongkaew, Medhi (1994) 'Income Distribution in East Asian Developing Countries: An Update', *Asia Pacific Economic Literature*, November, 8 (2).

Lee, K. H. (1986) 'Malaysia: The Structure and Causes of Manufacturing Sector Protection', in Findlay, C. and Garnaut, R. (eds), *The Political Economy of Manufacturing Protection: Experiences of ASEAN and Australia* (Baltimore: Johns Hopkins University Press).

Lin See Yan (1992) 'The Savings–Investment Gap, Financing Needs, and Capital market Development', in Teh Hoe Yoke and Goh Kim Leng (eds), *Malaysia's*

Economic Vision: Issues and Challenges (Kuala Lumpur: Pelanduk Publications).

Merican, Malek (1992) 'The Employees' Provident Fund and Its Investment Policies', in Teh Hoe Yoke & Goh Kim Leng (eds), *Malaysia's Economic Vision*: Issues and Challenges (Kuala Lumpur: Pelanduk Publications)..

MITI (Ministry of International Trade and Industry) (1994) *Malaysia International Trade and Industry Report* (Kuala Lumpur: Government of Malaysia).

Osman-Rani, H. and Piei, Mohd. Haflah (1990) 'Malaysia's Industrialization and Trade: Issues, Options and Strategies', *Jurnal Ekonomi Malaysia*, 21/22.

Osman-Rani, H. and Salleh, Ismail (1994) 'The Public Sector', in Jomo, K. S. (ed.), *Malaysia's Economy in the Nineties* (Kuala Lumpur: Pelanduk Publications).

Rasiah, Rajah (1992) 'The Role of Foreign Manufacturing Firms in Industrial Development: A Study of Malaysia', Ph.D. Thesis, University of Cambridge.

Salleh, Ismail and Osman-Rani, H. (1991) *The Growth of the Public Sector in Malaysia* (Kuala Lumpur: Institute of Strategic and International Studies Malaysia).

Shari, Ishak and Zin, Ragayah Mat (1990) 'The Patterns and Trends of Income Distribution in Malaysia, 1970–1987', *Singapore Economic Review*, April, 35 (1).

Sheng, Andrew (1984) 'Growth of the Malaysian Economy – Some Issues for the 1980s', in Lim Lin Lean and Chee Peng Lim (eds), *The Malaysian Economy at the Crossroads* (Kuala Lumpur: Malaysian Economic Association and ORSB).

Tan Tat Wai (1984) 'Trends in Malaysian Economic Development', in Lim Lin Lean and Chee Peng Lim (eds), *The Malaysian Economy at the Crossroads* (Kuala Lumpur: Malaysian Economic Association and ORSB).

World Bank (1993) *The East Asian Miracle: Economic Growth and Public Policy* (New York: Oxford University Press).

3 Macroeconomic Perspectives of the Malaysian Economy

M. Zainudin Saleh

INTRODUCTION

The high growth achieved by Malaysia in the 1970s continued into the early 1980s. The recovery from recession in the mid-1980s had led the country out of its worst growth period since Independence. The main impetus came from rapid expansion of the export-oriented industrial sector and strong manufactured exports. Along with growth and low inflation, national consumption and investment increased and the current account of the balance of payments recorded a surplus. Private investment expanded rapidly in industrial activities, notably in manufacturing, construction, petroleum exploration and production as well as export-oriented industries. The development policy is to strengthen further the internal resilience and competitiveness. Policies and strategies to sustain the momentum of rapid growth would continue to be implemented to meet the country's objective of growth with equity in line with the national aspiration of a caring industrialised society.

CHANGING ROLE OF THE PUBLIC SECTOR – FROM PUBLIC ENTERPRISES TO PRIVATISATION

In tandem with the growing economy the role of the public sector had expanded rapidly. Table 3.1 (all figures and tables are in the Statistical Appendix to this chapter) shows that the share of public sector expenditure on consumption and investment of GNP increased from 25 per cent in the early 1970s to a peak of 35 per cent in the early 1980s and averaged at 26 per cent in the late 1980s and early 1990s. In addition, before the 1980s, in line with the growth of public enterprises, the government played an increasingly active role in the economic management of the nation. For example, the share of public investment to GNP rose from 7.8 per cent in the early 1970s to 17.3 per cent in the early 1980s. However, after the recession, with Malaysia confronting twin deficit problems – the overall public sector fiscal deficit and the current account deficit of the balance of payments – and mounting foreign debts, a privatisation policy was adopted in the early 1980s to ease the government's financial burden.

With respect to the role of public sector in the economy, it can be divided into three phases. In the first phase, the early years after Independence, the role of government was limited to the provision of basic infrastructural facilities and the creation of an economic environment which was suitable for private investment. It made no direct attempt to involve itself actively in economic activities. However, the 1969 racial riots convinced the government of the urgency of certain major structural changes required in the share of national wealth.

The second phase started with the launching of the Second Malaysia Plan and the New Economic Policy in 1970. In this respect, the government insisted that public investment, besides providing the infrastructures and social environment to stimulate private investment, would also become a dynamic force in the economic life of the country through active and direct government participation in industrial and commercial enterprises (Government of Malaysia, 1971, p. 66). In this period there has been expansion and proliferation of so-called quasi-government corporation or public enterprises empowered to invest government funds, either as equity capital or as loan finance. When the recession hit the economy in late 1970s or early 1980s the government began to realise the extent of its financial burden. Specifically, Malaysia was confronted with the twin deficit problem – the overall public sector fiscal deficit deteriorated from RM3.5 billion or 8 per cent of GNP in 1979 to a peak of RM11 billion or 19 per cent of GNP in 1982, and at the same time deficit in the current account of the balance of payments increased to an unprecedented high of 14 per cent of GNP in 1982 as against 1 per cent in 1980. To finance this deficit Malaysia borrowed heavily from the international capital markets, resulting in a rapid accumulation of external debt from RM10 billion in 1980 to RM24 billion in 1982 or 41 per cent of GNP (ibid., 1994a, p. 229). These phenomena, mainly due to the world recession and falling commodity prices, had forced the government to re-examine critically its development policy.

The third phase which started in the early 1980s gave a bigger role to the private sector in the economy. With the Malaysia Incorporated concept, by which every citizen is an employee of a big corporation in Malaysia, and is responsible for the survival and prosperity of the corporation, it was hoped that the private sector would play an increasingly significant and important role in developing and managing the economy.

This approach depicted the intention of government to reduce its involvement in the economy. For example, by selling public enterprises to the private sector – privatisation – it was hoped that they would become less politicised, more efficient and be able to provide higher quality products and services.

THE NEW DEVELOPMENT POLICY – THE WAY FORWARD

The ultimate objective of Malaysian development policy is to achieve a fully developed country status in its own mould by the year 2020. This is popularly known as Vision 2020. It dictates that Malaysia should not only be developed in an economic sense but is also fully developed in all dimensions, economically, politically, socially, spiritually, psychologically and culturally. It must be fully developed in terms of national unity and social cohesion, in terms of growth and distribution, in terms of social justice, political stability, government administration, quality of life, social and spiritual values, national pride and confidence. In short, the term 'development in its own mould' covers all aspects of improvement in social welfare and life. Furthermore, a competitive Malaysian economy should be able to sustain itself over the long term, must be dynamic, robust and resilient. It must mean, among other things (Mohamad, 1991):

a. a diversified and balanced economy with a mature and widely based industrial sector, a modern and mature agricultural sector and an efficient and productive and equally mature service sector;
b. an economy that is able to adapt quickly to changing patterns of supply, demand and competition;
c. an economy that is technologically proficient and increasingly technology-intensive, and is able to adapt, innovate and invent;
d. an economy that has strong and cohesive industrial linkages – backwards and forwards;
e. an economy that is advanced in information technology and has a wide range of industrial and business information, driven by skills and diligence;
f. an economy with high and increasingly improved productivity with regard to every factor of production;
g. an enterprising economy with a high degree of entrepreneurship which is self-reliant and outwardlooking;
h. an economy led by an exemplary work ethic, quality consciousness and the quest for excellence;

i. an economy characterised by a low cost of living and low inflation;
j. an economy that is subjected to the full discipline and rule of market forces.

GROWTH WITHOUT INFLATION

The question of the relationship between growth and inflation has always attracted attention from academicians, politicians, and public practitioners at least since David Hume. The relationship has long been examined theoretically and empirically. For example, Professor A.P. Thirlwall (1974, p. 17) once wrote: 'If it is true that growth might have been faster in developing countries had they been willing to pursue slightly more expansionist policies, there is no reason in principle why it should be more difficult for monetary and fiscal policy to maintain, say a 6 percent rate of inflation than a 3 per cent rate of inflation.'

In Malaysia inflation has been the prime concern among politicians, policy-makers and members of the public. The superb economic performance since recovery in 1987, which recorded economic growth in the range of 7–9 per cent per annum, has led to a growing worry over inflationary pressure. Monetarists argue that money is the sole cause of inflation. With Fisher's classical equation of exchange, price level is linked to money stock under the assumption that velocity of transaction is stable and money is considered an exogenous policy-controlled variable. Modern quantity theorists argue that money only affects prices in the long run; in the short run it affects output. The Keynesian school, on the other hand, take the view that inflation results from the interaction between demand and supply forces in an imperfect market. With markets being imperfect, prices are determined as a mark-up over unit cost and are sticky downwards. Economists from the structuralist school argue that inflationary pressure in developing countries was the result of various rigidities and inelasticities in economic environment. Supply rigidities, complemented by an already imperfectly competitive market, that is, the high concentration ratio in key industries, not only make prices rigid downward, but also induce prices to go up as firms exploit their market power in the face of rising demand.

Monetarists argue that higher inflation is always associated with a higher variability of inflation which consequently lead to variability in output growth. This implies that lower inflation reduces price uncertainty in the market, thus a reduction in the inflation rate would have a positive impact on output growth. On the other hand, non-monetarists believe that, up to a certain point, inflation is helpful in allocating resources. Keynesians, for example, believe that inflation would redistribute income from an income group with a low propensity to save to an income group with a higher propensity to save, thus inflation could raise national saving (ibid., 1994, p. 288). Seigniorage works best under a low inflation environment and since it could provide government with a source of revenue, growth prospect would be better. However, this argument holds only under the specific assumption of predictable and stable prices.

An econometric study, conducted by the central bank of Malaysia on 71 countries – 23 industrialised and 48 developing – suggests that the inflation–growth relationship of the industrialised countries differs from that of the developing countries. Inflation seems to affect growth positively in developed countries but negatively in developing countries. Furthermore, the more inflation fluctuates, the slower growth will be in developing countries (Government of Malaysia, 1994a, p. 78).

Since the economy recovered from the recession in 1986, the inflation rate averaged at 2.5–4.7 per cent per annum. In the absence of direct external influences (such as high imported inflation in the early 1970s) this was considered high according to Malaysian standards. The inflation was due to several factors. Excellent economic growth during the period 1986–93, averaged at about 7.5–8.5 per cent per annum, led to a substantial increase in aggregate domestic demand. During the period the aggregate investment and consumption grew at annual rates of 16 per cent and 11 per cent respectively. At the same time, the inflow of foreign investment created an additional demand for labour causing increases in wages which contributed to cost pressures. Compounded with the already rising costs associated with institutional and supply rigidities and infrastructural bottle-necks, producers were forced to raise prices in order to maintain a reasonable mark-up. Furthermore, studies have shown that the Malaysian industrial market structure is highly oligopolistic. Certain industries are either controlled by less than four firms and by four firms which supply at least 70 per cent of total industry output. The high market concentration means producers have higher collusive powers and prices tend to be rigid downwards, thus encouraging price increases (Yusof and Phang, 1993). In addition, money growth folded the inflation rate. Some studies on the relationship between money growth and inflation suggest that in Malaysia the inflation rate has been highly influenced by the money supply growth rate, in particular M2. A study by the central bank showed that in the period 1970–92, M1 and M2 seemed to lead to inflation. Figure 3.1 (see Statistical Appendix) shows that in the period 1986–93 M1 and M2 expanded at annual rates of 17 per cent and 14 per cent, respectively, causing inflation to run around 3.3 per cent yearly. Due to data constraints, M3 was tested for the period 1974–92 but the result was not statistically significant. It should be noted that the results are merely an indication of the long-run relationship, not a forecast of the short-run movements of money and inflation (Government of Malaysia, 1994a, p. 80).

In Malaysia, it has been government priority that rapid growth is achieved and sustained with low inflation. As inflation has the adverse effect of reducing the real income of consumers, inducing pressures for wage increases, if not accompanied by productivity improvement, it would adversely affect the competitiveness of the economy, particularly in the international market. In early 1994 the Prime Minister even stated that attempts should be made to try to achieve a higher growth rate with a zero rate of inflation. Based on the purchasing power parity, the so-called Mahathir's theory of deflation argues that if prices in all parts and income groups of the economy could be reduced at the same rate, then all economic units enjoy the same purchasing power – no one is worse off or better off. In addition, the economy will grow with exports being more competitive.

The objective of achieving higher growth with low inflation was depicted by the monetary and fiscal policies. Monetary policy in Malaysia has always meant to combat inflation. In the early 1990s, the large inflow of short-term funds resulted in an upward pressure on the price level. To contain these inflows within a manageable level, as well as discourage speculative trading in the ringgit, the government adopted measures which included (ibid., 1994b, p. 30):

1. Increasing the statutory reserve requirement of the commercial banks, finance companies and merchant banks in order to absorb the excess liquidity in the banking system.
2. Redefining the eligible liabilities base of the banking institutions to capture all inflows of funds that are abused. In this respect, the banking institutions are required to keep an estimated RM1 billion in additional reserves and about RM2 billion in additional liquid assets with the central bank.
3. After deducting inflows which are trade related or genuine investments, the net external liabilities position of each bank is subject to a ceiling specified by the central bank. This measure is to contain the inflows of short-term capital at a manageable level at all times.
4. Under the Exchange Control Act 1953, all residents are prohibited from selling short-term monetary instruments to non-residents. These instruments include Bank Negara bills, treasury bills, government se-

curities (including Islamic securities) with a remaining maturity of one year or less, Cagamas bonds with remaining maturity of one year or less, bankers' acceptances and negotiable instruments of deposits.

5. The commercial banks are required to place the ringgit funds of foreign institutions in a designated non-interest bearing current account maintained with the central bank.

The measures taken led to a significant reduction in the inflows of short-term capital, depicted by the reduction in the outstanding vostro account balances of foreign banks held with local commercial banks. In addition, the convergence of domestic and international interest rates together with the appreciation of the ringgit discouraged interest rate arbitrage and speculation in the foreign exchange market.

Tight monetary policy is complemented by prudent fiscal measures to further reduce excess demand and remove price pressure in the economy. The main objective of the fiscal policy in Malaysia is to promote a sustained economic growth with low inflationary pressure, mainly as counter-cyclical measures, and to implement various programmes to reduce poverty and effectively restructure Malaysian society with the implementation of the New Economic Policy.

To expand domestic productive capacity and offset the effect of the world recession, as experienced in the seventies and which had threatened to slow down growth, in the early 1980s the government pursued an expansionary counter-cyclical fiscal policy. This led to large public sector outlays and proliferation of public enterprises whose main objectives were to spearhead the country's further diversification into heavy industries. As a result public expenditure grew at 22 per cent in 1980 as compared to an average of 7 per cent two years before. Consequently, public investment increased from 12 per cent of GNP in 1980 to 19 per cent in 1982 (ibid., 1994a, p. 229).

However, starting in mid-1982 and due to world recession, the government had scaled down public investment by reducing unproductive investments and checking the cost-effectiveness of national projects. National priorities were reranked such that they were consistent with domestic resources availability and a prudent recourse to external borrowing. By restraining expenditure on supplies and services, subsidies and recruitment the growth of Federal Government expenditure was significantly reduced during 1983–5. Beginning in the mid-1980s – in line with privatisation policy – the direction of public policy was to reduce the role of government and promote the private sector as the main engine of growth. Therefore, the development expenditure allocation under the Fifth

Malaysia Plan (1986–90) was scaled down to RM62 billion from an actual expenditure level of RM79 billion in the Fourth Plan. The fiscal measures also included further consolidation and rationalisation of activities and the financial position of the non-financial public enterprises (NFPEs), restraining public sector spending and introduction of new initiatives to increase revenue collection. As a result, the government's financial position improved, as reflected by better revenue collection and continued consolidation of the public sector. Consequently, the government was able to allocate additional resources in absolute terms, amounting to RM104 billion under the Sixth Malaysia Plan (1991–5).

INDUSTRIAL DEVELOPMENT

The rapid growth achieved in the 1970s had transformed the Malaysian economy from one dominated by the agricultural sector to one with the industrial sector, particularly manufacturing, playing an increasingly important role. In 1970, 1980 and the early 1990s the respective share of manufacturing output to GDP was 13.9, 19.6 and 29 per cent. Furthermore, the manufacturing sector was increasingly driven by export-led growth rather than import substitution. By 1993 manufactured exports contributed about 71 per cent of total exports while the export of major agricultural commodities accounted for only 12 per cent. More significantly, the share of manufactured exports will increase very rapidly during the 1990s, so that by the year 2000 its share will reach about 82 per cent of total exports (ibid., 1991, p. 80).

Since Independence in 1957 policies on industrial development in Malaysia can be broadly divided into four periods;

1. *Import substitution period 1958–68*: After the introduction of the Pioneer Industries Ordinance in 1958 import-substitution industries were encouraged.
2. *Export-oriented period 1969–80*: In 1968 the government introduced the Investment Incentives Act by which various incentives were used to promote export-oriented industries. This period also saw the introduction of the Industrial Coordination Act in 1975 as an addition and revision to the previous act. In this period, through industrialisation, the government was trying to achieve the twin objectives of the New Economic Policy launched in 1971.
3. *Second round import–substitution period 1980–5*: This period coincided with the Fourth Malaysia Plan in which the second round import-substitution period and heavy industries were emphasised.

4. *Industrial Master Plan period 1986–present*: In 1985 the Industrial Master Plan was launched. The plan detailed various liberalisation measures to attract more investments into the manufacturing sector. During this period emphasis on heavy industries was continued and the latter part of this period was highlighted by the emphasis of the development of small- and medium-scale industries.

The import-substitution period was characterised by various policies to promote industrial development, giving the private sector an active role in the process while the role of the government was only supplementary. The government was only maintaining the economic environment which was conducive to the private sector to play an active part in industrial development. The major instruments to promote private investments included the granting of tax holidays, the establishment of industrial estates, the provision of necessary services and infrastructures, and the imposition of tariff protection for import-substitution industries.

In the first phase of import substitution (IS), the strategy was to broaden the industrial base, diversify the economy, reduce excessive dependence on imported consumer goods, utilise some domestic natural resources, and more importantly, to generate more employment opportunities. The strategy has been particularly successful in the renewable resource-based industries such as tobacco, furniture, rubber products, wood products, food and beverages. Nevertheless, since some IS industries were based on imported raw materials and intermediate products or components, the end result was a low-value added ratio and poor linkage effects with the rest of the sector.

The fiscal incentives offered in this period tended to favour the larger companies. This encouraged the establishment of manufacturing companies employing relatively more capital-intensive techniques, partly making manufacturing employment growth lag behind output growth. At the same time, in a number of cases, the strategy also attracted less efficient manufacturers into the industry. However, while imports of consumer goods have declined, relatively as well as absolutely, the imports of investment and intermediate goods increased somewhat more proportionately.

Realising the limitations of a small domestic market, beginning in the late 1960s, industrial policy has shifted from an inward-looking to an export-oriented approach. This was particularly apparent since the beginning of the 1970s with the establishment of the free trade zones (FTZs). Direct foreign investments (DFI) were given an important role not only because they were expected to provide capital, management and industrial technology, but also access to foreign markets. These multinational corporations had given the impetus for export-oriented growth by maintaining and improving international competitiveness through product standards and quality, as well as marketing opportunities overseas.

The second round of IS which started in the early 1980s emphasised the production of consumer durables, intermediate inputs and capital goods. In order to enjoy economies of scale these goods were produced in large quantities utilising more capital and skill-intensive methods of production. At the same time, the continued export-expansion strategy underwent a shift from labour-intensive manufactures to more capital and technology-intensive products. Such products included machinery, motor vehicles, petrochemicals, and other resource-based industries in which the country was expected to have comparative advantage.

THE INDUSTRIAL MASTER PLAN

Any medium- and long-term policy to transform the country's industrial structure requires technology absorption and advancement, fulfilment of overseas demand and exploitation of opportunities in the global business environment. The deepening and broadening of the industrial base, for example, requires acquisition of high and new technology. It was in this context that the Industrial Master Plan was launched in 1985 to provide a medium- and long-term policy framework to foster the development of a more diversified and intergrated manufacturing sector. The main thrust of the IMP was an outward-looking industrialisation strategy, emphasing export-led growth, diversification of the industrial base and rationalisation of the industrial structure.

The principal objectives of industrial development set by the IMP are as follows (ibid., 1986, p. 19):

a. to accelerate the growth of the manufacturing sector to ensure a continued rapid expansion of the economy and to provide a basis for meeting the social objectives consistent with the New Economic Policy;
b. to promote opportunities for the maximum and efficient utilisation of the nation's abundantly endowed natural resources; and
c. to build up the foundation for leap-frogging towards an advanced industrial country in the information age, by increasing indigenous technological capability and competitiveness.

The IMP recognised twelve industry groups for the purpose of industrial planning and policy implementation during the plan period, with seven categorised as resource-based industries (RBIs) and five as non-resource-based industries (NRBIs). The RBIs were rubber products, palm oil products, food processing, wood-based, chemical and petrochemical, and non-ferrous metal products and finally non-metallic mineral products. On the other hand, the NRBIs were electronic, electrical and transport equipment, machinery and engineering products, ferrous metal (iron and steel) and finally textiles and clothing.

Of the RBIs, the rubber products, the wood-based, tin-based and palm-oil based industries were classified as export-oriented, whereas the petrochemical and non-metallic mineral based industries were classified as domestic market oriented industries. Of the NRBIs, the electronics as well as the textiles and clothing industries were identified as export-oriented, whereas the transport equipment, the iron and steel, and the non-ferrous metal-based industries were regarded as domestic market oriented industries. The food processing, machinery and engineering industries were considered as composite industries, respectively, consisting of diversified products, some with export orientation and some with domestic market orientation.

The export-oriented strategies of the manufacturing sector have led to the rapid growth of the economy. Realising that the manufacturing sector is still narrowly based, the government has continued to focus its strategies on industrial widening and deepening to achieve greater value added and linkages. Backward integration, especially in the electronics, transport, basic and fabricated metal industries, is promoted and at the same time greater linkages through downstream activities are also encouraged, especially for the resource-based industries such as wood and rubber products as well as chemicals and petrochemical products.

To create greater interlinkages and ancillary support among industries the government has also made a concerted effort to promote the development of small- and medium-scale industries (SMIs). By making SMIs the reliable manufacturers and suppliers of industrial inputs, machine parts and components and equipment used by larger industries and multinational corporations (MNCs), the dependence of large industries on imported parts and components can be reduced. This could scale down the currently relatively high import content of the country's exports, as reflected by the presently high ratio of intermediate goods to manufactured exports of 0.47:1 (ibid., 1994b, p. 29). In this regard, the development of domestic industries such as vehicle components and accessories, moulds and dyes, as well as engineering and metal fabrication, would be essential for greater industrial linkages.

To encourage linkages between domestic SMIs and foreign anchor companies the government has given high priority to Vendor Development Programmes (VDP). Under this arrangement, the foreign anchor companies provide the assurance of markets for the local SMIs (vendors) and the financial institutions provide the necessary financial support. By the end of July 1994, there have been 30 anchor companies working with 55 vendors under the supervision of the Ministry of International Trade and Industry. These Vendor Development Programmes cover a wide range of manufacturing activities such as plastic injection moulding, automotive components, metal stamping and fabrication as well as electro-plating.

In regard to its large contribution to total export, the competitiveness of the manufacturing sector is critical and every effort must be made to maintain and improve it. The unit labour cost which indicates the percentage of labour cost in total output showed an increasing trend from 0.080 in 1989 to 0.088 in 1991 (ibid., 1994c, p. 226). Therefore the government has regularly monitored the increase in labour cost to ensure it did not exceed productivity increases. Given the increasing globalisation of the domestic economy and intense competition in world markets, industrial policies after the IMP must therefore be strategically charted to ensure the continuance of the nation's drive to achieve the status of an industrialised country by 2020. Thus the future policy thrust should be in the areas of higher domestic value added, high skill and technology-intensive industries, to increase SMI participation, domestic investment as well as reinvestments and expansion of the manufacturing export base and diversification of export markets.

INDUSTRIALISATION FOR THE FUTURE – TOWARDS THE DEVELOPMENT OF HI-TECH INDUSTRIES

The emphasis on heavy industries led the government to recognise the importance of developing high-technology industries to pave the way for the achievement of the status of an industrialised nation. The emphasis has been given even greater attention lately, particularly under the Sixth Malaysia Plan and the coming Seventh Malaysia Plan scheduled in 1996. After the recovery during late 1980s, with rapid growth and acute labour shortages, notably in large-scale agricultural estates, construction and manufacturing sectors, the need to push further towards high-technology industries is becoming increasingly necessary. In addition, other labour surplus economies such as Vietnam and the People's Republic of China are also industrialising themselves by inviting foreign investors to help build their economies and Malaysia will therefore no longer be able to compete for labour intensive products against these countries in international markets. Furthermore, in order to remain efficient and competitive in rapidly changing world trade, industries in Malaysia also has to restructure themselves so that technological advancement could flourish easily.

After the launching of the Industrial Master Plan in 1985, a committee was set up to formulate an Action Plan for Industrial Technology Development (APITP) in 1987. The APITD had identified several structural weaknesses relating to the state of technological development which included weak science and technological infrastructures, inadequate industrial technology and the lack of a human resource base to support the latter. The APITD outlined several strategic thrusts to encourage the development of industrial technology and provide an environment conducive to technological betterment. These strategic thrusts included upgrading the development of key emerging technologies, strengthening institutions and mechanisms for technological development and encouraging invention, innovation and technological advancement. The key industries designated for intensified industrial technological development are microelectronics, automated manufacturing technology, information technology, the aerospace industry, advanced materials and biotechnology (ibid., 1994b, p. 76).

At present, the electronic and electrical industry is one of the most important manufacturing activities in the economy. As electronics forms the foundation for many high-technology processes and products, it is part of the country's industrial policy to encourage the domestic electronic industry to upgrade its technology and to advance into the area of microelectronic and automated manufacturing. Despite the long presence of the electronics industry, the linkages with local industries are still weak and the level of local content in electronic products remains low.

Information technology (IT) is one of the fastest growing industries in the country, particularly in the 1990s. In the early 1990s Malaysia spent about one per cent of its GNP, equivalent to RM1.5 billion, yearly on information technology. With superb economic growth and a rapid rate of computerisation, the market for IT is expected to expand more strongly in the future. Since the IT industry is closely related to the electronics and telecommunication industries the rapid development of these industries will help to foster growth of the IT industry.

In Malaysia, the aerospace industry has started to emerge only in recent years. It started by the manufacture of light aircraft and aircraft components; with the hope that some day Malaysia will be able to manufacture her own air carrier. In 1991, Composite Technology Research Malaysia (CTRM) was established for the manufacture of aircraft and to act as a vehicle for the acquisition of aerospace technology. In addition, the aerospace industry is expected to provide opportunities for the development of components related to the engineering and avionic service industries, as well as the development of advanced materials technology. To develop composite materials CTRM formed joint ventures with local as well as other foreign composite material companies. For example, in a joint venture with PETRONAS, CTRM formed Eagle Aircraft Malaysia (EAM), which then acquired 100 per cent ownership of Eagle Aircraft of Perth, Australia. Other measures to support the development of the composite materials industry also have included the establishment of an Advance Materials Research Centre (AMRC) at Kulim High-Tech Park in which a directory on researchers, equipment and research activities in the area of advanced materials was made available.

HUMAN RESOURCE DEVELOPMENT

The rapid economic growth in a fast changing global environment has created an increasing demand for both skilled and unskilled workers, exceeding the new entrants in the job markets. The intense competition among employers for labour by offering better wages and benefit has created greater pressure on wages, as well as a higher incidence of job hopping and staff pinching, notably from public sector to private sector. In 1994, wages of all levels of employees in the manufacturing sector increased by 6.7 per cent during the first seven months, whereas productivity only increased by 2.2 per cent resulting in a 4.4 per cent increase in labour costs. Even though manufacturing wages comprised only about 7 per cent of the total sales value of manufactured goods, the increase in the unit labour cost would make Malaysian products less competitive in the domestic and international markets (ibid., p. 32).

The thrust of human resource development policy as envisaged in the Second OPP is to meet the objective of growth and equity. Since the economy requires a good supply of skilled and technologically proficient labour, greater emphasis will be given to the development of educated, well-trained, productive and flexible manpower. The Second OPP (ibid., 1991, pp. 169–70) states:

> The future growth of the economy will place greater demand for the high quality labour force which is versatile and which adapts quickly to a changing industrial environment. A skilled and productive workforce is a prerequisite to maintaining a favourable investment climate and the

competitive edge of Malaysian products in the world market. To meet this demand, the education and skill delivery system will be made more responsive to the requirements of a dynamic labour force.

Within the context of the Second OPP employment targets of achieving full employment by the year 2000 (with unemployment at 4 per cent), a total of 2.4 million new jobs will have to be created (ibid., p. 161). The services sector is expected to play a critical role, with the wholesale and retail trade, hotels and restaurants subsectors providing the principal catalyst with 34.3 per cent of the new jobs, while the manufacturing sector too will be relied upon to absorb more job-seekers during the period (providing 36.1 per cent of the new jobs).

The general shortage of skilled and professional workers is reduced by allowing recruitment from abroad. Except for a few cases, since Malaysia is abundant in unskilled and semi-skilled workers, the inflow of foreign unskilled and semi-skilled labour is controlled to a level such that the excess domestic labour could be absorbed. To help achieve this, the labour-intensive manufacturing activities and projects are encouraged in the relatively labour-abundant, less industrialised regions, particularly the eastern corridor states of peninsular Malaysia as well as Sabah and Sarawak. This relocation would not only enable employers to get cheap labour but also reduce the regional economic imbalances in the country. Various incentives, such as pioneer status and investment tax allowances are given to industrial projects in these regions.

To help generate a more skilled workforce, the government, under the Ministries of Human Resources, Youth and Sports, Public Enterprise and the People's Trust Council (MARA) as well as the industrial management training programme, has allocated funds to train the personnel of R&D agencies such as the Standards and Industrial Research Institute of Malaysia (SIRIM), the Malaysian Agricultural Research and Development Institute (MARDI), the Palm Oil Research Institute of Malaysia (PORIM) and the Malaysian Institute of Micro-Electronic System (MIMOS).

Despite the changes in intersectoral shares, the agricultural sector is undoubtedly still crucial in terms of employment absorption. In 1990, for instance, it was estimated that slightly more that 1.8 million people were in agriculture out of the total working population of 6.6 million. Although its share had decreased to 27.8 per cent in 1990 from 31.3 per cent in 1985, the percentage share in 1990 was still the largest, followed by the manufacturing sector with 19.5 per cent (ibid.). Basically, labour absorption has increased through the expansion of the non-agricultural or urban-based sectors. Even though this trend creates a problem of labour shortage in agriculture, it nevertheless increases labour mobility from the rural sector. This trend will undoubtedly become more apparent with the increasing pace of industrialisation, such that by the year 2000 employment in the agricultural sector is expected to decline, reducing its share in total employment to 20.0 per cent. This is in stark contrast to the more robust sectors such as manufacturing which indicated the fastest annual growth rate of 5.2 per cent during the 1991–2000 period.

BALANCE OF PAYMENTS – STRONG EXTERNAL BALANCE

For a very open economy like Malaysia, where foreign trade is one of the major influences on economic activity, the balance of payments position plays a crucial role in the economic life of the nation. The basic strength of Malaysia's balance of payments rests in the merchandise account which, except during 1981–2, had consistently been in surplus annually since the 1950s, reaching its peak of RM14 703 million in 1987. In the early 1990s, the average surplus was RM6333 per annum. This permitted the country to pay for its imports of both intermediate and capital goods necessary for domestic investment, as well as consumption goods to meet the rising standard of living. However, the surpluses in the trade balance were partially offset by a persistent deficit in service payments and transfers, resulting in a deficit in the current account during the early 1960s, 1971–2, 1974–5, the early 1980s and 1990s. The deficit in the current account was offset by the surplus in the capital account, which was mainly due to substantial long-term capital and, to some extent, short-term capital inflows from abroad. The Malaysian balance of payments had been running a surplus since the 1960s, except in 1961, 1967, 1981–3 and 1988.

CURRENT ACCOUNT

Since Independence, the contribution of the manufacturing sector to export earnings has been increasingly significant. Its contribution to total export increased from 12 per cent in 1970 to 74 per cent in 1993. Between 1970 and 1993, the average growth rate of manufactured exports was 22 per cent per annum, making the manufacturing sector the leading export earner in the 1990s. The growth of manufactured exports is reflected in the changing structure of the manufacturing industry in Malaysia. The leading activity in the early 1990s has been electrical machinery, appliances and parts which contribute most to exports of manufactured goods; about 61 per cent in 1993 as compared to the leading activities in the early 1970s which were food, wood and petroleum products. In 1970, the respective shares of those activities to the manufactured exports were about 15, 15 and 26 per cent. This shows a trend in which Malaysia is moving from light to heavy industries. In the long run, these high technology and capital-intensive industries will not only change the nation's manpower and financial requirements, but also its imports, production and export configurations.

Even though its significance has decreased over time, until the late 1970s the agricultural sector still remained the most important source of export earnings. However, as the economy entered the 1980s, agricultural significance has been decreasing. The rates of growth in agricultural export during the 1970s and 1980s were 16 and 2 per cent, respectively. In the 1990s, the value of agricultural export was falling. In the 1960s, Malaysia's export was highly dependent on only two commodities, namely, rubber and tin; making the economy very vulnerable to changes in the external market. In order to reduce this heavy dependency, the government diversified the agricultural sector and the effects can be seen particularly in the decreasing percentage contributions of rubber and the increasing contributions of timber and palm oil to the export sector in the 1970s compared with those of the 1960s. In the 1980s and 1990s, heavy emphasis on industrial development had caused exports to be led by manufactured products.

The government had identified six primary commodities, namely, rubber, palm oil, sawlogs, sawn timber, tin and petroleum. The palm oil industry has also shown a tremendous performance in terms of the growth of its output during 1970s. This rapid increase in output was due to the continuation of large government land development programmes and the replacement of rubber with oil palm in estate and smallholder replanting. The government industrialisation policies gave support for further development of the 'downstream' processing of palm oil products. As for timber, the sustained demand for tropical hardwoods and semi-hardwoods had led to a steady growth of timber export. Since 1980 the value of tin export has shown a decreasing pattern. This was partly the result of the economic diversification policy in 1970s and mainly due to the gradual depletion of tin reserves and falling prices. Nevertheless, as far as the mining sector is concerned, the decreasing trend in tin production has been offset by the emergence and development of the petroleum industry notably in the early 1970s. This industry has shown a tremendous rate of growth. Between 1970 and 1990, the export value of petroleum increased fifty-two fold. This high growth mainly occured for two reasons; the first being the discovery and exploitation of oil along the east coast of Peninsular Malaysia, especially in the late 1970s and early 1980s, and off-shore oil off Sabah and Sarawak, where production started to increase tremendously in the late 1960s and 1970s. The second reason has been that the price of petroleum was increasing tremendously especially in the 1970s and early 1980s. In the late 1980s the global recession put a downward pressure on the petroleum price and it improved somewhat in the 1990s.

Importing has grown at 14.4 per cent per annum during the period 1970–93. There has been a changing structure in the import sector in the last two decades. In the 1960s, the biggest proportion of imports was in consumer goods; but as the economy entered the 1970s and thereafter, the proportion of consumer goods to gross imports has decreased and the shares of investment and intermediate goods have increased. In 1970, the respective shares of consumption, investment and intermediate goods were 29, 25 and 35 per cent; but in 1993 the respective shares were 16, 41 and 43 per cent, indicating that intermediate goods dominated import demand.

The decline in the proportion of consumer goods in gross imports was the result of the import-substitution policy implemented during the 1960s. This policy particularly encouraged the growth of industries which processed most of the beverages, tobacco, sugar, dairy products, biscuits, edible oils, grain and rice, which were previously imported. Most of the imported consumer goods were food and consumer durables. The largest proportion of imports of intermediate goods was for the manufacturing industry. This was associated with the continued expansion of more capital-intensive and sophisticated industries, especially vehicle assembly and automobile manufacturing, electronics, chemicals, foods and plastics. For construction activities, the main imported products were construction materials and components. Most of the investment goods imported were metal products (including machinery), and together with transport equipment, this import was associated with high growth in private and public investment

The services account of the Malaysian balance of payments has been running at a deficit since the 1960s, which means that there have been more payments abroad for services rendered by non-residents than the receipts from abroad for services rendered by residents. The services account mainly consists of payments and receipts for freight and insurance, other transportation, travel, investment income and government transactions. For certain years the services account deficit tends to increase over time. Since 1965, the item that experienced the largest deficit has been investment income. The large part of this, which is due to non-residents, consists of profits and dividends on foreign investment in Malaysia, and the remainder is the payments on foreign loans.

Even though the size of Malaysian equity participation in the corporate sector has increased over the years of development, foreign investment will continue to play a vital role in the future economic development of the nation, especially in the expansion of the manufacturing sector which most requires foreign technology and expertise. Therefore, the absolute level of investment income payments is expected to increase with the level of foreign investment, even though their relative importance may decline over time. The second largest item which causes the deficit in the services account is freight and insurance. Most of these payments are incurred in connection with imports. Therefore, increases in import volume as well as increases in freight rates have caused increases in net payments of freight and insurance, especially since Malaysia does not have a large merchant fleet. This means that a large part of its international trade is carried out in foreign vessels. Passenger transportation for international travel also depends mostly on foreign ships and aircraft. Due to various efforts by the Tourist Development Corporation to encourage foreigners to visit Malaysia, particularly through Visit Malaysia Years, the travel item has been in surplus since 1990.

To reduce service deficit various measures (ibid., 1994b, p. 33) have been taken including:

a. encouraging local companies to invest abroad and repatriate investment income to Malaysia;
b. increasing the reinvestment allowance to encourage companies to reinvest their profit in Malaysia;
c. increasing the nation's capability in free on board (fob) and exporting on a cost, insurance and freight (cif) basis. This is done by transforming the domestic freight forwarding industry into multimodal transport industry;
d. increasing the retention of reinsurance premiums in the country by allowing financially strong foreign reinsurance companies to operate locally;
e. encouraging tourism and exports of other services which would increase receipts of foreign exchange from royalties, contracts and professional services;
f. providing fiscal incentives to encourage parents to send their children to local institutions of higher learning rather than overseas.

The transfer account had only been in surplus since 1988. Most of the deficits before 1988 were accounted for by the net payments of pensions to retired personnel of the civil service, private enterprises and maintenance money for relatives abroad. These payments were partially offset by net receipts of intergovernmental grants for defence, development and training of personnels.

THE CAPITAL ACCOUNT

Except in 1987–8 the balance on long-term capital has been positive since the 1960s. The growth rate of this balance has been increasing, especially after 1970, due to an increasing inflow of foreign direct investment, resulting from various incentives given by the government. These had always been revised and modified occasionally to suit the needs of foreign investors. The deficit in 1987–8 was caused by decreasing long-term capital inflows due to an economic slowdown.

The long-term capital account consists of net inflows of both official and private capital. The official capital takes the form of loans from abroad to the government and some non-financial public enterprises.

The loans were mainly used to finance various development projects such as the Muda Irrigation Scheme, the East–West Highway, the Jengka Triangle Land Settlement Scheme, the Temenggor Hydro-Electric Project, the Butterworth Deepwater Wharves and the Pergau Hydro-Electric Project. Specific project loans were usually obtained from international development banks such as the Asian Development Bank, the World Bank, foreign governments or foreign official development finance institutions such as the Overseas Economic Cooperation Fund of Japan or the Kreditanstalt fur Wiederaufbau of the Federal Republic of Germany.

There had also been a reduction in foreign assets held by the government and statutory agencies abroad, which was partly offset by the government's subscription to various international organisations. This also caused an additional net inflow of official long-term capital.

The net private long-term capital also has been running a rising surplus since 1965. Much of the private capital inflows now represented new capital flowing in from abroad and retained profits of foreign companies resident in the country ploughed back for reinvestment.

In the 1960s, mainly due to lower profitability in the rubber and tin-mining industries, which consequently caused a smaller amount of profits to be reinvested, the inflow of private long-term capital tended to decline. However, in the 1970s, because of the acceleration in growth of domestic activity and the good performance of the export sector, corporate investment increased. The increased investment levels can be seen in manufacturing, exploration for and production of oil, copper mining and large reinvestment in the traditional plantation and mining sectors. In the 1990s, the superb economic growth had increased the inflow of direct foreign investment. All these factors contributed to the increasing balance on the private long-term capital.

The private financial capital represents the short-term capital; invested originally for a period of one year or less. The balance on private financial capital consists of net borrowing or lending by the commercial bank in connection with short-term trade financing. In the case of Malaysian branches of foreign banks, it includes borrowings from their head offices to supplement their resources from Malaysian sources. In the 1970s, this balance showed that there had been more net outflow than net inflow, arising mainly from investment abroad of some of the export earnings of the National Petroleum Corporation (PETRONAS). However, as the economy entered the 1980s, this account showed a positive balance, particularly in the 1990s due to substantial inflows of foreign fund. These inflows were encouraged by sound economic fundamentals, large interest rate differentials in favour of Malaysia, bouyant activities in the local stock market and expectation of further appreciation of the ringgit (ibid., 1994a, p. 88).

The favourable balance of payments position since the 1960s has led the net external reserves of the central bank, comprising gold, foreign exchange, reserve position with the International Monetary Fund (IMF) and holding of SDRs, to accumulate. During the period 1970–93, the reserves have grown at 28 per cent per annum. The fluctuations of the external reserves reflect mainly that the fluctuations were due to variations in the prices of and demand for Malaysia's major exports and net inflow of short-term and long-term private capital. For instance, due to good performance of merchandise exports and inflows of foreign capital in the late 1980s and early 1990s, the net external reserves of the central bank increased for the fifth consecutive year to a new peak of RM76 435 million (equivalent to SDR20 879 million) at the end of 1993 (ibid., p. 309).

Statistical Appendix

Figure 3.1 Monetary growth and inflation, 1974–93

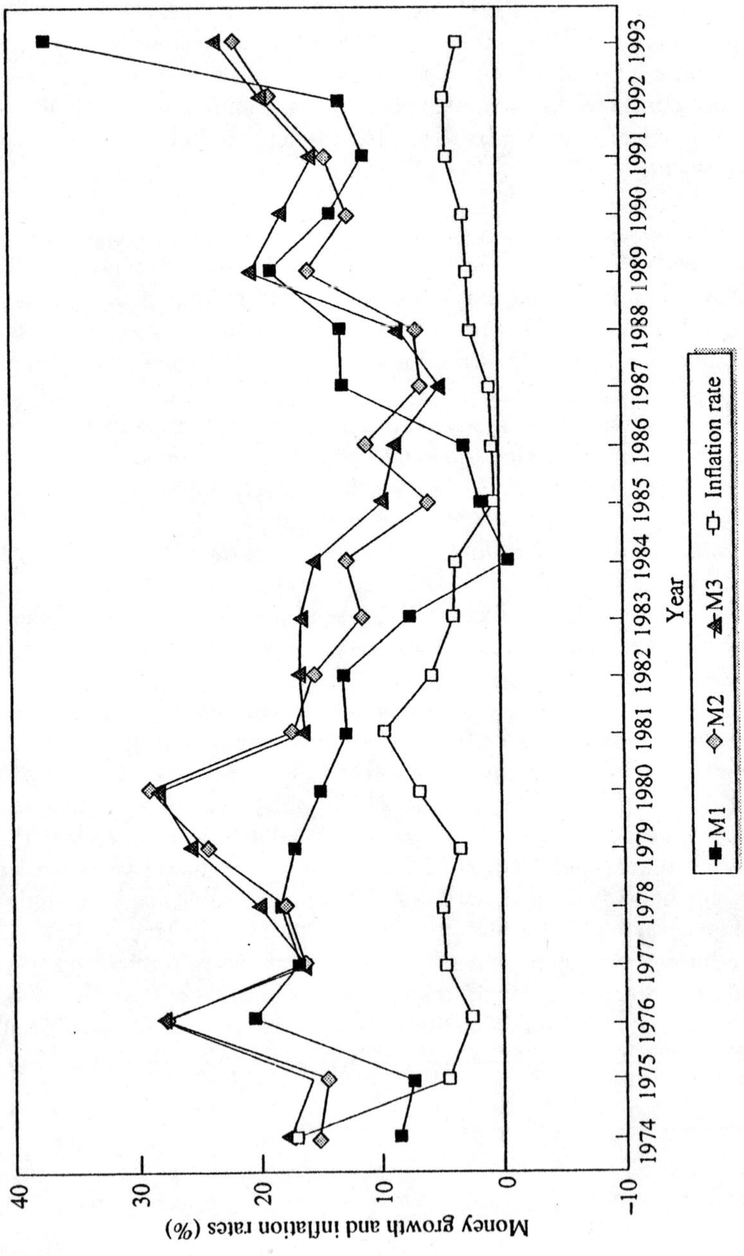

Table 3.1 Expenditure in Gross National Product at current prices (percentage of GNP)

	1971–5	*1976–80*	*1981–5*	*1986–90*	*1991–3*
Consumption	77.7	69.5	72.5	69.2	69.0
Private	60.2	53.1	55.1	53.6	54.8
Public	17.5	16.4	17.4	15.6	14.2
Investment	24.4	27.4	36.3	29.0	37.0
Private[1]	16.6	17.4	19.0	18.0	25.0
Public	7.8	10.0	17.3	11.0	12.0
Net Foreign Trade	–2.1	3.1	–8.8	1.8	–6.0
GNP	100.0	100.0	100.0	100.0	100.0
Gross National Savings[2]	20.8	30.0	27.5	30.8	31.0

[1] Includes inventories
[2] Gross capital formation +/– current account in the balance of payments
Source: Central bank of Malaysia, Treasury and Department of Statistics.

Table 3.2 Growth in manufacturing production, 1990–95 (percentages)

Industry		*Annual growth rate*			*Average annual growth rate*	*Average annual growth rate*
	1990	*1991*	*1992*	*1993*	*1991–3*	*1994–5*
Resource based	9.4	7.9	8.0	9.7	8.6	10.7
Food manufacturing	0.7	13.1	11.9	9.0	11.3	7.0
Oil and fats	9.5	–16.3	3.3	12.5	–0.9	5.7
Beverages	14.5	1.8	4.7	–10.0	–1.4	2.3
Tobacco manufacturing	7.2	1.1	–5.1	–7.5	–3.9	2.2
Wood and cork products (excl. furniture)	14.3	5.2	10.9	21.4	12.3	13.4
Industrial chemicals	1.9	15.6	2.8	8.5	8.8	12.6
Other chemical products	11.0	10.5	14.3	6.2	10.3	10.7
Petroleum refineries	13.8	6.3	3.7	13.0	7.6	7.9
Rubber remilling and latex processing	–5.1	–4.7	2.3	1.5	–0.4	2.0
Rubber products	18.0	19.8	15.4	20.2	18.4	14.0
Manufacture of plastic products	22.6	12.2	17.1	13.5	14.2	13.4
Glass and glass products	7.5	13.2	6.2	–5.0	4.5	7.8

Table 3.2 *continued*

Industry	*1990*	*Annual growth rate* *1991*	*1992*	*1993*	*Average-annual growth rate 1991–3*	*Average-annual growth rate 1994–5*
Non-metallic mineral products	21.0	19.7	10.2	6.5	12.0	15.2
Non-ferrous metal basic industries	8.0	–1.1	16.4	1.8	5.5	11.0
Non-resource based	25.2	22.7	13.3	15.7	17.2	13.3
Manufacture of textiles	11.4	5.9	15.6	25.2	15.3	9.2
Wearing apparel (excl. footwear)	4.4	0.3	4.6	2.0	2.3	4.8
Iron and steel basic industries	14.2	13.4	19.0	22.5	18.2	17.5
Fabricated metal products	18.6	18.7	43.4	38.4	33.1	14.7
Electrical machinery, apparatus, appliances and supplies manufacture of machinery (excl. electrical)	14.7	64.6	33.9	–2.0	29.3	9.9
Electrical machinery	33.7	28.8	11.5	15.0	18.2	14.4
Transport equipments	32.5	17.1	–6.2	4.0	4.5	11.2
Total	15.7	13.9	10.5	12.5	12.3	11.9

Source: Government of Malaysia (1993), p. 108.

Table 3.3 Export of manufactured goods, 1990–3 (RM million)

Industry	*1990*	*1991*	*1992*	*1993*	*Average Annual Growth Rate, 1991–3*
Resource based	8286	9925	11565	14926	21.7
Food	1966	2173	2241	2684	10.9
Beverages and tobacco	95	165	203	196	27.3
Petroleum products	1285	1194	1551	1651	8.7
Chemicals & chemical products	1468	1880	2305	2470	18.9

Table 3.3 *continued*

Industry	*1990*	*1991*	*1992*	*1993*	*Average annual growth rate, 1991–3*
Rubber products (excl. rubber footwear)	1354	1803	2099	3383	35.7
Wood products	1347	1787	2273	3522	37.8
Non-metallic mineral products	771	923	893	1020	9.8
Non-resource based	33914	47234	53190	65297	24.4
Textiles, clothings and footwear	3907	4913	5149	6723	19.8
Manufacture of metal	1577	1892	2199	2018	8.6
Electrical machinery, appliances & supplies	26502	37006	41645	52228	25.4
Transport equipment	1928	3423	4197	4328	30.9
Other manufactures	4633	6608	8011	5126	3.4
Total	46833	63767	72766	85349	22.1
Percentage of national gross exports	58.8	67.5	70.2	71.0	

Source: Government of Malaysia (1993), p. 110.

Table 3.4 Balance of payments, 1990–5 (RM million)

	1990		*1993*		*1995*	
	Value	*% of GNP*	*Value*	*% of GNP*	*Value*	*% of GNP*
Merchandise balance	7093	6.4	13227	8.4	15382	7.7
Exports	77458	69.9	116979	73.6	145175	73.1
Imports	70365	63.5	103752	65.2	129793	65.4
Services balance	–9723	–8.8	–12876	–8.1	–12397	–6.2
Freight and insurance	–3837	–3.5	–4290	–2.7	–4961	–2.5
Other transportation	–25	0.0	–71	0.0	234	0.1
Travel	632	0.6	796	0.5	1722	0.9
Investment income	–5072	–4.6	–7748	–4.9	–8030	–4.0
Government transactions	–3	0.0	39	0.0	47	0.0
Other services	–1418	–1.3	–1602	–1.0	–1409	–0.7

Table 3.4 continued

	1990		*1993*		*1995*	
	Value	*% of GNP*	*Value*	*% of GNP*	*Value*	*% of GNP*
Transfers balance	147	0.1	160	0.1	250	0.1
Current account balance	–2483	–2.3	511	0.4	3236	1.6
Capital account balance						
Official long-term capital	–2836	–2.6	–519	–0.3	—	—
Corporate investment	6309	5.7	10500	6.6	—	—
Central bank reserves	27021	24.5	57000	35.8	—	—
Months of retained imports	4.1		6.1		—	—

Source: Government of Malaysia (1993), p. 36.

References

Ali, Anuwar and Saleh, M. Zainudin (1994) 'Pembangunan Perindustrian di Malaysia', in Ali, Supian and Saleh, M. Zainudin (eds), *Rancangan Malaysia Keenam – Prioriti Pengukuhan Negara* (Bangi: Universiti Kebangsaan Malaysia Press).

Government of Malaysia (1971) *Second Malaysia Plan, 1971–75* (Kuala Lumpur: Government Printers).

Government of Malaysia (1986) *Industrial Master Plan, Executive Highlights* (Kuala Lumpur).

Government of Malaysia (1991) *The Second Outline Perspective Plan, 1991–2000* (Kuala Lumpur: National Printing Department).

Government of Malaysia (1993) *Mid-term Review of the Sixth Malaysia Plan* (Kuala Lumpur: Government Printers).

Government of Malaysia (1994a) *Bank Negara Malaysia, Annual Report, 1993* (Kuala Lumpur).

Government of Malaysia (1994b) *Economic Report, 1994/95* (Kuala Lumpur: Ministry of Finance).

Government of Malaysia (1994c) *International Trade and Industry Report* (Kuala Lumpur: Ministry of International Trade and Industry).

Hisashi Yokoyama and Tamin, Mokhtar (eds) (1991) *Malaysian Economy in Transition* (Tokyo: Institute of Developing Economies).

Mohamad, Mahathir (1991) *Malaysia: The Way Forward* (Kuala Lumpur: Centre for Economic Research, Malaysian Business Council).

Saleh, M. Zainudin (1991) *A Structural Model for Malaysian Balance of Payments, 1962–82* (New York: Garland).

Taylor, Michael and Ward, Marion (1994) 'Industrial Transformation since 1970: The Context and Means', in Brookfield, Harold (ed.), *Transformation with Industrialisation in Peninsular Malaysia* (Kuala Lumpur: Oxford University Press).

Thirlwall, A.P. (1974) *Inflation, Saving and Growth in Developing Economies* (New York: St Martin's Press).

Thirlwall, A.P. (1994) *Growth and Development – with Special Reference to Developing Economies* (London: Macmillan).

Yusof, Zainal Aznam and Phang Hooi Eng (1993) 'Determinants of Industrial Market Structure in Malaysia, 1970–90, *Bank Negara Malaysia Discussion Paper No. 22* (Kuala Lumpur: Bank Negara).

4 Microeconomic Approaches to Socio-economic Development in the Third World

Supian Ali and Mohammad Anuar Adnan

INTRODUCTION

The current interest in socio-economic development in the Third World in general, and in the East Asian region in particular, revolves around the perplexing issue of why the East Asians seem to be successful while debunking the textbook models of development, preferring instead to improvise on their own philosophies and societal needs.

The economic performance of the East Asian countries over the last two decades has been spectacular. This picture was totally different in the mid-1960s when Gunnar Myrdal confidently wrote *The Asian Drama* (1968). Subtitling his great work as 'An Inquiry into the Poverty of Nations', Myrdal drew oblique attention to the industrialised West and the chronic poverty in the Third World and in South Asia in particular. His institutional theory of development did not get off the ground here and above all he doubted whether the democratic states of Asia have the right political will to carry through large-scale socio-economic reforms as successfully as in the West or even in the socialist countries. Of course, he did not live to see that his pessimism was largely misplaced especially in the case of East Asia. The East Asian countries hitched their economic dreams not to that of Europe but to that of Japan. They brushed aside Protestant ethics inherent in Western economic thought and loudly declared their preferences for home-grown social values instead.

THE EAST ASIAN ECONOMIC SYSTEM

The East Asian NIEs, Taiwan and South Korea, and the city-states of Hong Kong and Singapore, and their neighbours such as Thailand and Malaysia can be considered as diverse advocates of the alternative approach to development. Their initial conditions and rates of progress were far from similar. Taiwan and South Korea were poor in natural resources, but rich in human capital with surplus labour. Malaysia and Thailand were, on the other hand, rich in natural resources but initially poor in human capital.

Taken as a whole these countries are ardent followers of *laissez-faire*. But there are those who believed that they too have benefited from interventionist government policies. However complex their social structures, these countries displayed the right capacity to adapt to changes quickly. Their governments are flexible and succeeded in creating the right ruling elites to execute these changes, which are invariably tied to political visions based on general consensus. Asian societies are not individualistic and they have long harnessed group dynamics which relied on clan and family ties and appeared to be non-optimal organisations to Western eyes.

However, there are certain common domestic policies which enabled the East Asians to develop faster than the other Third-World countries (Shinichi, 1993). First, the government practises an open-door policy both for international trade and foreign direct investment. Secondly, government policies are oriented to export-led economic growth. Thirdly, the foreign exchange rate is maintained below the purchasing power parity level for price-elastic export products to boost their sales and curb imports, as well as to encourage capital inflow.

In addition, these East Asian economies displayed large doses of common characteristics which include:

a. high rate of capital accumulation;
b. high rate of saving;
c. appropriate transfer of technology;
d. quality human resource;
e. export-oriented industrial strategies;
f. conducive to foreign capital inflow;
g. sound fiscal and monetary policies;
h. growth with fair income distribution;
i. privatisation with declining public sector;
j. relative political stability.

Capital and Saving

There is no doubt that capital accumulation in the region is high relative to other Third-World countries. The East Asian capital formation ratio to GNP, for instance, increased from 12.6 per cent (for Indonesia) in the 1960s to as high as 39 per cent in 1990 (see Table 4.1). Singapore and China shared this

Table 4.1 Rates of capital accumulation and saving in selected Asia-Pacific and Latin American economies, 1965–90

	GDP per capita 1990 ($)	*Rate of capital accumulation*				*Rate of saving*			
		1965–72	*1973–8*	*1979–83*	*1990*	*1965–72*	*1973–8*	*1979–83*	*1990*
Industrial market economy									
Japan	23 801	31.9	35.9	32.0	33.0	30.8	33.6	36.8	34.0
NIE									
Singapore	12 706	36.7	34.9	40.4	39.0	23.6	32.8	35.6	45.0
Hong Kong	12 304	36.0	—	—	28.0	29.0	—	—	33.0
Taiwan	7 905	26.2	30.6	32.4	—	23.1	29.3	37.0	—
South Korea	5 693	24.1	29.0	30.0	37.0	14.9	24.9	23.7	37.0
Developing economies									
Malaysia	2 368	19.6	25.7	33.4	34.0	20.8	27.2	26.3	33.0
Thailand	1 402	23.8	25.4	25.3	37.0	21.3	23.6	20.5	34.0
Philippines	709	20.9	28.6	29.6	22.0	17.1	23.9	23.3	16.0
Indonesia	582	12.6	20.6	23.0	36.0	6.9	18.8	20.1	37.0
Giant economies									
China	325	—	—	33.6	39.0	—	—	33.2	43.0
India	336			23.0					20.0

Table 4.1 *Continued*

	GDP per capita 1990 ($)	Rate of capital accumulation				Rate of saving			
		1965–72	1973–8	1979–83	1990	1965–72	1973–8	1979–83	1990
Latin American economies									
Venezuela	2 920	29.1	35.4	26.2	9.0	29.8	36.1	29.3	29.0
Argentina	2 350	20.4	24.6	20.5	9.0	20.3	26.2	17.9	16.0
Mexico	1 860	21.3	23.4	26.1	20.0	19.2	20.2	24.2	19.0
Brazil	1 810	25.6	28.1	22.5	22.0	24.0	24.0	17.6	23.0
Chile	1 320	15.3	15.3	17.2	20.0	13.0	11.9	7.0	23.0
Ecuador	1 160	18.6	26.4	24.2	19.0	11.3	20.4	20.5	22.0
Colombia	1 139	19.0	18.8	20.0	19.0	15.4	19.1	17.2	25.0
Peru	1 090	16.7	16.0	17.0	23.0	15.2	11.4	13.5	23.0

Note: Figures for Taiwan are for 1970 instead of 1965, and those for Singapore are for 1982 instead of 1983.
Source: *World Development Report, 1985, 1986, 1992*; national statistical yearbooks.

high magnitude. Meanwhile, the saving ratio was as low as 6.9 per cent (Indonesia) in the mid-1960s, and as high as 45 per cent (Singapore) in 1990. Notice that the corresponding ratios for Latin American countries were not as impressive. The high saving ratio for Singapore and Malaysia originated from the forced saving system channelled through their respective Central Provident Fund and Employees Provident Fund. On the other hand, Taiwan's high rate of saving was due to accumulated funds held by the government. Besides the government held funds, the East Asian private household savings are also high. Thus almost all the East Asian region growth phenomenon is traceable to these high ratios of capital formation and saving rates during the last three decades. The exception here is the Philippines which have experienced a string of natural disasters.

Productivity and Efficiency

However, there is no guarantee that rapid growth will follow once the rate of capital accumulation is high. Capital must first be used efficiently. The incremental capital–output ratio (ICOR) index is used to capture the state of capital utilisation here. Table 4.2 shows ICOR and growth rates for the Asian region and Latin America.

During the two periods shown, 1965–73 and 1974–83, most East Asian countries showed rising trends in their ICOR. The rise, however, is moderate, for example, Taiwan, from 2.6 to 3.7; South Korea, from 2.4 to 4.0; Malaysia from 2.9 to 4.0; and Indonesia, from 1.6 to 3.1. These moderate rates indicate that a number of countries in the East Asian region, for instance, Taiwan, have successfully adopted modern technology. In the case of South Korea, it managed to register a marginally higher ICOR, although having per capita income lower than Taiwan. This is due to South Korea's deliberate preference for heavy industries. It should be noted in passing that under normal circumstances ICOR rises as per capita income rises. The Philippines might be an exception here because its ICOR is comparable to that of Japan although its income level is nowhere near that of Japan. Interestingly enough the rates of capital accumulation in East Asia although not uniform show a similar growth pattern. In contrast, India's ICOR is seen to be higher than that of Japan despite its low income level. This is a reflection of India's inefficient use of capital as is also the case in the Latin American countries, such as Argentina, Chile and Peru.

Constraints in Agriculture

In East Asia, productivity efforts in the past have been concerned with enhancing the efficiency of capital utilisation and reducing costs especially

Table 4.2 International comparison of incremental capital–output ratio, 1965–83

	Growth rate (1965–73)	*1965–73* rate of accumul.	ICOR (1965–73)	Growth rate (1974–83)	*1974–83* rate of accumul.	ICOR (1974–83)
Industrial market economy						
Japan	9.8	30.0	3.1	4.3	22.7	5.2
Asian NIE						
Singapore	13.0	36.7	2.8	8.2	37.6	4.6
Hong Kong	—	—	—	—	—	—
Taiwan	10.1	26.2	2.6	8.5	31.5	3.7
South Korea	10.0	24.1	2.4	7.3	29.5	4.0
ASEAN–4						
Malaysia	6.7	19.6	2.9	7.3	29.1	4.0
Thailand	7.8	23.8	3.1	6.9	25.4	3.7
Philippines	5.4	20.9	3.9	5.4	29.1	5.4
Indonesia	8.1	12.6	1.6	7.0	21.8	3.1
Giant economies						
India	3.9	18.3	4.7	4.0	23.2	5.8
South Asia						
Pakistan	5.4	16.3	3.0	5.6	15.9	2.8
Sri Lanka	4.2	16.1	3.8	5.2	23.1	4.4
Burma	—	—	—	5.5	15.8	2.8
Nepal	—	—	—	3.7	13.8	3.7
Bangladesh	—	—	—	5.2	9.4	1.8
Latin America						
Argentina	4.3	20.4	4.7	0.4	22.6	56.4
Brazil	9.8	25.8	2.6	4.8	25.3	5.3
Chile	3.4	15.3	4.5	2.9	16.3	5.6
Colombia	6.4	19.0	3.0	3.9	19.4	5.0
Mexico	7.9	21.3	2.7	5.6	24.7	4.4
Peru	3.5	16.7	4.8	1.8	17.5	9.7
Venezuela	5.1	29.1	5.7	2.5	25.8	10.3

Source: World Development Report, 1985 and 1986; national statistical yearbooks.

within its agricultural sector. Resources have now been channelled increasingly to non-agricultural sectors, although agriculture still absorbs a large proportion of the workforce. Agriculture's share in GDP is on the decline but in many East Asian countries rural and agricultural regions are still important political constituencies which governing parties can ill afford to neglect.

Thus governments have continued to pursue vigorous agricultural development policies, including land reforms, food self-sufficiency, diversification and poverty eradication. With greater economic growth farm diversification has brought progress to rural Thailand, Indonesia, Malaysia and Bangladesh. Massive infrastructural improvement and price policies were implemented. Regional irrigation projects have played an equally important role in producing double cropping of rice harvests.

Constraints in Industrialisation

Resource constraints quickly surfaced with rapid industrialisation, shortage of capital and labour became a constant bugbear of development. Various constraint patterns emerged across East Asia. For instance, Taiwan experienced rapid industrialisation with decreasing farm workers but increasing farm size, thanks to previous land reforms. On the other hand, we find a rapid industrialisation pattern which causes rural–urban migration of the labour force without completely wiping out the commercial plantation sector. This is typical of Thailand, Malaysia and Indonesia.

At another level of development we find those city-states of East Asia which are becoming power-houses of development, focusing on total productivity enhancement encompassing quality of life, socio-economic development, human resource development, that is, material aspects which almost all of the East Asian economies aspire to achieve in the shortest possible time.

VARIETIES OF ASIAN POLICIES

The most successful examples of Asian industrialisation, namely Japan and South Korea, do not strictly follow the conventional Western model. Similarly, specialisation and comparative advantage are not religiously adhered to in some of the Asian countries. For instance, Taiwan and South Korea are poor in natural resources, but with a labour surplus and rich in human capital. In the 1950s they had implemented an import-substitution strategy, but by the 1960s they had shifted their industrial strategy to primary export production. During these two decades they produced labour intensive non-durables as expected of them. However, in the two following decades they shifted their emphasis to capital-intensive products at competitive prices to the rest of the world.

East Asian economies are open economies with liberal international trade policies on the whole. But they have also implemented interventionist policies, low rates of monetary growth giving rise to low inflation and positive real rates of interest. The 'night watchman' function of governments is remarkably free from the adverse effects of successive changes in political leaderships. In fact the stable political environment here, despite occasional havoc in some parliaments, has helped to depoliticise the market system.

South Korea and Taiwan best illustrate the East Asian model of implementing both interventionist and liberal free market policies simultaneously without adverse effects or overt clashes of political ideologies. Thailand, Malaysia and the Philippines followed them with considerable success too. But Malaysia is unique. The presence of government is seen and felt at every corner and in many aspects of everyday life despite professing an open door economy.

Similarly, growth management in the East Asian region is hardly uniform. At the country level, a variety of policies can be found. In Taiwan, for instance, it undertook tight fiscal policies combined with budgetary deficits during the early phases of development. After 1984 it generated budgetary surpluses for most of the decade (Ranis, 1991). As for South Korea, budgetary deficits were limited to be around below 1 per cent of GDP. Thus whether during periods of booms or depressions governments in these two countries exercised restraints.

Government intervention in markets seemed to have promoted rather than inhibited the welfare-oriented growth in Taiwan, South Korea, Malaysia and Singapore. However, this comment certainly cannot be extended to all Third-World countries. For instance, interventionist policies in India failed to promote growth with distributional justice. Growth also failed to take off in Pakistan and Bangladesh even though they have relatively smaller doses of government intervention. It can be concluded that it is the flexibility of the government that is important here, not its absolute size to meet the challenges of growth with distribution.

Sometimes inflexibility can contribute to heavy costs as when macroeconomic policy fails to deliver microeconomic effects in the market economy. The experience of Malaysia here is a case in point. (World Bank, 1989, p. 46).

Since 1982, the Malaysian public policy dilemma has been how to cure its external and internal imbalances without at the same time endangering its economic growth. Various combinations of fiscal and monetary policies have been tried and they succeeded in bringing down inflation rates. But the cost has been rising public debt, and a slower growth rate, although it was impressive by outside standards. It is apparent that counter-cyclical public expenditure policy could not be used to raise growth rate in a sustained fashion. Efforts in response to external shocks by changes in public expenditures had created inflexibilities in the whole economy. This created new problems affecting wage fixation in the private sector. As the government sector in Malaysia assumed wage leadership, downward stickiness in nominal wages coupled with low inflation rates brought about a surge in wages in the manufacturing and services sectors way above their productivity increases.

This wage spiral has also happened in South Korea and Singapore. But in South Korea rising unit labour costs have been offset through exchange rate policy, hence preventing any decline in its international competitiveness (see Table 4.3).

Unfortunately, Malaysia's real exchange rate followed the yen–US dollar exchange rate movements rather than responding to Malaysia's terms of trade and global competitiveness. With this wage demand on the rise, the share of wage income in the total national income also rose and consequently profit declined. During the 1985–7 downturn Malaysian and foreign businesses pulled back their investment although there was no shortage of liquidity in the market. As profits fell, mobile local capital took flight overseas.

The Malaysian government quickly reversed its macroeconomic policies and immediately implemented microeconomic measures to correct the imbalances. These include liberalisation of industrial licensing, weeding out of red tape in administrative procedures, rationalisation of banking procedures, introduction of privatisation and reduction in corporate taxes. Above all the government cleared the way for the setting up of channels of positive interactions between the public and the private sectors with the latter to lead in industrial development.

In the field of income distribution the role of government is still important. This entails structural changes in the economy involving the redistribution of productive assests and entitlements. By providing social goods and services benefiting human resource development of the disadvantaged groups, this exercise in social engineering is not a zero-sum game. In the beginning it was feared that this would interfere with private enterprise and affect economic growth and curtail all round efficiency, but the Malaysian model disproved that.

The assumption of the neo-classical economists is that income growth and income inequality are bonded in a tight two-way causal relationship. If growth takes place, its benefits will accrue to the already privileged class, comprising the high savers, the investors and the entrepreneurs in society.

Table 4.3 Manufacturing unit labour costs in East Asia (1980=100)

	1981	*1982*	*1983*	*1984*	*1985*	*1986*
Unit labour cost in domestic currency						
South Korea	108.1	126.2	131.2	145.4	147.8	163.0
Taiwan	113.9	121.9	132.7	128.5	126.4	124.8
Singapore	111.9	131.9	140.0	151.0	134.1	n.a.
Hong Kong	108.8	130.7	116.0	132.0	127.4	n.a.
Malaysia	109.7	125.3	154.8	178.3	169.9	153.9
Thailand	110.8	109.9	114.9	121.4	n.a	n.a
Exchange rate (LC/US$)						
Korea	112.1	120.4	132.7	143.2	145.1	135.4
Taiwan	102.3	108.6	109.9	110.6	105.0	88.4
Singapore	98.7	99.9	99.6	102.8	101.7	n.a
Hong Kong	112.5	122.0	157.1	156.6	156.8	n.a
Malaysia	105.8	107.3	107.7	114.1	118.6	115.8
Thailand	106.6	112.3	115.4	132.6	n.a	n.a
Unit labour cost in US$(A/B)						
Korea	96.4	104.8	98.9	101.5	101.9	120.4
Taiwan	111.3	112.2	120.7	116.2	120.4	141.2
Singapore	113.4	132.0	140.6	146.9	131.9	n.a
Hong Kong	96.8	107.1	73.8	84.3	81.3	n.a
Malaysia	103.6	116.8	143.8	156.3	143.3	132.9
Thailand	104.0	97.9	99.6	91.6	n.a	n.a

Source: World Bank (1989), table 2.6, p. 12.

The underprivileged and the grassroots in society will not gain anything at the beginning of the growth process, and only very much later if at all. The Malaysian model is an exception.

Development strategies here are based mainly on promoting human capital formation and infrastructure development. Strange as it may seem the government played an unconventional dual role, one as an active facilitator of growth benefiting the private sector and the ruling elites, and second, as an active guardian of the assetless poor majority which formed its political backbone. It has succeeded in this dual role for nearly four decades now. Skilled jobs and asset acquisition by the underprivileged are provided by the government through the education system and specially created unit trusts and financial institutions. The latter strategy espoused by the Malaysians somehow paralleled the neo-classical assumption that access to assets will promote growth. But the Malaysians succeeded in accumulating assets without having to depend too much on interest-charging financial institutions.

In trying to break out from the neo-classical requirement of efficiency criterion superseding egalitarian development, Malaysian policy-makers have to shift their thinking and philosophical roots to ensure the achievement of Malaysian social justice. After that they also have to make or renew various social contracts with economic actors and pressure groups of various persuasions. Interlinkages are created to establish agreements covering consumer and producer groups, their property rights and entitlements; technology and skill usage in industries, wage fixation and interest rate guidelines; official and vernacular language policies and curricular development in the public education system. These socio-economic policies are important because social and political strife on petty issues can break out here and put a break on growth. Instead, cooperation is emphasised. Parties involved have shown moral commitment in their dealings not just in the political arena but across institutions and in the market at large (Huq, 1994).

ASIAN PHILOSOPHIES

Even countries as capitalistic as Japan have national goals based on moral values, and not on 'yen' alone. Likewise, the deep-seated Confucion culture in China, Taiwan, South Korea, Thailand, Hong Kong and Singapore has influenced the corporate and national goals of these countries, emphasising various degrees of assimilation of neo-Confucian dynamism. This and other types of non-Western world-view are now emerging in Malaysia and Indonesia, such as the integrative world-view of *Hablum Minallah* (inner relations to God) and *Hablum Minannas* (outer relations among fellow men) (Choudhury, 1994). International cooperation based on mutual help and non-exploitative stance flowed from these Asian spirits. This is best illustrated by the spirit of the ASEAN nations. The ASEAN 4 nations (namely Malaysia, Indonesia, the Philippines and Thailand) have long pursued an outward-looking primary oriented development strategy. Now they are pooling their combined resources to create triangular growth regions. However, to succeed they have to depend on technical know-how and capital from other countries, such as Japan and the United States. On the other hand, South Korea, Taiwan, Hong Kong and Singapore had pursued outward industry-oriented development, necessitating the inflow of foreign capital and technology. There is a considerable gap between ASEAN 4 and the NIEs of Asia, but they have all formed interactive links with each other.

GLOBALISATION

In the post-Cold War era, the barriers between countries have come down. With globalisation the interdependence of East Asia, Europe and America is enhanced. It has an important impact on methods of production and technology as these can move rapidly from the industrial countries across the globe. In the past foreign direct investment via multinational companies had created economic enclaves in developing countries producing goods for Western home markets. Multinational companies which spearheaded capitalist globalisation do not have to cater for local needs. In fact they think globally and respond to local requirements only when this suits their management strategies. In such a situation local companies which aspire to develop their comparative advantages have embarked on cooperative strategies in order to interlink with world corporate leaders. Taiwan and Indonesian aerospace industries and the Malaysian national automobile industry are perhaps pertinent examples here. The twenty-first century will no doubt introduce more sophisticated technologies into the East Asian markets and only those with durable strategic alliances with foreign corporate giants can hope to keep abreast with the best in the world.

In short, the future will see more competitive adaptation, cooperation and shifting comparative advantage, and developing countries will be dominated unless they can interlink with powerful partners in their region. This is already happening now in the post GATT era with respect to ASEAN countries when confronted with the New World Economic Order, whereby world economic superpowers (not just the United States) are feverishly involved in their own regrouping and strategic actions on trade to ensure their continued oligopolistic shares of world trade. The fear of losing hegemony worldwide makes these superpowers advocate the resurrection of Bretton Woods institutions to effect structural adjustments in their favour forever. This includes privatisation, price stability of primary commodities, population and environmental controls, etc., and the eventual rise of neo-mercantilism.

PRIVATISATION

The controversial nature of privatisation, as already noted above, is a powerful instrument of social engineering in some developing countries, much to the chagrin of the neo-classical purists.

The mainstrean argument supporting privatisation is that it increases efficiency, profitability and productivity. Similarly, it will reduce public debt and increase government revenue by the sale of state enterprises, and the reduction of subsidies to ailing public enterprises. On an organisational level, privatisation will introduce corporate culture and modern management instead of the 'muddling through' techniques of everyday public administration. All this will ensure that government intervention in the economy will be minimal and corruption in public agencies reduced.

The arguments against privatisation are often based on ideological reasons. Public sector trade unions fear that privatisation will result in lay-offs, reduction in wages and the silencing of trade union members' right to protest over conditions of work and income security.

The above arguments are far from exhaustive. But on the ground, the implementation of privatisation in developed and developing countries is full of adaptations to local needs. The much touted efficiency inducing quality of privatisation is ephemeral and clouded with value judgements. There are many examples of parts of the public utilities and services which were hived off to be privatised to ensure profitability, leaving behind the rest which continue to drain the public purse. Even after being privatised, the problem of adequate capitalisation is not easily solved by resorting to local financing. However, in some developing countries where the open flotation of shares of newly privatised companies is practised, there is the risk of foreign control taking them over.

For example, in Malaysia the initial share offer of the Malaysian International Shipping Corporation to private individuals was confined to Malaysians only to avoid owership complication. Similarly, Singapore arranged for a wide selection of foreign investors from various countries when it embarked on its private sector enlargement. Another example occurred in 1985 when the Malaysian Airlines System was privatised, allowing the government to retain a special 'golden share' to safeguard the national interest. Foreign participation was only confined to a small share by the Brunei Government.

Despite this token foreign interest in local privatisation, it is still true that the government still want to continue to control and safeguard their former agencies and services by holding golden shares and the right to appoint key personnel on the board of directors. Arguments in support of productivity and efficiency can be sacrificed to suit political ends. This is increasingly so in countries like Malaysia where privatisation of giant agencies is treated as an instrument of social engineering to benefit the formerly assetless majority and train them to seize global business opportunities. This twist to the neo-classical model of privatisation is not welcome in some quarters but it is readily accepted by others, especially when it became a fortuitous policy stance to halt the severity of the crowding-out effects in the later half of the 1980s.

CONCLUSION

The arguments in the preceding sections are not meant to imply that mainstream economics cannot offer insight into growth processes in Third-World countries and East Asian countries in particular. Development processes in these regions are in fact products of interlinkages of various factors whose inquiry cannot fruitfully be organised along mainstream economic analysis. The following chapters will put into sharper focus this alternative method of analysis.

Referencess

Choudhury, M.A. (1994) 'Why Cannot Neo-Classicism Explain Resource Allocation and Development in the Islamic Political Economy?', Seminar Paper delivered at the Faculty of Economics, Universiti Kebangsaan Malaysia, Bangi. Now appearing in E. Ahmad (ed.) *Islamic Perspectives of Economic Growth and Privatization* (Herndon, VA: International Institute of Islamic Thought).

Huq, Ataul (1994) *Malaysia's Economic Success* (Kuala Lumpur: Pelanduk Publications).

Myrdal, Gunnar (1968) *The Asian Drama* (Harmondsworth, England: Penguin).

Ranis, Gustav (1991) 'The Role of Government: Comparative International Experience', in Haque, Irfanyul (ed.), *International Competitiveness* (Washington DC: World Bank), pp. 69–82.

Shinichi Ichimura (1993) 'Policies for Economic Development', *APO Productivity Journal* (Tokyo: Asian Productivity Organization) Spring, pp. 106–33.

World Bank (1989) *Malaysia: Matching Risks and Rewards in a Mixed Economy* (Washington DC: World Bank).

5 Privatisation as an Instrument for National Policy and Socio-economic Restructuring

Uzir Abdul Malik

INTRODUCTION

Privatisation which is currently a worldwide phenomenon has been justified on several grounds, from increasing public enterprise efficiency to creating a free enterprise economic system. In Malaysia, where it was made a national policy in the mid-1980s, it was regarded as an instrument of national policy and socio-economic restructuring. As an instrument of national policy it was aimed at reducing the financial and administrative burden of the government, improve the efficiency and productivity of public enterprises and facilitating economic growth. In the case of socio-economic restructuring, the main role of the privatisation policy is to help achieve the objectives of the New Economic Policy (NEP) and subsequently of the Economic Policy for National Development (EPND).

It should however, be noted at the outset that privatisation as loosely defined has been practised by the Malaysian Government long before it became popular in the early 1980s. This was in the form of works contracted out to private individuals and enterprises by government departments and ministeries. However, privatisation as generally accepted is said to have taken place only when there is a transfer of management with or without ownership of enterprises which are run by government due to actual or potential market failures. In addition, it should also have the effect of denationalisation and liberalisation of the market forces (Cook and Kirkpatrick, 1988). Moreover, as illustrated subsequently, privatisation has its own definition in the context of Malaysia and is being practised in various forms.

This chapter intends to look at several key policies of the Malaysian Government and examine the extent to which the privatisation policy fulfils the objectives of these policies. The main policies are those aimed at socio-economic restructuring, namely, the NEP and the EPND. To the extent that privatisation is a response to too much public intervention, the role of the public sector in economic and social development will also be discussed. This will also include the policy to reduce public expenditures and the public debt.

PUBLIC SECTOR AND DEVELOPMENT

Since achieving independence in the late 1950s and until fairly recently, the Malaysian Government has played an increasingly important role in the economic activities of the nation. This has actually been a global phenomenon and it is true not only for the welfare economies of a number of countries in Europe but also of many less developed countries (LDCs) of Asia, Africa and Latin America. The public sector was engaged in providing essential services such as roads, electricity and water supply and also in running nationalised industries. Thus until quite recently, the public sector has been generally regarded as the engine for growth for most of the LDCs.

The Malaysian Government could be said to have been destined to play a very active role in the development of the economy. Prior to its independence in the late 1950s a study was conducted by the World Bank in Malaya to assess the national economy and the areas needed for development. This report forms the basis of the first national Five-Year Plan. Since then the Malaysian Government has been guided by eight Five-Year Plans, starting with the First Malaya Plan in 1955 to be followed by the Second Malaya Plan in 1961. In 1966, with the formation of the Malaysian Federation, the current plan then was called the First Malaysia Plan and this Five-Year Plan followed one after another until the current Sixth Malaysia Plan covering the period 1991–5.

In the post independent period of the late 1950s and the decade that follows, the public sector was mainly involved in the development of infrastructures and filling in the gaps left by the colonial administration. A great deal of emphasis was given to education and strengthening the internal security of the country against communist insurgencies (Salleh and Osman Rani, 1991). As a result of these efforts, by the end of the First Malaysia Plan, as shown in Table 5.1, government expenditure reached a level of 23.7 per cent of GDP. The increasing role of the government in generating growth and development and the lack of dynamism in the private sector during the decades that followed resulted in ever bigger public sector involvement, until public expenditures peaked to 47.8 per cent in 1981. Although government expenditures declined after that, the

Table 5.1 Federal Government expenditure and revenue, 1970–90 (as percentage of GDP)

Year	Total expend.	Current expend.	Capital expend.	Total revenue	Current balance	Overall balance
1966	23.2	16.6	6.6	17.1	0.82	–4.6
1967	23.9	17.8	6.1	18.2	0.41	–6.1
1968	22.8	17.0	5.8	17.9	0.92	–5.7
1969	21.7	16.6	5.1	18.0	1.40	–4.9
1970	23.7	17.8	5.9	19.7	1.97	–3.8
1971	26.8	18.5	8.3	18.7	0.15	–8.1
1972	30.2	21.6	8.6	20.5	1.04	–9.6
1973	23.9	17.9	5.9	18.2	0.31	–5.6
1974	27.0	18.9	8.1	21.0	2.07	–6.0
1975	31.4	21.9	9.5	22.9	0.97	–8.5
1976	29.1	20.8	8.3	21.9	1.17	–7.1
1977	32.6	22.9	9.7	24.0	1.12	–8.6
1978	31.0	21.2	9.8	23.3	2.11	–7.7
1979	31.5	22.3	9.2	23.3	1.03	–8.2
1980	40.4	26.3	14.1	26.9	0.60	–13.5
1981	47.8	28.0	19.8	28.2	0.21	–19.6
1982	44.5	26.6	17.9	26.7	0.00	–17.8
1983	39.9	26.4	13.5	26.7	0.03	–13.2
1984	35.0	24.9	10.1	26.2	1.26	–8.6
1985	34.6	25.9	8.7	27.2	1.35	–7.4
1986	38.0	28.2	9.8	27.4	–0.08	–10.6
1987	39.9	33.2	6.7	29.8	–0.03	–10.0
1988	39.0	32.9	7.9	31.1	0.23	–5.9
1989	42.2	34.3	10.6	34.9	0.61	–7.3
1990	44.1	34.1	13.5	37.2	3.04	–6.9
1991	46.0	36.3	11.1	39.5	3.19	–6.5

Source: Ministry of Finance, *Economic Report* (various issues).

public sector in Malaysia is still considered relatively big in comparison to its level of economic development (World Bank, 1983).

It is important to note here that in the case of the Malaysian Government, public expenditure plays a role not only of generating economic growth and development but also acts as an instrument of economic restructuring and social engineering. This was best illustrated by the introduction of the New Economic Policy (NEP) in the early 1970s. The NEP was prompted by the need to balance the inequitable distribution of wealth and economic opportunities between the major ethnic groups in the country, a legacy of the colonial era. Specifically, it has a two-pronged objective of eradicating poverty irrespective of race and correcting the economic imbalance between the indigenous Bumiputera and the non-Bumiputera. This intervention by necessity requires government initiatives in establishing agencies and corporations at the federal and state levels and other acts of empowerment to increase Bumiputera participation in business and commercial activities. This act of positive discrimination entails the commitment of fairly large government funds. Since internal sources were quite limited at this stage of the country's development, the government has had to resort to external borrowings. A substantial amount was in the form of Federal Government guarantees for external borrowings of state governments and their agencies. These two issues will later be discussed separately under the New Economic Policy, government expenditures and national debt burden.

PRIVATISATION IN MALAYSIA

The privatisation policy in Malaysia was largely in response to rather unfavourable international and domestic situations. At the international level, the years preceding the early 1980s were a period of low commodity prices although the nation was burdened with high national debt. At the national level, the decades of development policy and government intervention in the economy since Independence in the late 1950s have greatly enlarged the government's machinery and financial responsibility. As such the advent of privatisation during this period was considered as a convenient vehicle for ameliorating these situations. It was more of a political decision than a decision based on the neo-classical need to bring about greater market participation in the economy. It was also convenient, as indicated later, to act as a vehicle to enable certain groups to make rentier gains to improve their socio-economic status (Jomo, 1992). In order to allow this to happen, privatisation needs to be streamlined within a policy framework. This was initially in the form of a Privatisation Guideline to be followed later by a national privatisation policy document called the Privatisation Masterplan. Administratively, the policy is to be under the jurisdiction of the Privatisation Unit of the Prime Minister's Department, which very much reflects its importance to the current administration.

Privatisation has been defined by the Privatisation Masterplan drawn up by the Economic Planning Unit of the Prime Minister's Department as 'the transfer to the private sector of activities and functions which have traditionally rested with the public sector' (Economic Planning, 1985). In order to qualify as a privatisation exercise, the Masterplan outlines three essential components in the transfer, namely:

1. A transfer of management responsibility.
2. A transfer of assets (with or without liabilities) or the right to used assets.
3. A transfer of personnel.

This is rather too broad a definition because traditionally in the context of the Western democratic system to which Malaysia largely subscribes, the function of government or the public sector is mainly to provide law and order. But this tradition has changed with the change in economic thinking.

As defined by the Masterplan a privatisation exercise must necessarily involve the transfer of at least one of the components stated above. However, strictly for its purpose it should entail the transfer of at least components (2) and (3) above.

The privatisation exercise in the 1980s was rather slow, involving few big public enterprises, the main one being the Malaysian Airlines System (MAS) in 1985. These are mainly the public market sector enterprises. It is interesting to note at this stage that there was not much thought on deregulation and the liberalisation of particular industries. Although there was divestment in equity through flotation of MAS shares in the capital market, the market structure of the airline industry remained largely unchanged.

Objectives of Privatisation

Privatisation in Malaysia, as indicated earlier, is the government's response to specific international and national economic situations. However, in formulating its policy other objectives were also included. The overall objectives of the formalised policy as outlined in the Masterplan are as follows:

1. To relieve the financial and administrative burden of the government: the resources thus freed could be used to bring about more effective government and meet distributional objectives more efficiently.
2. To improve efficiency and productivity of economic activities: this is brought about, through greater competition, less governance and better work performance.
3. To facilitate economic growth: this is to be achieved through greater private sector participation in development activities. The higher

returns that are expected to be achieved could be used to generate higher growth for the economy as a whole.

4. To reduce the size and presence of the public sector in the economy. This is largely related to objective (1) above. However, the government intends to go beyond this and have the economy increasingly led by the private sector.
5. To help meet the National Economic Policy Targets. This is facilitated by the restructuring process of privatisation. Both ownership of capital and management functions could be diverted to the intended group, namely the Bumiputeras.

Privatisation within a Broader Policy Framework

Privatisation according to the Privatisation Masterplan is supposed to be implemented within the broader national policy framework of economic liberalisation. This means, as indicated earlier, that the private sector is intended to play a major role in the economy and that government intervention will be minimal and largely supportive in nature. There will also be continuous efforts towards deregulation in order to allow as much competition as possible in the privatised industries. In cases where there exist natural monopolies, regulation would be introduced to safeguard consumer interests. However, to date competition in the privatised industried has been fairly limited, except possibly in the telephone industry where a number of companies have entered the market with services for cellular and mobile phones. The high capital cost of many of these industries has acted as barrier for new entries and thus entrenched the monopolistic position of the privatised concerns.

The government is also fully aware that a full-fledged privatisation programme would affect other sectors in the economy. There will be an expanded demand for professional inputs which are scarce in a developing country like Malaysia. To overcome this problem, there needs to be a re-evaluation of the educational system and the training programme. Towards this end the government has encouraged the establishment of private colleges and twinning programmes between these colleges and their counterparts overseas. More local higher education institutions have also been established including universities in Sarawak and Sabah.

In addition to the above, there will also be an expanded demand on equity and debt capital. Since capital is necessarily limited in the country there could be a crowding out effect on capital by the private sector for other purposes. To avoid this the government has undertaken steps to promote investment, especially within the Bumiputera sector. The latter is served by the establishment of trust schemes called Amanah Saham Nasional or National Shares Trust and Amanah Saham Bumiputera or Bumiputera Shares Trust. Indirectly, privatisation has also expanded the capacity of the local capital market. This has been illustrated by the increase in volume traded in recent years as well as interest shown by international investors.

Criteria for Privatisation

There are a number of considerations that can be examined as criteria for privatisation and these are as follows (Economic Planning Unit, 1985).

1. *Profitability* In order to consider a project for privatisation, the interested party has to show the government that it is a profitable venture.
2. *Benefits exceed costs* This is largely an economic criteria and must take into consideration the costs and benefits to various interest groups. The benefits and costs that need to be considered are both financial and non-financial and both quantifiable and non-quantifiable.
3. *Feasibility of fragmentation* This criteria is meant to gauge the competitiveness of a project that is proposed to be privatised. The economies of scale within the industry and its technological intensity are part of this consideration.
4. *Social objectives* Social objectives need to be spelt out especially in terms of the effects of privatisation such as product pricing on the lower income group. The effects of the exercise on existing employees should be given special consideration.

Method of Privatisation

There are several options for making privatisation proposals of public entities. They range from total sale of public assets or equity to just management contract. The following are some of those recommended by the Privatisation Masterplan.

1. *Sale of equity or assets*
   Sale of equity method involves the transfer of all three organisational related components, namely, assets (together with or without liabilities), management responsibility and also personnel. This transfer of equity may be complete or partial depending on the role the govern-

ment wants to play in the privatised entity. Sale of assets, however, may not involve all the three components mentioned above.

2. *Lease of assets*
   In this case privatisation involves the transfer of rights to use the assets of a public entity for a specific period of time in return for a certain payment. Normally this method is used for rather large assets that have strategic value such as airports and seaports Acquisition of these assets, however, could be arranged towards the end of the lease.

3. *Management contract*
   This method utilises the management expertise of a private concern for managing a government entity in lieu of a fee. There may or may not be a transfer of personnel. However, it definitely does not involve the transfer of government assets.

4. *Build, operate and transfer (BOT) and build operate (BO)*
   This method basically involves a concession period whereby the private concern has a right to collect revenue. As the term denotes BOT involves building a facility, operating it and collecting revenue from the services rendered and finally transferring it back to the government. The BO method is basically the same as BOT but does not involve the transfer of the facility at the end of the concessionary period. This method of privatisation is popular for infrastructural and utility projects such as roads and water supply.

5. *Management-buy-out (MBO)*
   This method involves the buying of a government concern by the management itself. It involves transfer of assets and equity to the existing management. So far this method has only involved government-owned companies listed under the Company's Act.

As of February 1994, as shown in Table 5.2, 94 public entities or projects have been privatised or corporatised. Out of these, more than 50 per cent have involved the sale of assets and equities.

GOVERNMENT EXPENDITURES AND THE NATIONAL DEBT BURDEN

Among the prime movers of the Malaysian Government's privatisation policy are the reduction of public expenditure and the national debt burden. Although these were the intentions, they do not prove to be con-

Table 5.2 Malaysia: number of privatised projects as of February 1994

No. of method	*Project*	*Percent of total*
Build operate (BO)	3	3.2
Build, own and operate (BOO)	5	5.3
Build, operate and transfer (BOT)	13	13.8
Sale of equity	37	39.4
Sale of assets (SA)	12	12.8
Lease and lease sale (LLS)	8	8.5
Management contract (MC)	5	5.3
Management buy-out (MBO)	3	3.2
Corporatisation (C)	8	8.5
Total	94	100

Note: Corporatisation is also regarded as part of privatisation process although it may not necessarily lead to sale of equity or assets.
Source: Privatisation Unit, Prime Minister's Department.

sistently implemented. As shown in Table 5.3, the administrative expenditures of the government in terms of annual rate of growth have increased from 1975 up to 1980. In the early 1980s, when the privatisation policy was first initiated, the general trend showed that the expenditure growth rates were decreasing. However, after 1987 the trend was more or less the reverse. The same trend could also be seen for the development expenditures except that, for a number of years, the actual amounts had in fact decreased and thus given negative annual rates of growth.

One possible explanation for the above characteristics in the government's administrative and development expenditures is that the impact of the privatisation policy was greater on development than on current administrative expenditure. Secondly, the more important public entities such as the Tenaga Nasional Berhad (TNB) and the Telecom Malaysia Berhad (TMB), the main and biggest utilities in the country, were only privatised in the early 1990s. Their effects on expenditures during that period are somewhat noticeable as show in Table 5.3.

The other area which the privatisation policy aims to alleviate is the national debt burden of the government. These debts are derived from both

Table 5.3 Administrative and development expenditures of the Malaysian Government, 1975–94

Year	*Administrative expenditure (RM million)*	*% Change per year*	*Development expenditures (RM million)*	*% Change per year*
1975	4900	—	2123	—
1976	5828	18.93	2365	11.40
1977	7398	26.93	3205	35.52
1978	8041	8.69	3762	17.38
1979	10040	24.86	4136	9.94
1980	13617	35.63	7194	73.94
1981	15686	15.19	11023	53.22
1982	16671	6.27	11485	4.19
1983	18374	10.22	9670	–15.80
1984	19806	7.79	8407	–13.06
1985	20062	1.29	7142	–15.05
1986	20075	0.06	7559	5.84
1987	20185	0.55	4741	–37.28
1988	21812	8.06	5231	10.34
1989	24832	13.84	7696	47.12
1990	27105	9.15	10734	39.48
1991	28296	4.39	9565	–10.89
1992[1]	32075	13.35	9724	1.66
1993[2]	32315	0.75	9831	1.13
1994[3]	33285	3.00	13351	35.81

Notes: [1] Estimated actual
[2] Latest estimate
[3] Budget allocation
Source: Various Treasury Reports.

internal and external sources. Table 5.4 shows the external debt of the Malaysian Government for the period 1975–93. Generally, it can be stated that market loans and project loans in the 1970s were probably quite small. However, in the 1980s market loans have increased tremendously with the peak being reached in 1986 with an outstanding loan of about RM20.3 billion. After this year there was a gradual decline but loans remained fairly high compared to the 1970s. This was also generally true in the case of a project loan except that it peaked slightly later in 1991.

In general, it could perhaps be said that the privatisation policy had no discernible effect on external loans. In fact the decade of the 1980s saw a fairly high gearing of external loans, reaching a peak of RM28.3 billion in

Table 5.4 External debt of the Malaysian Government (RM million)

Year	Market loans	Project loans	Suppliers credit	IMF loans	Total
1975	1348	1077	—	—	2425
1976	1468	1388	—	—	2856
1977	1628	1721	—	—	3349
1978	1778	2081	—	—	3359
1979	2208	2335	—	—	4543
1980	2184	2663	—	—	4847
1981	4790	2966	—	—	7756
1982	9036	3375	119	—	12530
1983	12271	3868	754	828	17721
1984	14652	4673	820	703	20848
1985	16299	5681	825	263	23068
1986	20310	6986	1012	—	28308
1987	18940	7692	997	—	27629
1988	17265	7925	732	—	25922
1989	16375	7253	554	—	24182
1990	16182	8125	419	—	24726
1991	16693	8468	257	—	25436
1992[1]	12862	7978	109	—	20949
1993[2]	11635	8198	1	—	19825

Notes: [1] Estimated actual
[2] Latest estimate
Source: Various Treasury Reports.

1986. One possible explanation of this phenomenon is that the 1980s were also a period of high economic growth in the Malaysian economy. Thus, although there was a decrease in the external loans for the privatised entities, this was more than offset by the increase in loans for other development projects.

In the case of internal debt the trend was more straightforward. The 1980s and the early 1990s, as shown in Table 5.5, was a period of continuous growth of internal debt mostly in the form of government promissory notes. Thus the privatisation policy has almost no effect on economising the need for funding by the government from internal sources. As discussed above, this was mainly driven by the high growth rate of the economy and the need to secure funds, especially from internal sources in order to avoid currency fluctuations as dictated by the market as well as possible currency appreciations by foreign governments.

Table 5.5 Internal debt of the Malaysian Government (RM million)

Year	Treasury bills	Investment certificates	Government promissory notes	Other loans	Total
1975	1401	—	7355	—	8756
1976	1711	—	8681	—	10392
1977	1780	—	10497	—	12277
1978	1510	—	11958	—	13468
1979	1490	—	14459	—	15949
1980	1490	—	16770	—	18260
1981	1790	—	20561	—	22351
1982	2290	—	25978	—	28268
1983	2790	100	30037	1028	33955
1984	2490	200	33090	995	36775
1985	2790	200	36681	1141	40812
1986	3000	300	41302	1097	45699
1987	4000	500	48794	1502	54796
1988	4320	1000	55831	1946	63097
1989	4320	1000	58213	2230	65763
1990	4320	900	62106	2662	69988
1991	4320	900	65263	3171	73654
1992[1]	4320	1000	66642	4121	76083
1993[2]	4320	2000	67016	5065	78401

Notes: [1] Estimated actual
[2] Latest estimate
Source: Various Treasury Reports.

NEW ECONOMIC POLICY

The New Economic Policy (NEP), as indicated earlier, was a long-range policy covering the period 1970–90 with the view of eradicating poverty and restructuring society to bring about national unity. It was the first attempt of the Malaysian Government in social engineering and in direct response to the racial riots of 1969. The social and economic imbalance prior to the NEP was considered unacceptable to the Malays as the main indigenous group in the country. In terms of employment, the Malays were concentrated in the agricultural sector within which over 70 per cent of households were in poverty. The other major racial group, namely the Chinese, was mainly in the mining, manufacturing and construction sectors, where the number of poor households account for only 9 per cent of the total figure (Government of Malaysia, 1976).

The distribution of wealth was also skewed towards the other non-indigenous groups. In terms of share capital owned in 1970, the Malays and Malay interest owned only 2.4 per cent of equity capital, the Chinese owned 27.2 per cent, the Indians 1.1 per cent, others 6.0 per cent whilst the majority of 63.3 per cent was held by foreigners. In the non-corporate industrial sector which comprises manufacturing, mining and construction, ownership of fixed assets reflects very much the employment structure, with the Malays owing only 2.3 per cent of the assets compared to the Indians 2.3 per cent, Chinese 92.2 per cent, others 0.8 per cent and foreigners 2.4 per cent. Even in the non-corporate sector of modern agriculture, where the government has played a very active role in promoting Malay participation, the Malays owned 47.1 per cent; Chinese 32.8 per cent; Indians 10.1 per cent, of the acreage under cultivation.

In order to correct the above imbalances, the NEP adopted a two-pronged approach in order to eradicate poverty among all Malaysians and restructure Malaysian society so as to eliminate eventually the identification of race with economic function and geographical location. The first prong of the NEP would concentrate on increasing access to land, physical capital, training and other public facilities to all racial groups especially the poor. The second prong was targeted mainly at the Malays and aimed to allow them to participate more actively in the modern sectors of manufacturing and commerce, while at the same time encouraging the other racial groups to take a more active role in the modern agricultural sector.

The NEP was to be implemented in the climate of accelerated economic growth so as to ensure that the 'restructuring of the racial composition of employment and wealth ownership is to be effected in ways which do not deny opportunities to others as well' (ibid., p.8). This precondition for socio-economic restructuring was rather a tall order for the Malaysian Government, considering that the country then had only achieved its independence just over a decade ago and was still largely an agricultural and resource based economy.

The decade of the first half of the NEP (1971–80) was considered as a period of rapid economic growth and structural change in Malaysia (ibid., 1981). This was despite the fact that by the end of the decade the global economy was experiencing inflation and slow growth and was characterised by rising energy costs and increasing protectionism. During this decade, two Five-Year Plans were implemented, the Second Malaysia Plan (1971–5) and the Third Malaysia Plan (1976–80). The main policy objective of these two national development plans was the NEP, which was the promotion of national unity through the two-pronged objectives of eradicating poverty irrespective of race and the restructuring of society by eliminating the identification of race with economic functions.

The first decade of the NEP as indicated above was a period of rapid growth in the economy. Per capita income, in current prices, increased by nearly 12 per cent per annum or 4.9 per cent in real terms. This was brought about by the impressive growth of the economy which registered an annual growth of Gross Domestic Product (GDP) of 7.8 per cent per annum during the period. This high growth rate allows redistribution efforts to take place as planned by the government without depriving the opportunities of other ethnic groups.

Various development efforts were undertaken during this period to fulfil the NEP objective of poverty eradication. In the rural areas the main strategy was in new land development and targeted at in situ agriculture. The urban poor were provided with better public facilities and amenities including low-cost housing. In addition, facilities were made available to encourage the development of Malay entrepreneurship such as the provision of stalls and the necessary equipment.

The poverty eradication policies and programmes and the buoyant condition of the economy led to a decline in the incidence of poverty from 49.3 per cent in the beginning of the NEP period to 29.2 per cent in 1980. In terms of income distribution among the ethnic groups, although the Malay mean income continued to be below the natural average, its growth rate during this time was the highest compared with those of other ethnic groups. For the period considered, the gap between the Malay mean income and the national average was reduced from 34.8 per cent in 1970 to 32.7 per cent in 1979. However, it was noted that although there was much improvement in the level of absolute income for all the ethnic groups, much more needed to be done to remove the large income disparities between them (ibid.).

The other dimension of the NEP that needed to be fulfilled was the restructuring of society. This proved to be a much more difficult task to undertake since the initial distribution of human, physical and financial assets were largely in the hands of the other ethnic groups rather than those of the Malays. The government during this period concentrated its efforts on education and training programmes to enable mobility within and across economic activities, and also on the setting up of institutions that would provide the necessary facilities to allow Malay entrepreneurs to go into business as well as into various industries. These institutions included the Bank Pembangunan Malaysia Berhad (BPMD) or

Development Bank of Malaysia Limited, the Urban Development Authority (UDA) and the Majlis Amanah Rakyat (MARA) or Citizens Trust Council. In terms of ownership and control of wealth in the corporate sector, other institutions were created, such as the Pelaboran Nasional Berhad (PNB), the Kompleks Kewangan Malaysia Berhad (KKMB) and the Perbadanan Nasional Berhad (PERNAS). The main task of these institutions was to hold equity capital in trust for the Malays and other indigenous people with the final objective of handing over the shares to them. The low income level of these groups as well as their lack of entrepreneurial and business skills is making the restructuring process very slow and difficult.

The decade of the second half of the NEP (1981–90) spanned another two Five-Year Plans namely the Fourth Malaysia Plan (1981–5) and the Fifth Malaysia Plan (1986–90). The Fifth Malaysia Plan period was one of great variations, ranging from the most severe post-independent recession the country had ever experienced to that of boom conditions during the last three years. Overall performance of the Fifth Plan period had been quite commendable with GDP growth of 6.7 per cent per annum in real terms. Part of this remarkable performance was attributed to the government's privatisation programmes which consolidated the public sector and brought about a substantial reduction in its budgetary deficits (ibid., 1991a).

In terms of poverty eradication, the Fifth Plan had brought about a quite significant reduction in poverty especially in the rural areas, involving about 30 000 households. By the end of the NEP period in 1990 there still remained 619 400 poor households. Out of this, 143 100 households were within the category of hard-core poor. They were mostly located in remote traditional villages and settlements as well as in plantations, resettlement areas also known as new villages and in some urban areas. These households were considered within the poverty group not only because of their very low income but also due to lack of and access to basic services and amenities.

To what extent privatisation has really contributed to the NEP objectives is not really known. However, since most privatisation exercises require at least 30 per cent Bumiputera participation, they would enhance the inter-ethnic wealth redistribution objectives (Jomo, 1992). But a number of issues still remain to be addressed, among which are the deployment of such equity whether for short-term gains or for long-term developments and to what extent this has affected the status of Bumiputera participation in the corporate sector as well as in redressing the problems of poverty in general.

ECONOMIC POLICY FOR NATIONAL DEVELOPMENT (EPND)

The NEP expired after 1990 and was superseded by the EPND, which was aimed at taking over the NEP until the turn of the century. The EPND was deemed necessary in order to fulfil certain shortcomings of the NEP. The NEP has achieved its first objective of poverty eradication considerably. The level of poverty in the country was reduced from 49.3 per cent in 1970 to 17.3 per cent in 1987. However, as observed earlier, it is still high among the indigenous Bumiputera groups. In addition, there is also the problem of relative poverty because of the widening gap in income within communities and inter-communities and also between economic sectors and regions. The feelings of relative deprivation could be as serious as that of absolute deprivation if not given due attention. The second objective of the NEP regarding restructuring of economic activities and opportunities of the various ethnic groups proved to be more problematic. The objective was that by 1990 the Bumiputeras would hold at least 30 per cent of corporate equity with the non-Bumiputeras holding 40 per cent and foreigners 30 per cent. However, by 1988, without considering equities held by nominated and controlled companies, the Bumiputeras held only 19.4 per cent of common rate equity compared with 34.8 per cent for non-Bumiputeras and 24.6 per cent by foreign owned companies (Dasar Ekonomi untuk Pembangunan Negara, 1991).

In its implementation, the EPND still maintains the spirit of the NEP, in the sense that in its efforts to improve the relative position of the Bumiputeras it will not deprive others of their rights and opportunities. Guided by the National Constitution and the National Tenets or Rukun Negara the EPND has the following objectives (ibid.):

1. Continue the formation of a society that shares its welfare, remains united, just, equitable, peaceful and prosperous having a Malaysian identity and functions under stable political environment that is based on parlimentary democracy.
2. Eradicate poverty irrespective of race and correct economic imbalance between and within communities, sector and regions, on the basis of the acceptance that the Malaysian society, which is made up of different communities, is a reality that must be accepted in all development plannings, and their implementations, which have as their objective the distribution of wealth and opportunities equitability and effectively.
3. Involve all parties to strive more effectively so as to avoid abuses and improve the achievements of the two-pronged objectives of the original NEP towards all communities for the sake of all citizens.

4. Strengthen the moral and spiritual values as well as upgrade the self-reliance and defensive spirits of the citizens through more effective development of human resources.
5. Encourage economic development that is healthy and sustainable and advanced on the basis of science and technology, to a position to face the challenges of development in international economies so that Malaysia will emerge as a nation that is advanced and dynamic.

The above objectives are to be achieved within the 1990s and beyond. In order to achieve them a doubling of income per capita and its redistribution is needed by the end of the decade. This would be possible if the Gross Domestic Product (GDP) grows at about 9.0 per cent per year. To achieve this an Income Doubling and Distribution Plan (IDPP) was mooted and a few scenarios were outlined to support it. These took into consideration factors such as the growth rates of the OECD countries, the progress of GATT agreements and the success of the privatisation plan within the country.

In terms of the eradication of poverty, the EPND takes cognisance of absolute as well as relative poverty. First of all, it intends to redefine the Poverty Income Level (PIL) to take account of changes in prices, expenditure patterns of consumers and the ordinary as well as the expected standard of living. Certain groups have been identified as still having a high incidence of poverty by the end of the NEP period, namely, fishermen, farmers, small holders, estate workers, hawkers and residents in original and new villages.

For these groups certain courses of action need to be undertaken to ensure that they are provided with basic amenities, such as proper housing, water supply and education for their children. More importantly, they are to be given facilities such as landownership, interest-free loans, production equipment and proper marketing channels for their produce.

The end of the NEP period showed a widening of relative incomes between communities as well as within communities. The higher growth rates that are expected in the 1990s would worsen the situation if no mitigating measures were undertaken. This would include, among others, the redistribution of income sources to the low income groups in the form of land, equipment and ownership of shares, certain budget and fiscal measures to allow a bigger share to the low income groups and direct assistance to the poor.

The EPND has identified various measures to correct the imbalance between ethnic groups, sectors and regions, which are both general and specific in nature. At the general level, the concentration of Chinese in higher management in the private sector and Bumiputeras in the government sector needs to be rectified. The other minorities including Indians are also left behind in both sectors. At the regional level, the Bumiputeras in Sabah and Sarawak are also in the same position and therefore need to have greater participation. Specifically, there are numerous measures that need to be undertaken of which only a few could be outlined here. One of them is to create a Bumiputera Commercial and Industrial Community (BCIC) in order to accelerate Bumiputera participations in these sectors. These efforts would require a number of supporting measures such as the provision of opportunities and facilities to the intended groups and incentives to encourage non-Bumiputeras to help bring about such a community. Cooperative efforts among the various ethnic groups in the form of meaningful joint ventures are to be encouraged and monitored. The issuing of licences for the manufacturing, industrial and service sectors can act as monitoring devices for their implementation.

CONCLUSION

Malaysia can be said to be one of the few countries among the developing nations that has a formal policy on privatisation and which has used it as an instrument of national policy and socio-economic restructuring. It was initiated more on the basis of pragmatism than on political ideology. Like many other developing nations that have followed the path of public intervention in economic planning and development, the result was far below expectations and a burden to the national economy. There are evidences that the privatisation policy adopted by the Malaysian Government has lessened her financial and administrative burdens. Although studies on productivity and efficiency increases are limited, the privatised concerns are now operating in buoyant economic conditions and making a great deal of progress. To what extent they have contributed to economic growth, however, is yet to be determined.

The privatisation policy has played an important role in the country's efforts towards socio-economic restructuring. As a result of Bumiputera participation in the privatised concerns either individually or indirectly through Bumiputera trust funds, the Bumiputera share in the corporate sector has increased tremendously, although still below the targeted figure. Privatisation has also helped either directly or otherwise in achieving the other NEP objectives of poverty eradication and economic restructuring. In addition to being sources of employment to Bumiputera professionals, they have also increased Bumiputera participation in the commercial and industrial sector through equity ownership and management. Privatisation is targeted to play an equally active role in achieving the objectives of the EPND, especially in deepening and widening the inter-ethnic structural changes in the economy.

It is, however, important to note that the full benefits of privatisation would not be realised without deregulation and liberalisation of the affected industries. These have not been given as much emphasis in the restructuring exercise. The monopolistic and oligopolistic position of the privatised industries could adversely affect performance that would not be in the best interest of suppliers and consumers. There should not be a second round of market failures, because the process of privatisation can be said to be quite irreversible.

References

Cook, Paul Kirkpatrick, Colin (1988) *Privatisation in Less Developed Countries* (Hemel Hempsteald: Harvester Wheatsheaf).

Dasar Ekonomi untuk Pembangunan Negara (DEPN) (1991), (Kuala Lumpur: Laporan Majlis Perundangan Ekonomi Negara, Jabatan Percetakan Negara, 9 Februari).

Economic Planning Unit (Prime Minister's Department) (1985), *Guidelines on Privatisation* (Kuala Lumpur: Goverment Printer).

Government of Malaysia (1971) *Second Malaysia Plan, 1971–1975* (Kuala Lumpur: Government Printer).

Government of Malaysia (1976) *Third Malaysia Plan, 1976–1980* (Kuala Lumpur: Government Printer).

Government of Malaysia (1981) *Fourth Malaysia Plan, 1981–1990* (Kuala Lumpur: Government Printer).

Government of Malaysia (1986) *Fifth Malaysia Plan, 1986–1990* (Kuala Lumpur: Government Printer).

Government Malaysia (1991a) *Sixth Malaysia Plan, 1991–1995* (Kuala Lumpur: Government Printer).

Government of Malaysia (1991b) *Privatisation Master Plan* (Kuala Lumpur: National Printing Department).

The Economic Development of Malaya, Report of a Mission Organized by the International Bank of Reconstruction and Development (1960) (Baltimore: Johns Hopkins University Press).

Jomo, K.S. (1992) 'Privatisation in Malaysia: For What and For Whom?', paper presented at the Conference on Post-Privatisation Policy and Performance: International Perspectives, University of Bradford, England, 6–7 March. (mimeo: Faculty of Economics, University of Malaya, Kuala Lumpur, Malaysia)

Ministry of Finance (1990) *Economic Report, 1990/91* (Kuala Lumpur: National Printing Department).

Ministry of Finance (1991) *Economic Report, 1991/92* (Kuala Lumpur: National Printing Department).

Ministry of Finance (1992) *Economic Report, 1992/93* (Kuala Lumpur: National Printing Department).

Salleh, Ismail and Osman-Rani, H. (1991) *The Growth of the Public Sector in Malaysia* (Kuala Lumpur: Institute of Strategic and International Studies (ISIS)).

World Bank (1983) *World Development Report* (New York: Oxford University Press).

6 A Note on the Ethical Role that Money Can Play in Development: The Case of Malaysia

Abdul-Ghafar Ismail

INTRODUCTION

Strategies for the economic development of developing countries traditionally have emphasised larger foreign aids or capital inflows from industrialised countries. But these forms of assistance are in some cases insufficient to overcome the countries' fundamental problems.

Theoretical analyses of development also emphasise the lack of resources, such as physical capital, managerial capability, and other real factors, to the almost complete exclusion of financial factors. In this chapter, a different approach to the development problem will be discussed. Instead of emphasising the scarcity of capital, the chapter will focus on the ethical role of money in the development process of Malaysia, because it seems important to develop a distinct alternative view of the role of money, particularly the capital market in the process of development. This view is especially important in the expanding economy where high rates of savings and investment are required.

This chapter will be organised in three sections. The first section will discuss the ethical role of money, especially the capital market, in the development process. In section two, the factors that influence the funds raised in the capital market will be discussed. The conclusions concerning the effect of capital market in the conduct of monetary policy will be presented in section three.

THE ETHICAL ROLE OF MONEY

In the 1980s, much effort was focused on creating a modern and efficient banking system, which is now fairly well developed, following the deregulation efforts to provide greater freedom and become more market-oriented. These deregulation measures include the freeing of interest rate determination, relaxing lending guidelines on credit rationing, levelling the playing field for different financial institutions and development of the capital market.

As a result, the development of the Malaysian capital market has accelerated. It represented a relatively small part of the Malaysian financial system during the early stages of economic development in the early 1960s and 1970s. The banking system then provided the bulk of the financing of economic activities.

The capital market has since witnessed significant developments, both in qualitative and quantitative terms in the 1980s and early 1990s. In the 1980s, the capital market expanded mainly to cater for the needs of the public sector, where the bulk (about 75 per cent) of the new funds raised during this period was in the form of issuance of Malaysian government securities. However, in the 1990s, the funds raised in the capital market is predominantly held by the private sector, especially when the interest rate was allowed to be freely determined by market forces.

The above developments are parallel to the need of the government to provide infrastructure and public utilities. The capital market has to be activated in order to assist the process of economic development by mobilising medium and long-term funds to finance public development programmes and to fund private investment, as well as to assist the banking system in securitising its assets. At the same time, the capital market promotes private companies by providing intermediary facilities to raise funds for corporate investment and expansion, and in changing the ownership structure of companies.

The argument is that capital market operations are influenced by monetary policy, since the thrust of monetary policy has to ensure that adequate liquidity continues to be channelled for productive purposes, so as to sustain economic growth with moderate price increases. Therefore, the question arises as to what extent the ethical role of money, especially the capital market, plays in economic development (Ismail, 1993).

THE ROLE OF THE CAPITAL MARKET – THE MALAYSIAN EXPERIENCE

Apart from financial institutions, increasing attention has been paid to the capital market to accelerate the mobilisation of private sector savings. To a large extent, the development of the capital market holds the key to assisting the private sector in the financing of its investment. To ensure a well-balanced capital market in the future, the market is being developed along three lines. First, the stock market is expected to grow to meet the needs of investors and borrowers. To meet the demand from an increasingly sophisticated securities industry and to reinforce the supervision of the capital market, the government has to promote and ensure the orderly development of the capital market.

Second, a wider choice of financial instruments has been made available. This has been achieved partly through concerted efforts to develop the corporate bond or private debt securities market. Rating Agency Malaysia Berhad was set up to assess the creditworthiness of bond-issuing companies, hence facilitating bond issues. This would encourage more potential investors to raise funds directly from the market.

Third, trading of Malaysian Government securities in the secondary markets has been enhanced and deepened to further increase liquidity and allocative efficiency.

However, in line with the above measures, total net funds raised by both the public and the private sectors declined from RM14 743 million in 1990 to RM6450 million in 1993, as shown in Table 6.1. Funds raised by the public sector were less, but were compensated by the substantial increase in the amount raised by the private sector. Consequently, the share of the private sector in the total of new funds raised rose to 80.9 per cent in 1993, from 74.1 per cent in 1990.

The funds raised in the capital market are influenced by several factors (Bank Negara, 1993).

Corporate Securities Market

Funds raised by the private sector through new issues of quoted corporate securities (shares market) and private debt securities declined substantially by an average of –1.1 per cent from RM10 927 million in 1990 to RM5220 million in 1993 (see Table 6.1). This was largely due to the decline in the shares issued, especially in the absence of the privatised companies which had mobilised about 65 per cent of the equity market in 1992. However, the development of more active private debt securities took up 49.9 per cent of the new fund raised in 1993.

The share prices performance was more comforting. The KLSE composite index in 1993 closed at 1275 points, 152 per cent higher than the level at the end of 1990, as shown in Table 6.2. Similarly, the new KLSE EMAS index closed on a higher rate at 384 points, 193 per cent higher than the level at the end of 1990. The New Straits Times (NST) price indices followed in tandem setting new highs, with the mining, finance,

Table 6.1 Funds raised in the capital markets (RM juta)

	1990	*1991*	*1992*	*1993*
By public sector				
Government securities	5 141	3 500	3 800	1 600
less redemption	1 243	343	2 420	2 225
Equal net issues	3 893	3 157	1 380	–625
Investment certificates	–100	—	100	1 000
Malaysia Savings Bond	—	—	—	855
Net funds raised	3 816	3 157	1 480	1 230
By private sector				
Shares	8 649	4 392	9 181	3 245
Public issues	3 757	1 743	5 416	1 442
Right issues	4 419	2 158	3 438	1 177
Special issues	473	491	300	626
Private placement	—	—	27	—
Private debt securities	2 603	1 966	4 112	3 242
Conventional bonds	953	695	1 635	1 439
Convertible bonds	871	921	337	153
Islamic notes	379	350	25	—
Cagamas bonds	400	0	2 115	1 650
Less redemptions	325	125	991	1 267
Equal Net issues	2 278	1 841	3 302	1 975
Net funds raised	10 927	6 233	12 302	5 220
Total	14 743	9 390	13 782	6 450

Source: Bank Negara Malaysia (1993).

plantation and property shares rising sharply by 183.5 per cent, 123.8 per cent, 112.5 per cent and 99.1 per cent respectively, while the index for industrial shares increased moderately by 44.5 per cent.

During the same period, the total number of companies listed increased from 285 in 1980 to 413 at the end of 1993. As a result of the additional stocks from these new companies as well as the sustained price increases of shares, market capitalisation of the KLSE increased remarkably during the period, from RM132 billion in 1990 before ending the period at a record high of RM620 billion or four times the size of the Malaysian GNP.

In sharp contrast to the developments in the KLSE, trading on the Bumiputera Stock Exchange (BSE) was less active during the period. Although, the volume of shares traded on the BSE increased significantly by 65 times to 1.3 million units in 1993, compared with 19 974 units in 1990, in value terms, it increased by 54 times to RM1.5 million. The more modest trading was attributed to the absence of speculative activities which were generated by corporate developments of some listed companies. With the transfer of several companies of the BSE to the second board of the KLSE, the number of listed companies on the BSE has declined.

Therefore, a special share has been allocated to the Bumiputera community to invest in the capital market. The amount of these shares has increased from RM473 million or 5.5 per cent of the total shares in 1990 to RM626 million or 19.3 per cent of the total shares in 1993, as shown in Table 6.1. In addition, the unit trust industry has also been encouraged to invest in the capital market, particularly for the Bumiputera investors. The Bumiputera's investment is also channelled through the Amanah Saham Bumiputera (ASB) scheme as well as an Islamic-based unit trust, where the fund size accounted for 82 per cent of the industry aggregate. The total investment of the ASB scheme expanded tremendously to RM14.2 billion in 1993 from RM624 million in 1990. These investments are mainly in the plantation, industrial and finance counters.

Favourable monetary conditions in the 1990s have encouraged several large corporations with good credit standing to raise funds by way of issuing public debt securities. However, this market is still in its early stage of development. These instruments, with maturity ranging between from two to ten years, provide a wider range of instruments to investors to structure their investment portfolio. At the same time, they provided borrowers with alternative sources of financing, in addition to the traditional methods of bank borrowing and share issuance. Islamic public debt securities have also been introduced to provide a wider alternative for investment avenues. During the period, RM3242 million were raised in 1993 through these medium-term securities, compared with RM2603 million in 1990. The issues were mainly confined to the large companies.

Government Securities Market

Reflecting the favourable financial position of the Federal Government, total gross funds raised fell to RM1600 million in 1993 from RM5141 million in 1990. After adjusting for large redemptions, net funds raised in 1993 amounted to RM1230 million, or just one-third of the amount raised in 1990.

The bidding of Malaysian Government securities (MGS) depends on several factors, such as the expectations of interest rates in the future, the strong non-resident demand for ringgit-denominated assets, the high liquidity in the banking system and the relatively more attractive returns on government securities.

The issue of Bank Negara Bills and Malaysia Savings Bonds also provided an alternative source of investment for the banking systems to fulfil their liquid asset requirements. The major traditional holders of government securities, that is, the social security and insurance institutions, continued to increase their investment in MGS. The increase was largely to meet their statutory obligation to invest part of their funds in MGS (Bank Negara Malaysia, 1994) (see Table 6.2).

The market of MGS can be activated in the secondary market. The interest rates and the demand for such securities by financial institutions that have to meet statutory investment requirements are expected to induce the demand for MGS in the secondary market. An alternative source of investments for *Shari'ah*-based financial institutions has been introduced (*Shari'ah*=Islamic law).

The introduction of Malaysian Government papers through Malaysian Government securities, government investment certificates, Malaysia savings bond and Bank Negara bills are part of the government effort to promote savings and to educate Malaysians to become familiar with the concept of investing in bonds as well as an alternative of investment avenues.

Table 6.2 Kuala Lumpur Stock Exchange: key indicators

	1990	*1991*	*1992*	*1993*
Price indices				
Composite	506	556	644	1275
EMAS	131	141	162	384
Second Board	—	127	140	352
Industrial	—	1 062	1 088	2 030
Finance	—	2 187	2 703	8 760
Property	—	1 111	1 140	3 370
Plantation	—	1 061	1 118	3 573
Mining	—	204	179	858
PE ratio	25	24	23	48
Market capitalisation (RM billion)	132	161	246	620
No. of companies listed	285	324	369	413

Source: Bank Negara Malaysia (1993).

Privatisation

The ongoing policy of the Malaysian Government to reduce the role of government has resulted in restructuring and rationalisation programmes to improve efficiency for the continuing benefit of public enterprises. As privatisation remained an important part of the overall strategy to consolidate public sector finances, the government continued to monitor and streamline the activities and expenditures of these public enterprises to further strengthen their financial position to pave the way for their privatisation. In addition, a policy decision is made to privatise the dormant public companies and those facing serious financial problems in order to alleviate the financial burden of the government.

The implementation of the privatisation programme continued to be actively pursued in the 1990s, especially with the commencement of several infrastructure projects, such as the Kuala Lumpur International Airport and the Light Rail Transit. These projects would require substantial capital investment over the next several years. In addition, the manufacturing, transportation and services sectors have been earmarked to be restructured and prepared for privatisation.

The estimates indicated that the consolidated financial position of the non-financial public enterprises (NFPEs), which are dominated by the privatised companies, remained comfortable. Both operating and development expenditures have increased over the period. As shown in Table 6.3, the activities of the NFPEs expanded significantly during the 1990s, with total expenditure registering a growth of 5.1 per cent to RM37.9 billion in 1993.

With the expansion in operating expenditure outpacing the growth in revenue, the operating surplus of the public enterprises was slightly lower at RM7.6 billion in 1993. The sizeable operating surplus was attributed to a few large and viable NFPEs involved mainly in commodities, utilities and commercial services, such as Petroleum Nasional Bhd (PETRONAS), Telekom Malaysia Bhd, Tenaga Nasional Bhd, Malaysia LNG Sdn Bhd, Malaysia Airlines System Bhd dan Perbadanan Kilang Felda. A few of the other enterprises continued to suffer small losses.

Development of several large projects by the major public enterprises (mainly by the privatised companies) proceeded during the period – especially infrastructure and public utilities projects – to expand the industrial base and provide support to the rapidly expanding economy; for example, the expansion of transmission and distribution networks as well as the implementation of fast track power generation projects in order to keep pace with the growing demand for electricity by the industrial and commercial

Table 6.3 Consolidated NFPEs finance (RM billion)

	1990	*1991*	*1992*	*1993*
Revenues	38.4	41.3	42.4	45.5
Expenditure	32.7	33.4	34.6	37.9
Current surplus	+5.7	+7.9	+7.8	+7.6
Development expenditure	4.6	5.7	6.8	8.8
Overall deficit (–) /surplus (+)	+1.1	+2.2	+1.0	–1.2
% of GNP	1.0	+1.8	+0.7	–0.8
No. of NFPEs (unit)	50	46	44	42

Source: Bank Negara Malaysia (1993).

sectors. In order to cope with the rapid growth in container traffic, the national carriers (MAS and MISC) continued to acquire new aircraft and tankers as well as expanding capacity and upgrading their facilities. In the transportation sector, the double-tracking project involving the construction and electrification of a second line and installation of a modern signalling and communications system was implemented.

The impact of privatisation towards capital market development remained significant. The 15 existing privatised companies contributed close to a quarter of the market capitalisation of the KLSE. The two largest companies on the Exchange, namely Tenaga Nasional and Telekom Malaysia, are privatised companies. Together, they accounted for 16.4 per cent of total market capitalisation in 1993. Furthermore, of the 130 companies which made it to the billion ringgit mark at the end of 1993, ten were privatised companies. Similarly, the 15 privatised companies contributed significantly to total turnover, accounting for 2 per cent of units traded and 4 per cent of total value traded in 1993.

CONCLUSION

Given the reduction of government expenditure, the private sector is expected to assume the role as the main engine of growth in the 1990s. Given this trend, the capital market has been developed to help finance the future development of the Malaysian economy. As a result the number and range of financial institutions have expanded significantly to widen the choice of available financial instruments for both borrowers and investors. These financial instruments are held by the financial intermediaries which are required to hold a minimum of their liabilities in Malaysian Government papers. In addition, the liberalisation of the interest rate (monetary policy instruments) has resulted in less distortion in interest rate structure and yield curves and this has also facilitated further secondary trading of government securities in Malaysia.

From the above measures aimed at mobilising funds in the Malaysian financial markets, it is found that the monetary policy on interest rate liberalisation has kept interest rates historically low in Malaysia. This in turn has caused a substantial amount of funds to be directed into the KLSE market, Islamic outlets of investment and savings, and to encourage money supply for investors. It has also generated an effective diversification of financing away from public spending and towards private sector spending. This is a much required condition for realising privatisation. The net result of these changes has been an impetus on market transformation in Malaysia, a direction of change that has now become irreversible.

References

Bank Negara Malaysia (1993) *Annual Report (1990–1993)* (Kuala Lumpur: Bank Negara Malaysia).

Bank Negara Malaysia (1994) *Money and Banking in Malaysia*. 35th Anniversary Edition 1959–1994 (Kuala Lumpur: Bank Negara Malaysia).

Ismail, Abdul-Ghafar (1993) 'Bank Regulations and Monetarty Policy', *Malaysian Management Review*, 28, pp. 56–60.

7 Trade and Regional Integration in the Global Perspectives for Malaysia

Mohammad Haflah Piei

INTRODUCTION

There has been an emerging trend for a global revival of regionally based trading arrangements between economies of the world. This phenomenon has been increasingly referred to as the 'new regionalism'. Among the major regional trading arrangements which have recently taken effect are the North American Free Trade Area (NAFTA) the European Union (EU), and the Asean Free Trade Area (AFTA). All these regional arrangements had been negotiated and concluded almost concurrently with the recently concluded Uruguay Round of multilateral trade negotiation.

In addition there are several other regional arrangements that are currently being negotiated. In the Asia-Pacific region there is the Asia-Pacific Economic Cooperation (APEC) within which there are smaller subregional arrangements: the proposed East Asian Economic Caucus (EAEC), the Australian–New Zealand Closer Economic Relations Trade Agreement (ANZERTA or sometimes described in short as CER) and a number of growth triangles each comprising subregions of different neighbouring countries.

Against the above development, the question is how to ensure that the establishment of regional trading groupings and FTAs will complement and support multilateralism and not turn them into inward-looking economic blocs.

As far as Malaysia is concerned, the above development would create opportunities and challenges for the economy depending on the orientation of the arrangement. If it is for open regionalism, that is, regional effort with global orientation, that Malaysia would expect a certain amount of economic opportunities though she would be at a disadvantage *vis-à-vis* other participating members of the regional grouping. Nevertheless, if the regional grouping is to become more restrictive, inward-looking and discriminatory towards non-members, then the consequences would be detrimental to Malaysia's economic performance.

It is the aim of this chapter, first, to predict and assess the nature of the impacts that these regional economic arrangements could have on the Malaysian external trade performance, and second, to suggest trade policy options that Malaysia could adopt in the context of the changes in the global economies.

MALAYSIA'S EXTERNAL TRADE: A REVIEW

Malaysia, being an open economy, is heavily dependent on external trade for its economic development. Total external trade registered a significant and increasing share of its Gross Domestic Product reflecting the importance of international trade to the Malaysian economy. The share of merchandise trade which accounted for 73 per cent of Malaysia's GDP in 1970 had grown to 14 per cent in 1993.

With respect to the direction of Malaysia's trade, it remains relatively unchanged since 1970 with Japan, the US, the EU and ASEAN together remaining Malaysia's major trading partners. Together they account for about 75 per cent of Malaysia's total trade between 1970 and 1993 (Table 7.1). While the order of importance of these countries/regions as Malaysia's trading partners has changed over the period, their importance as major trading partners remains. For instance, countrywise, Japan, the US and Singapore remain the top three trading partners, each contributing about 20 per cent of Malaysia's total trade. Regionally, the role of the EU has declined remarkably, now accounting for only 13 per cent of Malaysia's total trade compared to 63 per cent in the case of the East Asian region represented by Japan, ASEAN, East Asian NICs and China. Trade with the NAFTA region has been about 19 per cent.

In terms of exports, while Singapore maintains its role as the most important export market for Malaysia, the US has overtaken Japan and the EU as the second most important export market for Malaysia, contributing about 20 per cent of Malaysia's export market in 1993 compared to about 15 per cent and 13 per cent in the case of the EU and Japan, respectively (Table 7.2). An important observation is the importance of the East Asian NIEs and China as a fast growing market for Malaysia's exports.

As in the case of exports, the EU, ASEAN, Japan and the East Asian NIEs and China were also the major sources of Malaysia's imports. In the 1970s the EU and ASEAN were the major sources of Malaysia's imports, each contributing 23 per cent of its import requirement followed by Japan accounting for 17 per cent of Malaysian imports, East Asian (10 per cent) and the US (9 per cent). Nevertheless, the relative importance of the EU

Table 7.1 Direction of trade by major markets

	1970		*1980*		*1990*		*1993*		*Average annual growth (%) 1971–93*
	RM million	*% share*	*RM million*	*% share*	*RM million*	*% share*	*RM million*	*% share*	
United States	1 039	11	8 137	16	26 720	17	44 485	19	18
European Union	2 050	22	8 634	17	23 418	15	31 153	13	13
UK	920	10	2 049	4	7 448	5	8 769	4	10
Germany	371	4	2 292	4	6 486	4	8 914	4	15
Japan	1 694	18	11 795	23	31 563	20	47 959	20	16
ASEAN	2 276	24	10 208	20	38 010	24	57 001	24	15
Singapore	1 434	15	8 138	16	29 852	19	44 193	19	16
East Asia	740	8	3 954	8	19 000	12	31 227	13	18
South Korea	145	2	987	2	5 711	4	7 731	3	19
Hong Kong	158	2	851	2	4 021	2	7 362	3	18
Taiwan	142	2	17 045	2	6 051	4	10 180	4	20
China	295	2	1 023	2	3 186	2	5 912	3	14
Others	1 652	17	8 895	17	20 054	12	26 813	11	13
Total	9 451	100	51 623	100	158 765	100	238 638	100	

Source: Statistics provided in Tables 7.1–7.4 all compiled from various UNCTAD Direction of Trade publications.

Table 7.2 Direction of Malaysia's exports by major markets

	1970		*1980*		*1990*		*1993*		*Average annual growth (%) 1971–93*
	RM million	*% share*	*RM million*	*% share*	*RM million*	*% share*	*RM million*	*% share*	
United States	671	13	4 609	16	13 487	17	24 631	21	17
European Union	1 047	20	4 962	18	11 863	15	17 549	15	13
UK	3 420	7	779	3	3 136	4	5 102	4	13
Germany	162	3	1 017	4	3 097	4	4 431	4	16
Japan	944	18	6 429	23	12 589	16	15 729	13	13
ASEAN	1 311	25	6 348	22	23 048	29	33 783	28	15
Singapore	1 113	22	5 385	19	18 052	23	26 307	22	15
East Asia	330	6	2 112	8	9 605	12	16 139	13	18
South Korea	134	3	569	2	3 677	5	4 155	3	16
Hong Kong	64	1	529	2	2 523	3	4 994	4	21
Taiwan	65	1	498	2	1 728	2	3 888	3	20
China	67	1	471	2	1 675	2	3 094	3	18
Others	860	17	3 712	13	9 054	11	3 383	11	13
Total	5 163	100	28 172	100	79 646	100	121 214	100	15

and ASEAN declined over the period 1971–93 (Table 7.3). By 1993, the share of Malaysia's imports from the EU had declined to 12 per cent while that of ASEAN to 20 per cent. On the other hand, the relative share of imports from Japan and the US had registered a remarkable increase during the same period. The share of imports from the US had increased by 7 percentage points to 17 per cent while that of Japan by 10 percentage points to 27 per cent in 1993.

In line with the rapid structural transformation that has taken place in the Malaysian economy during the last three decades, the structure of its external trade too has been undergoing a remarkable transformation. On the export side, the share of inedible crude material (mainly rubber, tin and timber), mineral fuel and lubricants had shown a steep decline from as high as 61 per cent in 1970 to only 19 per cent in 1993 (Table 7.4). Within this group of exports too the relative importance of rubber and timber had sharply declined and were taken over by petroleum and LNG which became dominant since the early 1980s. On the other hand, the share of manufactured exports (broadly defined as SITC 5–8) had registered substantial gains in its relative share, increasing from about 27 per cent of the total export to about 75 per cent by 1993. This reflects the rapid rate of industrialisation that had taken place in the economy since 1970.

Within manufactured exports, the machinery and transport equipment subsector had experienced rapid annual growth of 33 per cent between 1971 and 1993 with its share increasing from a meagre 2 per cent to 49 per cent of Malaysia's total exports. A large proportion of products in this subsector comprises electrical, non-electrical and electronic products and to a lesser extent transport equipment. Another subsector which had shown rapid increase has been the export of manufactured goods (SITC 8) which comprised mainly textile and clothing, footwear, rubber and plastic products.

If one were to analyse in further detail the composition of the electrical and electronic subsector one would observe that this too had experienced remarkable transformation as a result of the government's deliberate effort in diversifying and deepening this subsector in terms of its output as well as export structures. For instance, the proportion of electronic components declined from a high of 70 per cent in 1980 to 34.5 per cent in 1992. In contrast, the contribution of consumer and industrial electronics, comprising mainly television sets, radios, sound recorders, office machinery and telecommunication parts, had increased from 4 per cent in 1980 to 25.1 per cent in 1992. With regard to the import structure, this has changed from one of more broad-based imports to one emphasising imports of intermediate manufactured goods, machinery and transport equipment.

Table 7.3 Sources of imports by major markets

	1970		*1980*		*1990*		*1993*		*Average annual growth (%) 1971–93*
	RM million	*% share*	*RM million*	*% share*	*RM million*	*% share*	*RM million*	*% share*	
United States	368	9	3 528	15	13 233	17	19 854	17	19
European Union	1 003	23	3 672	16	11 555	15	13 604	12	12
UK	578	14	1 271	5	4 312	5	3 657	3	8
Germany	209	5	1 274	5	3 389	4	4 483	4	14
Japan	749	17	5 365	23	18 974	24	32 230	27	18
ASEAN	965	23	3 860	16	14 962	19	23 218	20	15
Singapore	320	8	2 753	12	11 800	15	17 886	15	19
East Asia	410	10	1 842	8	9 394	12	15 089	13	17
South Korea	11	2	418	2	2 034	3	3 576	3	29
Hong Kong	94	2	321	2	1 497	2	2 368	2	15
Taiwan	76	2	546	2	4 323	5	6 293	5	21
China	229	5	551	2	1 511	2	2 818	2	12
Others	792	18	5 183	22	11 001	14	13 429	11	13
Total	4 288	100	23 451	100	79 119	100	117 423	100	

Table 7.4 Export and import trade structure

	Export (% of total) 1980				*Average annual growth (%)*	*Imports (% of total)*				*Average annual growth (%)*
	1970	*1980*	*1990*	*1993*	*1971–93*	*1970*	*1980*	*1990*	*1993*	*1971–93*
Food, beverages, tobacco, oils and	12	15	12	9	14	21	11	7	5	9
Inedible crude materials, mineral fuels and lubricants	61	57	33	19	9	20	20	8	6	10
Manufactured goods, intermediate	23	14	9	12	11	25	25	24	23	15
Machinery and transport equipment	2	11	36	49	33	28	39	50	56	19
Manufactured goods, final products	1	2	10	10	28	5	4	5	6	16
Miscellaneous	1	1		1	12	1	1	5	4	21
Total	100 (5.2)	100 (28.2)	100 (79.6)	100 (121.2)	100 15	100 (4.3)	100 (23.5)	100 (79.1)	(117.4)	16

The preceding discussion shows that the topic of the increasing importance of Japan and, to a lesser extent, the East Asia NIEs as Malaysia's trade partners needs further exploration. The significance here is borne out by the rapid rate of economic integration that has been taking place in the East Asian region, which includes Japan, ANIEs, China and ASEAN. This is evident from the magnitude of intra-regional trade and investment, which represents a large and increasing proportion of the region's total trade since the 1980s. Malaysia and other ASEAN countries have been a major recipient of FDI from Japan and lately from the ANIEs. This has been part of the industrial restructuring process that has been taking place, first in Japan and later on in the ANIEs. Rising labour costs and a sharp appreciation of their currencies have forced these countries to relocate those industries that are fast losing their competitive edge. Initially, Japan had relocated the more capital and skilled industries to the ANIEs and the more labour intensive one to the third tier countries, ASEAN and China. This brings about an emerging investment-induced trade among Japan, the ANIEs and ASEAN countries, whereby the latter source their supply of intermediate products from Japan and export part of their final output to Japan. After a time lag, when the ANIEs have attained a higher level of technological capability, they would pass over the production activities that they had received earlier on from Japan to the third tier countries, mainly ASEAN, and move up the ladder of technological and industrial development. By then the ASEAN countries too would have been ready to receive these industries from the ANIEs and move out of the unskilled labour intensive production activities. This process of industrial development has been popularly called 'the flying geese' pattern within the region.

As Malaysia is increasingly being integrated into the region, its trade balance has been showing an increasing deficit with the region as a whole. This has been mainly due to a sharp increase in its trade deficit with Japan which cannot be sufficiently balanced by its growing trade surplus with the rest of the region. In short, Japan has not been importing enough of Malaysian exports to cover its imports of Japanese products which have experienced a sharp increase due to the rapid appreciation of the yen in recent years. To cover the regional trade deficit, Malaysia needs to export more to other regions, mainly the US and Europe. Hence the importance of these regions as Malaysia's export markets. It is crucial that the global trading system remains open and expanding not only to lock in the present high growth but also to ensure a sustainable future.

Nevertheless, recent development has been less assuring despite the conclusion of the Gatt round. This is especially critical as a bipolar structure in world trade seems to be emerging: in Europe with the EU, EFTA and European Economic Area (EEA), and the American Hemisphere comprising the North, Central and Latin America centring around the NAFTA and the South American Common Market (MORCOSUR). Concommitant with the new structure is the drift from a multilateral structure towards discriminating bilateral or regional solutions to trade conflicts or issues. East Asia's economies, which greatly depend on the global market, are yet to react to these developments in a formal way.

It is in the above context that Malaysia needs to evaluate each of the regional compacts and position itself in the most efficient way that would ensure growth and substainability of her export and economy.

AFTA: ANOTHER FUTILE OR FERTILE TRADE AREA FOR MALAYSIA?

Since its inception in 1967, the ASEAN member countries have taken several measures to achieve closer economic cooperation within the region. These include measures to liberalise intra-ASEAN trade through the ASEAN Preferential Trading Arrangement,[1] and regional industrial specialisation schemes to name a few.[2] The progress of these programmes had been insignificant and this had prompted the ASEAN countries to embark on a more ambitious and comprehensive effort to establish the ASEAN Free Trade Area (AFTA)[3] in 15 years commencing in 1993. Its main mechanism of implementation is through the Common Effective Preferential Tariff Scheme (CEPT),[4] which plans to reduce tariffs on all intra-ASEAN trade in manufactured goods to between zero and 5 per cent within 15 years starting from 1993.

Reduction of import duties under the CEPT was to be undertaken according to the Fast Track or the Accelerated Tariff Reduction Programme (ATRP) and the normal track programme. The fast track covers 15 product groups to be implemented earlier than the 15 years time frame. The import duties of these products were to be reduced to 0–5 per cent within seven to ten years only.[5] The rest of the products would be covered under the normal track basis through which import duties on them would be reduced to 0–5 per cent within 10–15 years starting in 1993.

Under the fast track, Malaysia is offering about 3251 items or 27.7 per cent of 11 746 total tariff lines. Under the normal track, Malaysia is offering 6895 items for reduction in import duties covering another 59 per cent of the total tariff lines. There was some delay in implementing the programme and it was only on 1 January 1994 that the Initial Package of Tariff Reduction came into effect. Under this package, Malaysia offered

3431 items to be effective from 1 January 1994 while the remaining items would be effective in 1996. Malaysian tariff reduction included a notional cut for 1993 and the tariff cut for 1994.

In adopting the ASEAN–CEPT, Malaysia has two proposed objectives. The first is to seek liberalisation on a regional basis as part of the ongoing strategy to diversify its export market as well as to upgrade global competitiveness. Second, it is to maintain Malaysia's attraction as a major foreign direct investment (FDI) destination in the region.

The importance of ASEAN to the Malaysian economy can hardly be exaggerated. ASEAN as a group remains the most important trading partner contributing about 24 per cent of Malaysia's total trade since 1970. Though more than 90 per cent of Malaysia's intra-ASEAN trade was comprised of its entrepôt trade with Singapore, the trend of Malaysia's trade with the other ASEAN countries has been encouraging. Between 1970 and 1973, ASEAN remained Malaysia's largest export market taking 25–29 per cent of its exports. On the import side, ASEAN had been contributing about one-fifth of Malaysia's import requirement during the period. As a result Malaysia continues to enjoy a trade surplus in her intra-ASEAN trade.

Major components of exports comprised crude petroleum, rubber, machinery and transport equipment. Imports were mainly machinery and transport equipment, manufactured goods, food and mineral fuel. Through the AFTA, Malaysia would be able to increase its manufactured exports to the region, especially technology and capital-intensive goods, such as electrical and electronic equipment and machinery. Malaysia would also be importing from the region and this would largely consist of intermediate imports for general Malaysian industries and consumer goods produced by labour-intensive manufacture.

As Malaysia is fast losing its comparative advantage in the labour-intensive industries, it can be expected that regional imports will significantly replace the domestic production of such labour-intensive goods as textiles and clothing. It is in this sense that the AFTA can be trade-creating for Malaysia with higher-cost domestic production being replaced by lower-cost ASEAN products.

Free trade among ASEAN countries would inject greater competition and efficiency into the production structure, within which member countries would compete among themselves in their own regional market before they could compete with others in the world market. This process would slowly render ASEAN products internationally competitive and make the region more attractive to foreign investors.

Against the above fertile prospects of AFTA for Malaysia, there remain several reservations that it needs to be wary of. First, the pace at which

AFTA has been implemented has been very slow and the effect of the regional trade liberalisation exercise would only be felt in the long term. In the meantime, the ASEAN countries have committed themselves to significant tariff reductions under the Uruguay Round of multilateral trade negotiations which were to take effect from 1 January 1995. At the present pace of the unilateral and multilateral trade liberalisation process, the chances are that AFTA will become redundant, if not irrelevant well before fruition. Second, by focusing too much attention and effort on AFTA, it may divert Malaysia's attention and resources from its trade and economic realities. One such reality is that Malaysia as well as other ASEAN countries owe their prosperity to extra-regional trade, and though AFTA may be an attractive proposition to Malaysia, it cannot become a substitute for the vast lucrative extra-ASEAN market. Thus Malaysian trade within ASEAN should not be at the expense of its extra-ASEAN trade. The current patterns of Malaysia's external trade is not expected to change very much under the ASEAN–CEPT scenario. In order to achieve this, AFTA should continue to liberalise its trade in greater depth and speed while at the same time lowering its discrimination against non-members. This would fit well with the kind of economic regionalism that would serve Malaysia best; that is, 'open regionalism' would strengthen its extra-regional linkages and extend its outreach by rendering its products internationally competitive.

Within the AFTA there is yet another very interesting experiment in the making for a closer economic relationship. It is the concept of the 'Growth Triangle', which brings together subregions in different ASEAN countries that are in close proximity with each other, to form a larger region with greater potential for development. The first to be established is the Singapore–Johore–Riau Growth Triangle (hereafter be referred to as SIJORI).[6] This has started to show some encouraging results. Differences in factor endowment and hence comparative advantages that exist in the triangle would ensure that the economies of the subregion would be complementary rather than competitive. This is a basic prerequisite for a viable regional economic integration. Located within the same economic space it makes good economic sense that these areas in the subregion harness their economic potential for their mutual benefit.

Prompted by immediate success of the SIJORI, several initiative growth triangles are currently being negotiated.[7] These may serve as a complementing role for an AFTA trade liberating exercise, at a much smaller and easier scale to manage, and more likely to produce significant positive effects within a shorter time period. The growth triangle, the IMT-GT in particular, and other subregional compacts have a potential role to ensure Malaysia's trade and investment competitiveness.

APEC: ANOTHER PROSPEROUS ECONOMIC COOPERATION FOR MALAYSIA?

Another issue that concerns Malaysia as much as the other ASEAN countries is the position that ASEAN should take within a wider economic cooperation, namely the Asian-Pacific Economic Cooperation (APEC). APEC was initiated by the then Australia Prime Minister Bob Hawke. As an economic entitity it represents a big economic power in the world economy, combining approximately 61 per cent of the world population and 73 per cent of the world total GDP. APEC brings together highly industrial economies, Japan (with a per capita income of about US$30 000) and the United States (with a per capita income of about US$23 000). It also includes the 'newly industrialised economics' such as South Korea, Chinese Taipei, Hong Kong and Singapore, as well as developing economies such as China and Indonesia with a per capita income that remains below US$1000.

The relationship between ASEAN and APEC would depend on whether they would compete or complement each other and whether APEC would render ASEAN irrelevant. It would also depend to what degree APEC would be able to allay ASEAN and to some extent the NICs' fear of the 'big brotherly' domination by the much strengthened United States within the NAFTA. Though it is too early to make a definitive assessment of the implication of NAFTA on Malaysia's (a well as other ASEAN countries) trade and investment, some element of the NAFTA provision appears to be restrictive.[8]

The removal of internal tariff and non-tariff barriers within the NAFTA member countries would enhance intra-regional trade in products of interest to Malaysia, such as textiles, clothing, footwear, electrical and electronic equipment, furniture, toys, games, marine products, vegetable oil and food, which could be substituted by NAFTA sources of supply thereby diverting trade to some extent. In addition, the reduction and elimination of tariffs and non-tariffs under NAFTA would give Mexican producers a competitive advantage for these products in the US market, as they constitute Mexico's major market. In 1993, 90 per cent of Malaysia's export to the US comprised machinery and transport equipment and other manufactured goods. Nevertheless, these discriminating effects may be cushioned to same extent by the trade liberalisation measures pursuant to the Uruguay Round agreement.

In terms of investment flow, the elimination of restrictions by Mexico on foreign investment under the NAFTA would attract investment from the USA and Canada, especially from companies that want to re-export their products to their home countries in order to take advantage of the lower rates in Mexico and unrestricted access to the NAFTA market. Hence Mexico could became a major production base which could have the effect of not only diverting investment from the USA and Canada but also from Japan, Europe and ANIEs.

The impact would be more far reaching considering that there has been strong commitment to expand NAFTA to other countries in the Western Hemisphere. The summit of the Americas held in Miami in early December 1994 could accelerate the pace at which NAFTA is expanded.

At the rate at which NAFTA is developing, it is natural that ASEAN members of APEC should be wary of the possibility of US domination of APEC. As a result, ASEAN countries would be more comfortable in APEC if the proposed East Asian Economic Caucus (EAEC), which was initiated by Prime Minister Mahathir Mohammad of Malaysia and was strongly endorsed by the rest of the ASEAN member countries, could take off. The ASEAN strategy will then be to promote itself as the core in a configuration of concentric circles with EAEC serving as the middle layer[9] that would protect ASEAN interests from the US domination of APEC and US 'aggressive unilateralism'.[10]

Despite the importance of EAEC to the ASEAN, the recently released Eminent Person Group's (EPC) second report commissioned by APEC and deliberated upon at the Bogor summit, chose not to mention it at all. Instead the EPG report urges APEC member countries to adopt as a long-term goal a 'free and open trade and investment in the region' starting from year 2000. Taking into account the diversity of the region, member countries would be given staggered duration to complete the exercise by the year 2020 by recommending a three-way differentiation in the timetable.

> As a general rule the more economically advanced economies should eliminate their barriers on the most rapid of the three schedules, perhaps in ten years. The NICs should liberalise on an intermediate timetable, perhaps in fifteen years. The developing member economies should aim to fulfil their obligation on the slowest schedule, say over twenty years. (APEC, 1994)

While this augurs well for the majority of the APEC countries, some other sweeping recommendations of the EPG report are not timely and appropriate. These include the early adoption of an APEC Concord on Investment Principles, creation of an anti-dumping and restricted business practices, an APEC dispute mediation service and harmonisation of national product standard and testing procedures.

Adoption of such proposals would push APEC a long way towards becoming a full-fledged bureaucratic organisation – a kind of regional world trade organisation. In its nascent state of development as an institution, it is unlikely that APEC could, and probably inappropriate that it should, take such a sweeping role. Such a function would duplicate the work of GATT, which is set to become the World Trade Organisation (WTO) in 1995. GATT already addresses dumping issues and operates a comprehensive dispute settlement mechanism on a global scale.[11] Furthermore, an APEC agreement on trade and investment would be tantamount to killing the goose that lays the golden eggs to the extent that it would generate complex rules and regulations, necessitating elaborate documentation and raising the transaction cost of doing business in the region.

The present pattern of East Asian regional trade and investment has occurred independently of any significant institutional integration agreement within the region. It is market driven and spearheaded by the private sector with official intervention limited to non-discriminating measures directed at facilitating trade and investment flows. While the report discusses in great length the 2020 vision of APEC, it fails to highlight the spark plug of Asian prosperity in the private sector. Do the region's entrepreneurs really care for APEC? This is vital as real economic integration will come about far more as the result of private investment decision than of official policy-making.

The concept of 'open regionalism', which will be the basis for creating 'free trade in the area' as opposed to a 'free trade area' in APEC, is yet another issue which is very controversial, contradictory and discriminatory, and regarding which developing APEC member countries must be wary of the motives of the developed members.

By open regionalism it means that APEC as a whole could extend its trade concession to all or some non-member developing economies on a reciprocal basis. This would serve as a positive and healthy incentive for these countries to accelerate the economic reform processes in order to meet the reciprocal obligation. Additionally, through the open regionalism concept, 'individual APEC economies could unilaterally extend the benefits of their APEC liberalisation to all economies either on a conditional basis, via the negotiation of free trade arrangements with them, or on an unconditional MFN basis'.

By offering liberalisation benefits to non-APEC countries on a reciprocal basis,[12] APEC poses a contradiction to the GATT principle of MFN treatment. It is even more appalling to note that APEC singles out the developing countries. Most developing countries (member or non-members) are not ready to reciprocate the offer due to their economic backwardness. These countries have mainly commodity-based industries, with uncompetitive, remote and backward manufacturing industries and are, therefore, in no position to open up their economies completely to foreign competition. Doing so would only destroy their industries and hamper their efforts for economic development and industrialisation. Any attempt to pry open their economies for the capturing of market by firms in developed countries would be unfair, discriminatory and unjust, particularly when the developing countries are not ready to do so.

By legalising the offer of APEC liberalisation benefit by member countries to non-member countries via the negotiation of free trade arrangements with them would pose several problem for APEC, as this would result in a proliferation of such negotiated FTAs. NAFTA had already accepted Chile into the agreement and later into APEC. Mexico and Chile have bilateral or plurilateral free-trade agreements with other countries in Latin America, and by virtue of the fact that Mexico and Chile are members of NAFTA, all the preferences that Mexico and Chile enjoy with NAFTA would have to be extended to other countries in Latin America, with which they have an FTA agreement. Some of these countries are non-APEC members. Similarly, Israel would have to be given the same treatment as it has an FTA agreement with the US. The accession of additional economies to NAFTA to include more Latin American economies would discriminate against the rest of the Pacific. It would be increasingly difficult to reconcile with assurances that the East Asian economies would not be damaged. It will only confirm Malaysia's and other APEC developing economies' fear of the US strategy to increase its domination of the APEC economies. This will come as part of the US effort to use APEC as a strong economic leverage in her dealing with the EU and perhaps Japan and other individual countries in APEC itself.

As far as Malaysia is concerned, its stance with respect to APEC has been clear, consistent and positive all along. It acknowledges the importance of APEC as its export market as well as its main source of imports and foreign investment. Malaysia is strongly committed to the process of trade liberalisation through her early ratification of the GATT Uruguay Round agreement. She would commit herself to further trade liberalisation through the APEC only at a pace and capacity commensurate with her level of development. To Malaysia the timetable for achieving free trade in APEC is only indicative and non-binding. Malaysia is of the opinion that whatever step is taken to facilitate the process, it must be based on what has been agreed with GATT. APEC in not mandated to force agreement of issues on members that are not covered by the GATT agreement. It is unfair on the part of the developed members of APEC, particularly the US, to force something that it failed to achieve in the GATT process.

Malaysia's reservation is based on her economic reality, which is also shared by many of the other APEC developing economies. The only difference is that Malaysia stated her reservation strongly and clearly by attaching an annexure to the declaration while others preferred to keep them to themselves. Even China, which had been critical of the proposed timetable, preferred to tag on with the rest without any reservation attached. It is in this respect that Malaysia had done a significant favour in protecting the interests of the developing members of APEC.

There is nothing to guarantee that the present developing APEC economies will be able to be on an equal footing with the developed members of APEC by the year 2020 even if the latter countries come to a standstill. For example, even if Malaysia were to grow at 7 per cent per annum until the year 2020 her per capita income would only be about US$16 000, which would be significantly lower than the estimated per capita income of the US at US$30 000 then. And Malaysia is not even the best economy in the APEC.

EAEC: EXCLUSIVELY ASIAN ECONOMIC CLUB?

Of the many proposals for regionalisation in Asia, perhaps the most publicised one is the East Asian Economic Group (now known as the East Asian Economic Caucus, EAEC) promoted by the Malaysian premier less than a year after APEC had successfully been initiated by Australia. It is envisaged as a loose consultative forum where East Asian economies consult each other on issues of common concern as and when the need arises. They would contribute to expanding cooperation among the region's economies and the promotion of an open and free global trading system.

Since the ASEAN countries adopted the EAEC as a caucus within APEC, the objective has been to ensure that the EAEC would complement both ASEAN and APEC, while at the same time it may help to allay the ASEAN and other East Asia developing economies' fear of the 'big-brotherly' domination of the US. Nevertheless, the US has a different opinion of the EAEC: successful and strong EAEC would anchor Japan in its natural constituency (East Asia) and prevent it from overly concentrating its industrial and investment activities in North America. The worst fear of the US is the possibility of Japanese domination of the EAEC – the fastest growing region in the World. As a result, at the APEC Forum in Seoul in 1991, the United States government led by the then Secretary of State, James Baker, had launched a direct and apparently successful attack against the initiative by labelling it as discriminatory, racist and in conflict with the APEC process.[13] The US rejection of the EAEC has been strongly backed by Australia, which feared for her possible isolation by both the US and the Asian-Pacific countries, partly due to the deterioration in her bilateral ties with Malaysia. Continued US political hagemony – enhanced by the end of the cold war and the disintegration of the Soviet Union – has dampened most other governments in the region, including Japan, from taking a more independent position which would offend the US Government. The absence of the Malaysian premier at the Seattle informal meeting in 1993 – where he could have continued 'lobbying' for the EAEC concept – may have unwittingly defined the EAEC as inimical of the APEC and thus foreclosed any further compromise. This largely explains the exclusion of the EAEC by the EPG report as well as at the Bogor informal meeting.

It would be very unfortunate if the EAEC proposal is to be abandoned without a full and serious consideration as to its merits not only to the economies in the region but also to the world economies at large. Over the last two decades or so, the countries in the region have been growing at a very rapid rate, such that the region has eventually assumed a new role as the group of the most dynamic economies in the world.[14] Rapid growth in the economies has been matched and reinforced by their strong trade performance characterised by their increasing contribution to world trade as well as intra-regional trade. The increase in intra-regional trade has also been followed by rapid growth in intra-regional investment flows. These development have led to the rapid emergence of a regional production system based on inter-regional foreign direct investment. The degree of production and trade integration already achieved by the economies in the region has created pressures for regional policy coordination that would facilitate further integration in the area. These policies that will enable the regionalisation process to develop further, extend well beyond trade liberalisation, and cover such issues as harmonisation operations, differences in domestic standards on safety and environmental protection, improvement in infrastructural facilities and standardisation of commercial legislation. In short, regionalisation in East Asia has created the need for a regional policy framework that would maintain the momentum of the regionalisation.

It is in the above context that the proposed EAEC should be evaluated especially by countries in the region. The US fear that the EAEC would develop into an exclusively Asian trade bloc that would threaten the global trading system seem to be exaggerated. The recent initiative for closer regional cooperation among the EAEC economies has been directed mainly towards open regionalism. There is a commitment to open market access and the recognition that the main export markets continue to be outside the region. While the acceptance by EAEC member countries has been lukewarm, it would be in their best interests to ensure that the EAEC option be strengthened and conduct itself in a manner that would facilitate but not frustrate the APEC process. By doing so, East Asian countries will still have the EAEC option to fall back on if at any time the APEC initiative fails to address their regional interest.

EEA: EXCLUSIVELY EUROPEAN AREA

While countries in the Asian Pacific are still divided and uncertain as to the best and acceptable form of regional arrangement for the alignment of member countries, their counterparts in the European community moved a big step forward in announcing the establishment of a single and unified market within the region as from 1 January 1993. It involves the free flow of goods, services, capital and labour within the community while maintaining a common external protection against imports from third countries. The potential benefits of the single market have led to many other countries in Europe to negotiate for arrangements that would allow them to participate in the Union. The EU's immediate neighbours, the European Free Trade Areas (EFTA), finally concluded an agreement in May 1992 to set up the European Economic Area (EEA), the world largest trading bloc, uniting over 350 million people in one of the richest areas of the global economy. Yet it is only a way-station; several countries that are now associate members of the EU, which lies at the heart of the EEA, are in the process of becoming full members. Several others, notably in East Europe, will be intensifying their ties with the group over the coming years. Regionalisation is thus expanding rapidly in Europe, raising questions for countries elsewhere and for the global system as a whole as to the effects of such a trend on their economies.

It is still too early to make a quantitative estimate of the effects of the European single market. Generally, the abolition of tariffs and other trade impediments on intra-EU trade would enhance discrimination against imports from non-EU countries. Products produced within the EU would be relatively cheaper than the products that are imported from non-EU sources, since the latter are still subjected to the EU common external tariff. This may result in the substitution of third-countries' imports by regionally produced products. Whether it would be trade creation or trade diversion, the fact is that third-countries' exports to the EU would be reduced depending on the percentage increase in their prices *vis-à-vis* regional products and their income elasticity of demand by the EU market. The formation of a large protected market may also divert investment from outside to within the EU.

On the positive side, rapid growth that may accompany the integration of the market may spill over to the third countries through increases in the regional demand for their imports. Rapid economic growth within the region will make the Union more open and reduce the protectionist pressure from within it. With a united market rather than the 12 previously fragmented markets, third-countries' exports need to conform to one set of national or harmonised standards rather than to the individual country's import regulations and rules. This would reduce the cost of exporting to the region and could finally increase demand for imports from the third countries. National quotas on several sensitive products may be converted into region-wide quotas. This would enable exporting third countries to utilise the quotas fully.

Nevertheless, during the first five years of its existence, the economic condition within the community has not been encouraging for a more liberal trade and economic policies towards the third countries. Economically, the region remained in recession since its downturn started in late 1991. With the exception of the UK, which showed signs of some economic recovery, most other member countries in the union are yet to recover. Unemployment, which has been on the increase, totalled around 17 million in 1993 and was estimated to reach 20 million in 1994. This increasing trend in unemployment is expected to continue in the near future. Having to face these economic problems the potential for a more protectionist and inward-looking EU cannot be discounted, as observed from a number of policy decisions taken recently.

The seriously affected industrial sector, such as the automobile, textile and clothing industries, had been seeking both assistance and protection against the import of similar products from third-world economies, which had succeeded in achieving competitiveness in the European market. The third countries had increasingly been accused of massive 'social dumping' – which means that a country is exporting in large quantities a product that is produced cheaply and under conditions that violate international labour, human rights and environmental standards. To curb the so-called 'social dumping', the EU has been urged to attach social clauses to international trade both at the multilateral and unilateral level. The GSP regime which was to be renewed at the beginning of 1995 will possibly include certain conditionalities linked to these social clauses.

The EU anti-dumping procedures, a mechanism to curb excessive imports to a point that causes serious injury to domestic industries, have undergone significant changes in recent years that, in effect, would make it easier to institute such a trade defensive mechanism. There has been a shift towards redefining the rule of origin which move away from the generally accepted notion of 'substantial transformation' to a more elaborate system of value-added measurement that could have the opposite effect. This move has an inherent bias against Malaysian products produced at low domestic value added, resulting in the in the product being ruled as of non-Malaysian origin. As a result, the product would not only be ineligible for GSP treatment but would also be subjected to the EU's anti-dumping investigation. Among the products that have been subjected to anti-dumping procedures which are of interest to Malaysia are compact disc players, CTV sets, microwave ovens, bicycles, wristwatches and clockworks.

Other policy measures and proposals that would adversely affect Malaysian exports include environmental measures and sanitary and phytosanitary measures. The introduction of the eco-label awarded to products, which have adopted specific environmental criteria set by the EU as well as eco-packaging aimed at reducing the environmental impact of packaging waste and encouraging lower consumption of raw material and power, will have a major impact on the production, marketing and distribution of most products. This will have a bearing on Malaysian exporters who would have to adjust their manufacturing process so as to meet eventually the requirements of the EU's future directive on environmental standards.

Our discussion on the likely scenario and effect of the EU on Malaysia's external trade prospects has shown that the EU's trade and economic policies in the short and medium term is expected to be increasingly restrictive. A country like Malaysia would increasingly be placed on a level similar to theirs and this would mean getting Malaysia to make more commitments in the international trading system.

CONCLUSION

Our discussions in this chapter point to the emergence of several regional trading arrangement among the world economies, despite the successful conclusion of the Uruguay Round. In Europe, events are fast moving in a direction of regional pan-European agreement between an enlarged European Union and the other nations of Europe which might take the form of a vast free-trade area. In the Americas, the tendency is for NAFTA to be expanded to include other economies in the Western Hemisphere in what is now known as the Organisation of the American

States. At the recently concluded Bogor informal meeting, APEC leaders had agreed to form a free-trading area within APEC member countries by the year 2020. In addition, there are several other smaller regional compacts within these three blocs of countries.

Being in the top 20 trading nation in the world, there is an urgent need for Malaysia to position herself in the proper perspective to ensure that her present growth path can continue within the new global trading configuration. High on the priority list of policy responses is Malaysia's commitment to ensure the successful implementation of the GATT agreement. This requires an early ratification of the agreement and a smooth transition of functions and roles of GATT to its successor, the World Trade Organisation (WTO). In addition, Malaysia would have to assume active participation in terms of its obligation and responsibilities. Among these obligations are to be included Malaysia's commitment to liberalise her trade regimes and to make the necessary changes to a number of her domestic policies, including those in investment and in industrial policies to conform to the GATT requirements. To a certain extent Malaysia had carried out these obligation. These include the ratification of the GATT agreement, offers of tariff concessions, changes in her anti-dumping rules, amendments to her trade-related investment measures, stricter enforcement of her copyright law, and so on. Most of these measures were taken unilaterally and well in advance of the GATT schedule.

The priority placed on the GATT trade liberalisation process has several merits in the sense that it is the most appropriate body to deal with most of the present-day trade issues. In addition, the GATT liberalisation measures may act as a buffer to mitigate some of the adverse and discriminatory actions of a country or group of countries such as the EU and NAFTA.

With respect to the AFTA, Malaysia's position should be supportive in as far as AFTA strengthens her extra-regional trade competitiveness and the region's attractiveness to DFI – the two objectives set out earlier on. This could only be accomplished if AFTA moves faster in speed and substance than that of GATT, if it is to remain an attractive and feasible proposition to Malaysia. Failing this other alternatives should be promoted, including the development of several more growth triangles as well as expanding the region to cover the newly emerging economies in the area, such as Mynmar, Cambodia and Vietnam.

As far as the EAEC is concerned, Malaysia can still pursue the initiative, albeit with a smaller number of East Asian nations to start with. It must remain a loosely knit consultative forum within APEC and play the role that would facilitate and not frustrate the APEC process. By now, most of the East Asian leaders must have a clear understanding of the concept, rationale and the *modus operandi* of the EAEC. Yet these countries should not take any definitive stance until Japan makes the first move.

In Japan, the debate on this issue is still continuing, especially among the leaders, officials and recently amongst the public, fired by the recent campaigning by the Malaysian premier which was given extensive coverage by the Japanese mass media. Enthusiasm for the EAEC idea of 'Asia-first' seems to be rising among Japan's ruling circles and powerful business groups. Its most influential business organisation, the Kaidendren, is now considering a plan to urge the government to endorse the EAEC.

The above stance with respect to the EAEC should not be construed as Malaysia's reduced commitment to the rest of the APEC region. In the aftermath of the Bogor Declaration – where she had officially stated her reservation as an annexure to the Declaration – Malaysia should maintain her relations with the rest of the APEC member countries and continue her present trade liberalisation exercise either unilaterally or multilaterally. After all, the APEC liberalisation process will only start at the earliest in the year 2000. With or without APEC, economic relations with the US must be maintained as it represents a large export market for Malaysia, perhaps larger than the Japanese market. Malaysia should confront the NAFTA market, positively drawing on her earlier experience in coping with the European market, when it was first established.

Notes

1. The PTA was introduced in 1977 to expand intra-ASEAN trade through the granting of preferential access into each other's market. The instrument identified by the PTA include long-term quantity contract; purchase finance support at preferential interest rates; preference in procurement by government entities; extension of tariff preferences; liberalisation of non-tariff measures on preferential basis. For the detailed performance of the PTA see Piei (1985).
2. Among the regional cooperation schemes are included: the ASEAN Industrial Projects (AIPs), ASEAN Industrial Complementation, (AIC), the ASEAN Industrial Joint Ventures (AIJVs) which are all based on the concept of resource pooling and market sharing. The AIPs seem to be the least successful in view of the longer approval process by the ASEAN member states and the difficulty of identifying suitable projects which will conform with the priorities of the ASEAN member countries. The AIJVs have been the most successful, to date 21 projects have been granted AIJV status which enjoys a 90 per cent tariff cut when imported into participating countries.

3. For a succint review of AFTA see Imada, Montes and Naya (1991); Imada and Naya (eds) (1992); Lee Tsao Yuan (1994).
4. The CEPT replaces the trade preference scheme under the PTA, whereby ASEAN countries exchange tariff preferences for each other's products under the CEPT scheme; tariff and non-tariff barriers within ASEAN will be gradually liberalised to a fixed time-frame.
5. Under the fast track, tariffs will be reduced based on the following formulae: a. for products with import duties above 20 per cent, the duties will be reduced based on the formulae (x – 5 per cent)/10 years where x = existing duties; b. for products with import duties of less than 20 per cent and below the duties will be reduced, based on the (x – 5 per cent)/7 years where x = existing duties.
6. For a detailed examination of the SIJORI refer to Lee Tsao Yuan (1991).
7. Among them are included: The Indonesia–Malaysia–Thailand Growth Triangle (IMT-GT) or the Northern Growth Triangle and the East Asian Growth Area known as Brunei–Indonesia–Malaysia–Philippine Growth Areas (BIMP-GA). For a brief discussion on the IMT-GT see Piei (1994).
8. For example, the more stringent 'roles of origin' for textile and clothing and motor-vehicles (MITI, 1994).
9. Nevertheless, it proved difficult to sell EAEC to other East Asian economies on this basis. As Ariff rightly noted, there was no incentive for them to join the caucus if it is meant to protect the ASEAN 'core'. Indeed, every member would like to be part of the core not the periphery.
10. Even the First Eminent Persons Report of APEC (1993) has acknowledged that US 'agressive unilateralism' could undermine the open multilateral system.
11. In fact, APEC is trying to perform more than GATT. For example, regarding the safeguard mechanism, it will be more comprehensive in its coverage and more rigorous in its criteria and procedures than is now embodied in GATT.
12. It is more alarming to note that the very term 'reciprocity' has a very different meaning in US policy than it does within GATT. In the contest of US trade law, reciprocity refers to a policy in which a country seeks to achieve its objectives or enforce its rights by threatening or imposing sanctions on a bilateral basis (UNCTAD, 1994).
13. These criticisms have since been convincingly diffused. For a thorough rebuttal of these criticisms of EAEC see Nordin Sopiee (1992).
14. East Asia as a whole (excluding Japan) had achieved an average annual GDP growth of 8.1 per cent during 1987–91, surpassing the economic performance of the developed economies and other parts of the developing economies.

References

Alek, A. (1992) 'Pacific Economic Cooperation: Policy Choices for the 1990s', *Asian Pacific Economic Literature*, 6 (1).

APEC (1993) *A Vision for APEC: Towards an Asia Pacific Economic Community*. A Report of the Eminent Persons Group to APEC Ministers (APEC Secretariat Tokyo, Japan).

APEC (1994) *Achieving the APEC Vision: Free and Open Trade in the Asia Pacific*. Second Report of the Eminent Persons Group (APEC Secretariat Tokyo, Japan) August.

Ariff, Mohamed (1992) 'The Political Economy of the ASEAN Free Trade Area: A Commentary' in Imada, P. and Naya, S., *AFTA: The Way Ahead* (Singapore: ASEAN Economic Research Unit).

Asiaweek (1994) *An Agenda for APEC*, 21 September.

The Economist (1994) *APEC: The Opening of Asia*, 16 July and 12 November.

Imada P. and Naya, S. (eds) (1992) *AFTA: The Way Ahead* (Singapore: ASEAN Economic Research Unit, Institute of Southeast Asian Studies).

Imada, P., Montes, M. and Naya, S. (1991) *A Free Trade Area: Implications for ASEAN* (Singapore: Institute of Southeast Asian Studies).

Lee Tsao Yuan (1991) (ed.) *Growth Triangle: The Johor–Singapore–Riau Experience* (Singapore: ISEAS).

Lee Tsao Yuan (1994) 'The ASEAN Free Trade Area: The Search for a Common Prosperity', *Asian Pacific Economic Literature*, 8 (1).

Ministry of Finance, *The Annual Economic Report* (Kuala Lumpur: Ministry of Finance), various issues.

MITI (Ministry of International Trade and Industry) (1994) *Malaysia International Trade and Industry Report 1993* (Kuala Lumpur: MITI).

Nordin Sopiee (1992) 'Political Issues Associated with Economic Cooperation in East Asia', *ASEAN–ISIS Monitor*, 4, July–September.

Piei, Mohammad Haflah (1983) 'ASEAN: An Economic Evaluation of Its Effect, with Special Reference to the Malaysian Economy', Ph.D. Thesis submitted at the University of Lancaster.

Haflah Piei, Mohammad (1994) *The Northern Growth Triangle: A Malaysian Perspective* (Bangi Faculty of Economics, Universiti Kebangsaan Malaysia).

UNCTAD (1994) *The Newest Issues in US Trade Policy: The Domestic Politics of Trade and Its International Economic Consequences*, A Report Prepared for Project RAS/92/034 (Geneva United Nations Conference on Trade and Development).

Yam, T.K., Toh M.H. and Low, L. (1992) 'Asian and Pacific Economic Cooperation', *ASEAN Economics Bulletin*, 8 (3).

8 Political Economy of Development in Malaysia

B.N. Ghosh

INTRODUCTION

As is well known, economic development is the outcome of the interplay of many forces and relations, and as such it cannot be well treated singularly in the domain of pure economics. This is especially true in the case of Malaysia where the economic sphere has largely been dominated by political considerations, and the two have always had a large degree of interaction in determining the shape of things to come. In other words, this implies that the best method of studying development in a country like Malaysia is the political economy approach.

The main objective of this chapter is to explicate the development scenario of Malaysia in terms of its political economy. Economic development in Malaysia can be satisfactorily interpreted through the perspective of class analysis. In what follows, it will be shown that far more than anything else, respective class interest has been the main driving force in Malaysia to initiate and sustain the process of her economic development.

MAJOR INDICATORS OF DEVELOPMENT

The tempo of development of a country can be interpreted in various ways. One can think of, in this connection, at least three relevant dimensions of development: (i) structuralist dimension, (ii) quantitative dimension, and (iii) qualitative dimension.

Structuralist Dimension

Development invariably accompanies some progressive structural changes. These may be with respect to occupational changes, to changes in production structure, and/or to factor allocation, productivity or new exchange relationships. In the present section, I shall confine myself to the discussion of only a couple of structural changes in Malaysia to obtain the *prima facie* indication of the trend.

The thesis put forward by Sutcliffe envisages that a country is said to be industrialised if 25 per cent of its national product arises in the industrial sector, of which at least 60 per cent is in manufacturing, and at least 10 per cent of the country's total population is employed in the industrial sector (Sutcliffe, 1971).

In the case of Malaysia (in 1992), 40 per cent of GDP (at 1978 prices) came from the industrial sector consisting of mining, quarrying, manufacturing and construction; the contribution of the manufacturing sector alone was 65 per cent, and 24.6 per cent of the population of Malaysia was engaged in the industrial sector. Thus, if one applies the *Sutcliffe Criterion*, one can classify Malaysia now as an industrialised country.

Occupation Structure in Malaysia

In a meaningful sense, the occupation structure of a country can be regarded as the reflection of its degree of economic development. Economic progress is generally associated with certain distinct, necessary and predictable changes in occupation structure. Whereas the percentage of people depending on agriculture is very low in developed countries (DCs), it is very high in less developed countries (LDCs). Developed countries have a high percentage of people in non-agricultural occupations (80 per cent), but LDCs have a low percentage of people in such occupations (nearly 20 per cent). Most of the LDCs have nearly 70 per cent of the labour force in agriculture, and 30 per cent in non-agricultural occupations. Following the historical experience of DCs, one can describe the rate of economic development as the rate at which the 70:30 occupation ratio in LDCs is changed to approximately 20:80. The transfer of population from the agricultural to the non-agricultural sector must, of course, be accompanied by a rise in productivity in the former sector for providing food and raw materials to the latter sector. Needless to say, an upward change in agricultural productivity has to be accomplished with the help of many structural changes in the economy.

Colin Clark observes that a high average level of real income per capita is empirically found to be associated with a high proportion of the labour force in the tertiary sector (Clark, 1984, pp. 82, 395–97).

With economic development, perceptible occupational shifting takes place first from agriculture to industry and then from industry to the tertiary sector. Two main explanations are put forward for the shift of the labour force from agriculture to the non-agricultural sector. First, with the increasing real per capita income in agriculture, less is spent on consumption (because of low-income elasticity of demand for primary products). It follows, then, that the labour force engaged in agriculture must decrease. Second, output per capita may be increasing more rapidly in some sectors than in others. If average output per head in the primary industry is increasing, it would accelerate the movement of labour out of agriculture. The shift of the labour force initially takes place from agriculture to industry. But ultimately, the industrial sector is saturated, and hence people would be shifted to the tertiary sector where goods and services would be in demand. A.G.B. Fisher reminds us that shifts of employment towards secondary and tertiary production revealed by the census are an inescapable reflection of economic progress (Fisher, 1964, pp. 224 ff).

Structural change in the realm of occupation is very conspicuous in the case of Malaysia. As development proceeded steadily, an occupational shift in sympathy also followed suit in the right direction. This is evident from Table 8.1.

A cursory glance at Table 8.1 shows that within a period of two decades, Malaysia's occupational structure has changed tremendously. The primary sector which used to absorb 53 per cent of the labour force, now only contains less than 30 per cent. The 30:70 ratio of agricultural *vis-à-vis* non-agricultural occupations is *per se* a commendable achievement. Whereas the agricultural sector is undergoing the process of structural slimming, the secondary and tertiary sectors have started gaining weight. The industrial sector which accommodated 14.5 per cent of the labour force in 1970 was able to absorb nearly 25 per cent of the labour force in 1990. This demonstrates the continuous expansion of the industrial sector which is indeed a salutary sign of the rapid industrialisation of the country. This observation appears to be pretty convincing because there has been a simultaneous growth of productivity of the labour force employed in Malaysian industries. The industrial sector in Malaysia is

Table 8.1 Occupational structure in Malaysia

Sector	*Year (per cent of labour force)*		
	1970	*1980*	*1990*
Agriculture	53	40.6	29.9
Industry	14.5	22.7	24.6
Services	32.5	36.7	45.5

Source: Compiled from Ministry of Finance, *Economic Reports*.

poised for further expansion: the saturation point for labour employment is as yet far away. There is a similar story regarding Malaysia's services sector. Productive absorption of labour is rapidly taking place in the tertiary sector. Whereas the tertiary sector employed only 32.5 per cent of the labour force in 1970, the percentage went up to 45.5 in 1990. Obviously, both these sectors are growing in importance and are expanding with increasing labour productivity. However, it must be noted that the nature of the tertiary sector in LDCs is entirely different from that of DCs.[1]

All this boils down to the fact that the labour-deficit economy of Malaysia can perform splendidly in the matter of acceleration of economic growth if it can supply more labour, even by importation, to these two growth-centred sectors.

Occupation structure is an index of economic progress. Considered by this index, Malaysia can now be regarded as a developed country albeit not highly developed (Ghosh, 1994). It will be regarded as highly developed when its occupational ratio changes from 30:70 to 20:80. One can rationally expect that, all being well, this desideratum could possibly be achieved in the early years of the twenty-first century. Be that as it may, one can clearly visualise that in the field of sectoral occupations, structural changes have been very progressive in Malaysia.

Quantitative Dimension

In quantitative terms, development, more particularly growth, can be measured by the growth rate of GNP per capita. In this regard, Malaysia's achievement is indeed remarkable. It had drastically increased from US$360 in 1970 to US$3265 in 1993. It is the same story for GNP which had risen from US$3881 million in 1970 to US$57 574 million in 1993. The GDP growth rate (1970 prices) had gone up from 5 per cent in 1970 to 8.0 per cent in 1993.

Although the labour force has grown steadily over the years, the employment growth rate has been around 3 per cent per year, overtaking the labour force growth rate. The unemployment rate as a percentage of the labour force had steadily declined from 7.8 per cent in 1970 to 4.0 per cent in 1993. Saving (investment) as a percentage of GNP had increased from 16.5 (22.3) in 1970 to 30.3 (35.1) in 1990.

A spectacular result has been achieved in the case of poverty alleviation. Absolute poverty in Malaysia had been reduced from 49.3 per cent in 1970 to 15.0 per cent in 1990, and the rate of inflation had grown moderately from nearly 2 per cent in 1970 to nearly 4 per cent in 1994 (see Table 8.2).

Table 8.2 Growth/development indicators of Malaysia

	Particulars	*1970*	*1980*	*1990*	*1991*	*1992*	*1993*
1	GNP (US$) (million)	3 881	23 573	40 861	44 923	51 112	57 574
2	GNP per capita (US$)	360	1 713	2 301	2 471	2 966	3 265
3	GNP growth rate (%)	5.0	7.4	9.4	8.7	8.5	8.0
4	Manufacturing production index (1988 = 100)	—	—	132.1	150.4	169.0	191.0
5	Saving (as % GNP)	16.5	—	30.3	—	—	—
6	Investment (as % of GNP)	22.3	—	35.1	—	—	—
7	Employment grow rate (%)	3.3	—	3.4	—	—	—
8	Unemployment (% labour force)	7.8	5.6	5.6	4.3	4.1	3.5 (1994)
9	Absolute poverty (%)	49.3	—	15.0	—	—	—
10	Inflation rate (%)	1.8	6.8	3.1	4.4	4.7	4.0 (1994)

Source: Government of Malaysia, *Economic Planning Unit Publications* (Kuala Lumpur), various issues.

A cursory glance at Table 8.2 reveals the very impressive quantitative growth pattern of Malaysia with the average growth rate of more than 8 per cent per annum at present.

Qualitative Dimension

The qualitative dimension of development in Malaysia has been no less impressive than its quantitative counterpart. Quality of human life in Malaysia has registered continuously perceptible improvement since 1970 (see Table 8.3).

It is intriguing to analyse the qualitative dimension of life in a bit more detail by formulating a composite human quality of life index. The studies by Morris D. Morris (1979), and by the UNDP (1990) can be said to be incomplete and rather slipshod (Ghosh 1995). Hence, to gauge the relative

Table 8.3 Indicators of quality of life in Malaysia

	Indicators	*1970*	*1993*
1	Literacy rate (%)	60.2	78.5
2	Population per doctor	4302	2656
3	Life expectancy (years)	63.5	71
4	Infant mortality rate (per 1000 live births)	39.4	15
5	Calories intake	2170	2774
6	People per television	45	6.9
7	People per telephone	59	5.8

Source: EPU and *Asia Newsweek* (1993).

position of Malaysia among the ASEAN countries, an attempt has been made to construct a Human Quality of Life Index (HQLI) by taking into account seven important aspects on which such an index can *prima facie* be presumed to depend.[2] These are: literacy rate, population per doctor, life expectancy, infant mortality, calorie intake per day per person (average), population per television and population per telephone (Table 8.4). In a way, I have made an attempt to capture the elements of traditionality as well as the modernity of human life in some developing economies of South East Asia. My choice has fallen unequivocally on the newly emerging ASEAN countries around South East Asia. I have chosen the six ASEAN countries which have had not only a similar demographic temperament but also some affinities in the problems of development. These countries are Singapore, the Philippines, Brunei, Malaysia, Thailand and Indonesia.

The data for the study have been collected from various multilateral sources: reports, studies, journals and books. These data pertain to the year 1993. The methodological base of the study is a rather simplistic conceptualisation. Every variable has been presented in the form of an index across the countries. Then, a horizontal summation of the indices for each country gives us the composite index for the country as a whole. And on the basis of the total indices score of each country, ranking has been assigned to each country (Table 8.5).

A cursory glance at Table 8.5 reveals the fact that Malaysia is doing rather well in the development of the quality of human life. In a six-country study, she is in third position. Singapore, however, is doing marvellously well. Brunei, which scores the second position in HQLI, is excellent in certain respects. Malaysia is still lagging behind in the literacy

Table 8.4 Indicators of quality of life in ASEAN countries

Country	*Literacy rate (%)*	*Population per doctor*	*Life expectancy*	*Infant mortality*	*Calories intake*	*People per television*	*People per telephone*
Singapore	91.0	711	74	5	3 198	2.7	2.0
Philippines	93.5	1 016	65	34	2 375	24.4	52.5
Brunei	85.1	1 323	74	8	2 837	2.6	3.8
Malaysia	78.5	2 656	71	15	2 774	6.9	8.8
Thailand	93.0	4 361	69	28	2 316	9.2	28.5
Indonesia	81.5	11 641	60	61	2 750	18.2	107.7

Source: Various multilateral reports, journals and books and *Asia Newsweek* (December 1993).

Table 8.5 Human Quality of Life Index (HQL)

Country	*Value of composite index*	*Ranking*
Singapore	9 523	1
Brunei	5 769	2
Malaysia	3 316	3
Philippines	1 960	4
Thailand	1 461	5
Indonesia	756	6

Source: Estimated by the author.

rate, the infant mortality rate, life expectancy, and even in the doctor–population ratio as compared to those of Singapore and Brunei. In all these directions, Malaysia needs to catch up, and this will indeed necessitate Herculean efforts through proper allocation, family planning and welfare.

DIALECTICS OF DEVELOPMENT

The amazing economic rate of growth (around 8 per cent per annum) which Malaysia has been experiencing can best be explained by the political economy of class relations in the country, an analysis of which will be pursued at some length in this section.

The high growth rate of the Malaysian economy has been made possible by a sort of calculative collusive class alignment among the three present prominent classes in Malaysia – the bureaucratic class, the capitalist class and the working class.[3] Such alliances have been made possible because of the fact that as development takes place each of these classes stands to gain positively. The role of each class is a positive sum game. A common class interest has been the basis of Malaysia's accelerated rate of growth. The genesis of this commonality of class interest is easy to unfold to the students of Malaysia's economic history.

The class structure that Malaysia has now is in fact the modified version of the class structure that obtained in the colonial period. However, after the attaining of Independence in 1957, the importance of the land-owning class gradually diminished in Malaysia. The reasons are not far to seek. First, the policy of the government was to develop the country rapidly, and it was thought that an unbalanced strategy of development would do the trick because the productivity of the industrial sector, as experiences of developing countries suggest, far outstrips the productivity of the agricultural sector. The paradigm shift in the strategy from agriculture-based development to industry-based development contributed to the gradual but slow demise of the importance of agriculture.

However, for quite a long time till 1970, the primitive accumulation had to be based on agriculture as industrial development was still in its nascent stage. But since 1980, when capitalist development had already taken off, a marked trend in the movement of men and materials from agriculture to industry became conspicuous. As a result, occupational structure, as we have discussed above, changed in favour of the industrial sector. This was accompanied by the terms of trade that also went in favour of the secondary sector – which is to be expected in a developing economy. The transfer of resources including manpower from agriculture to industry took place in consequence of the relatively higher productivity in the secondary sector and also because of lesser demand for labour in producing food and fibre in the primary sector in a developing country like Malaysia. All this contributed to the decreasing importance of agriculture in Malaysia's development. For instance, Malaysian agriculture which contributed 30.8 per cent of GDP in 1970 had its share reduced to only 15 per cent in 1993. However, it must not be forgotten that this is the very natural corollary of the process of economic development.

Malaysia's strategy of economic development is based on the Preobrazhensky model of squeezing agriculture for the extraction of surplus and not the Bukharin type of strategy of ameliorating agriculture. The landowners in the 1980s experienced unequal benefits favouring large and medium farms. This was evident from the Gini Coefficient of concentration of land ownership.[4] For most of the farmers, agriculture was unremunerative and poor households were in perpetual debt. The World Bank report revealed that 70 per cent of the surplus generated by the poor farmers of the *Muda Scheme* was siphoned off the region (World Bank, 1982). All these facts contributed to the negative interest in land and agriculture in Malaysia in the 1980s, and class interest, if at all, was relegated to the background almost forever and agriculture indeed became alienated. This is borne out by the fact that in the post-Merdeka period, no significant land reform policy has been formulated in Malaysia.

Secondly, with the decline in the importance of agriculture in the national economy of Malaysia, the importance of the landed aristocracy (landowning class) also declined correspondingly. This happened in mainly two ways. First, with the rapid growth of the non-agricultural sector *vis-à-vis* the decline of agriculture, a large part of the agrarian labour force sought employment, temporarily or permanently, in the industrial sector for higher wages, better prospects of advancement, and better living/working conditions. Second, over the years, Malaysian agriculture experienced drastic structural changes. The growth of *latifundist* commercial farms owned by the government or by the private sector was indeed conspicuous. This type of agrarian structural change drastically reduced the number of landowners which contributed negatively to the growth of the agricultural class. Some of the small landowners had already sold their small parcels of land and converted themselves into industrial proletariats having no stake in the promotion of agrarian class interests. Moreover, in course of time, a section of landed aristocrats joined the ruling bureaucracy. Thus, with the growth of a capitalist system of development in Malaysia, the landowning class became almost a non-existent entity, and their contribution to the expanded capital accumulation process can be regarded as very marginal indeed, if at all significant.

As was adumbrated earlier, the renewed interest in industry and commerce created a new type of production relations. The movement of people from agriculture, coupled with the existing labour force in the non-agricultural sector, added to the generation of surplus labour in Malaysia in the 1970s when modern industries started operating. The increasing entry of the rural labour force into the urban labour market resulted in wage reductions for manufacturing workers after 1970 (Khoo and Said, 1979). This helped the capitalist class to generate a more absolute and relative *surplus value*. Gradually, the *organic composition of capital* increased in sympathy with the laws of motion of capitalist production.[5] The control of capitalists over workers became absolute in every sense of the term (Ai, 1984, p. 318). And all this was done under the impetus of the New Economic Policy (NEP) of 1970.

Since 1970, a new phase of industrialisation has started in Malaysia. A new type of committed, disciplined, cheap and loyal labour force began to emerge in the modern urban sector. The Malay labour force was wholly loyal to the state and the authorities (Roff, 1974, pp. 218). This was indeed a very strong factor in the growth of the capitalist system in Malaysia in subsequent years. The state (bureaucratic) policy in many ways helped the capitalist system to become entrenched. In fact, both bureaucratic and capitalist classes found a common interest in the growth of the economy in general and in the growth of a committed labour force in particular.

The capitalist class in the past badly needed the help of the state for optimising their goals of running business smoothly. This was true not only of the old native capitalists but also of the foreign capitalists, who became the front-line players in the Malaysian drama of development after 1970.

In the dependent type of capitalist development that Malaysia has been pursuing, foreign capitalists were given unbridled opportunities to run their houses in their own ways and remit huge amounts of profit to their homes every year. These capitalists did not have to face competition from the domestic economy of Malaysia, their market was growing and was protected by the state and they could easily tap the supply of cheap and disciplined labour. The comprador elements in the Malaysian bureaucracy who were exposed to foreign education and culture were ready at the first instance to extend help to foreign multinational capitalists.

In turn, the local bourgeoisie and the state were helped by MNCs in various ways. MNCs built up the capital-based infrastructure, introduced new technologies, absorbed the surplus labour of the economy, increased the volume of production, helped in the process of export promotion and contributed positively to the generation of surplus in the balance of payments. With their help, Malaysia was able successfully to introduce an outward-looking development policy from 1970 onwards.

After the 1969 race riots, Malaysian state policy was to acquire more strength and power.[6] The state wanted to repress all sorts of mass mobilisation in future. It invited foreign capitalists to thwart the growth of Chinese domestic capitalism which was supposed to be one of the principal reasons for increasing rural poverty in Malaysia. However, the apparent conflict between the state and the domestic private capitalists was not essentially on ethnic lines (Ai, 1984, p. 312). In fact in the domestic economy, the rate of growth of Chinese capital has really overtaken that of MNCs in recent years. The main goal of the state was to carry out the NEP Programme and to forge ahead with the process of capitalist accumulation. With this aim in view, the state extended all types of control to Bumiputera and non-Bumiputera capitalists, and advocated profitability as the criterion of running state enterprises (*New Straits Time*, 7 September 1981).[8] However, within the broad framework of the control mechanism, the MNCs were given a comparatively free hand to expand capitalist production, for, to the state, MNCs did not pose any internal threat to the government. Thus, there was a tacit understanding of a mutual nexus between bureaucracy and foreign capitalists after 1970.

The state wanted a stable government, mass support and sympathy. Just as the MNCs needed the state, the state in turn required their help for decreasing unemployment, for keeping the local labouring class happy and for contributing to the reduction of the inflationary spiral. In the 1960s, Malays were very poor and sufficient opportunities were not given to them to improve their economic position. Their economically depressed condition always remained a potential threat to the stability of the state.

Since 1970, a number of ameliorative measures have been adopted by the state to appease the working class and the poor, particularly the Bumiputeras. Since then, the state has become enormously powerful in Malaysia and is now able to coordinate market laws in a manner that can placate both the working and capitalist classes. The industrial working class is happy, for its income has increased quite considerably. The real wage which was RM303.75 per month in 1970 went up to RM506.67 in 1985 and the share of wages for the same period went up from 27.4 per cent to 32.0 per cent in value added (see Economic Planning Unit and Survey of Manufacturing Industry Reports). The capitalist class is contented because value added per worker has gone up by more than three times. This, however, does not imply that labour is being exploited. On the contrary, Malaysian labour has been witnessing a period of *labour aristocracy*, for the greater part of their increased productivity/income is due to capitalist efforts of increasing fixed assets per worker from RM7156 in 1970 to RM37 466 in 1985 (Economic Planning Unit Reports, 1968–86). In this connection, however, one should not lose sight of the fact that a very large part of the surplus value for foreign capitalists has possible been made by the exploitation of foreign labour in Malaysia.[9]

The peculiar circularity of causation seems to suggest that all the three classes gain simultaneously through economic development in Malaysia: the state as a benevolent dictator *à la* Mill is able to generate and earmark more and more surpluses for the poor and needy masses, thereby becoming more powerful and stable. The capitalists are generating more *value-added* surplus from labour and the local labouring class is experiencing not only better labour market relations but also enjoying a higher standard of living. This is perhaps the reason why the majority of the working class does not feel the need for trade unionism in Malaysia. Thus, all three classes are deriving direct benefits from economic development, and Malaysia today seems to possess a system of partnership type of controlled capitalist development.

CONCLUDING OBSERVATIONS

From what has been discussed earlier it becomes very apparent that in Malaysia development has been the outcome of a triangular class alliance. Class relations on the whole have finally emerged since 1970 as mutually beneficial and cooperative rather than contradictory and conflicting.

All three classes – bureaucracy, working class and capitalists – have been working close together to contribute to development and to share its gain. However, in the process, the state has emerged as the most powerful partner able to formulate correct policies and apply proper control mechanisms to maximise social welfare in terms of amelioration of poverty, maximisation of employment, and raising the income and standard of living of all classes of people.

In fact, without the paternalistic role of the state, much of the politico-economic stability could not have been infused in Malaysia, and the economic position of local industrial labour would perhaps have been proletarised and immiserised, for this is the usual consequence of full-blown capitalism. The greatest role of the Malaysian state has been to prevent the degeneration of capitalist development into one of pure capitalism. Malaysia today is indeed capitalist but without the unacceptable face of capitalism.

Notes

1. Whereas in DCs tertiary occupations are highly capital-intensive and high-income induced in LDCs, these are highly labour-intensive and poverty-induced occupations (Ghosh, 1991).
2. D. Morris has taken into account only three simple indicators, for example, life expectancy, infant mortality and literacy, and the UNDP study has also considered three indicators such as longevity, literacy and per capita income.
3. In our formulation here, bureaucratic class and state (government) have been used interchangeably, and the working class refers to industrial labour.
4. The Gini Coefficient showed a trend of unequal benefits favouring the rich and middle class. The coefficients increased from 0.354 to 0.383 to 0.4 for 1966, 1975 and 1976, respectively (Ismail, 1982).
5. Organic composition of capital refers to fixed capital–labour ratio. A high value of this ratio shows high capital intensity.
6. The state realised that stronger political and economic power was necessary to fully control the racial tensions. In fact, interracial tension was the manifestation of economic disequilibrium (Ali S. Husin, 1984, p. 30).
7. The Malaya perception of Chinese behaviour is summarised in the remark that 'the only thing straight about Chinese is their hair' (vide, Yun, op. cit, p. 306).
8. The state itself became capitalist and wanted to subvert the growth of domestic capitalist enterprises both by means of internal control and through the introduction of foreign MNCs.
9. Foreign labourers, particularly from Bangladesh and Indonesia, are rampantly exploited by some foreign MNCs in Malaysia. The monthly wages of such labourers are around RM250 to 300 whereas for the local labourers these are around RM600. Morever, very often, the foreign labourers have to work overtime without extra payment. They are treated like bonded labourers and they cannot leave the firm for their passports are impounded by the firms. Their living conditions are virtually not much different from those of domesticated animals.

References

Ai Hing Yun (1984), 'Capitalist Development', in Ali, S. Husin, *Ethnicity, Class and Development in Malaysia* (Kuala Lumpur: Persatuan Sains Social Malaysia).

Ali, S. Husin (1984) *Ethnicity, Class and Development in Malaysia* (Kuala Lumpur: Persatuan Sains Social Malaysia).

Clark, Colin (1984) *The Conditions of Economic Progress* (London: Macmillan).

Economic Planning Unit (1993) *The Malaysian Economy in Figures* (Kuala Lumpur: Government Printer).

Fisher, A.G.B. (1964) *Economic Progress and Social Security* (London: Macmillan).

Ghosh, B.N. (1991) 'Hypertrophy of the Tertiary Sector: Discussion', *Economic and Political Weekly*, February.

Ghosh, B.N. (1994) 'Occupation Structure in Malaysia', *Dewan Masyarakat*, January.

Ghosh, B.N. (1995) 'Quality of Human Life in Malaysia', unpublished paper.

Government of Malaysia (1979) *Survey of Manufacturing Industries (SMIs)* (Kuala Lumpur: Government Printer).

Government of Malaysia (1991) *Second Outline Perspective Plan: 1991–2000* (Kuala Lumpur: Government Printer).

Ismail, Z. (1980) 'Economic and Social Aspects of Padi Production', Seminar on Economics, Development and the Consumer (Penang: Consumers Association).

Khoo, K.J. and Said, Ikmal (1979) 'Labour and Wage Patterns in the Manufacturing Industries in Malaysia', paper presented at the International Symposium on Local Level Development Alternatives, University of Science, Malaysia.

Ministry of Finance (1993) *Economic Reports* (Kuala Lumpur: Government Printer).

Morris, D. (1979), *Measuring the Conditions of the World's Poor* (London: Pergamon Press).

Roff, W.R. (1974) *The Origins of Malay Nationalism* (Kuala Lumpur: University of Malaya Press).

Sutcliffe, R.B. (1971) *Industry and Underdevelopment* (London: Addison-Wesley).

UNDP (1990) *Report on Human Development Index* (New York: United Nations Development Programme).

World Bank (1982) *World Development Report* (Washington DC: World Bank).

9 Perspectives in Economic Growth and Development with an Application to Malaysia

Masudul A. Choudhury

The objectives of this chapter are to explain, first the concept and practice of economic growth in mainstream economics and to develop the Islamic perspectives of economic growth. Second, we will examine the policy questions associated with growth and development in the context of sustainability.

MEASUREMENTS OF ECONOMIC GROWTH

We have been hearing much these days about the economic miracle of East and South-East Asia, in which are the Muslim countries of Malaysia, Indonesia and Brunei. Yet each of these countries is found to enjoy different levels and structures of economic growth, even in the face of the high figures they are showing for the rate of change of output. Thus, the criterion of economic growth is being simply equated to its measurement by means of the time rate of change of real Gross Domestic Product. Another measure of economic growth used is the time rate of change of real per capita Gross Domestic Product.

Let us examine the various measures first.

1. Real rate of growth of GDP is defined by

$g = (1/q)(dq/dt)$, where $q = Q/p$ denotes real Gross Domestic Product at a reference point in time, with Q as nominal GDP and p as price level over time. In an extensive form,

$$g = (1/Q)(dQ/dt) - (1/p)(dp/dt)$$
$$= g_Q - g_p,$$

where g_Q denotes the rate of change of nominal output; g_p denotes the rate of change of price level as measured by one of the accepted price indexes. For example, p would denote the consumer price index or the GDP deflator. In other words, g_p denotes the rate of inflation, defined as the time rate of change of price level. Expressed in this way, the real rate of growth is seen to be negatively influenced by the rate of change of inflation, although the nominal GDP can increase in the face of price increase.

2. Real per capita rate of growth of GDP is defined by
$q^* = (1/(q/P))(d(q/P)/dt)$, where P denotes the population size at a reference point in time; q/P thus denotes the real per capita GDP.

In extended form the expression for g^* is

$$g^* = g_Q - g_p - g_P$$

where g_P denotes the time rate of change of population. In this form, the real per capita rate of economic growth is seen to be negatively affected by the joint increases in price level and population.

The above measures of economic growth do not take account of factors such as the quality of life, employment, distribution and environment. Above all, there is no consideration in these measures of economic growth of the *structure* of economic growth. The concept of structure points to how economic growth is being realised by means of sectorial and factor market shifts (agriculture, manufacturing and services) and how productivity changes are affecting factor markets. The most important issue of structure is to show how economic efficiency and distribution are being substituted or are being attained together, by means of underlying technological and institutional changes. The structure of growth thus has an important cause and effect relationship among factors such as the quality of life, social welfare and economic growth.

It is therefore seen that real or real per capita rates of growth do not provide measures of these well-being indicators. It is, thus inadequate to infer the advance of any economy simply by reading its rate of economic growth.

Recent studies have shown that there is a positive correlation between autocratic political regimes and the level of economic growth. While India continues to have low real rates of growth, yet she is the largest democracy today with a great degree of self-reliance in her economic activities. China has the highest rate of growth but is today one of the most autocratic nations, where human organs are extracted by killing jailed convicts for lucrative markets.

THE STRUCTURE OF GROWTH

To elaborate further on this important topic of the structure of growth, we first examine the relationship of economic growth with factors of production. This relationship is explained by means of the aggregate production function, which is a macroeconomic measure for the total quantity of goods and services efficiently and optimally produced in the economy.

There are two ways of treating the production function. These are the neo-classical and the Keynesian ways of studying the structure of growth.

Neoclassical View of the Structure of Growth

In the neo-classical sense, aggregate output as value added of all goods and services produced and payments returned to factors of production is an optimal quantity. It is also termed as potential output and is associated with full employment of factors in their own factor markets. In such a production relationship the problem of unemployment does not arise. Furthermore, factors are paid their *due* returns. Such due returns are equal to the marginal revenue products of the respective factors (Burmeister and Dobell, 1970).

All these can be written down as follows:

Let, $Q = f(L,K)$

with $\partial Q/\partial L > 0$, $\partial Q/\partial K > 0$, $\partial^2 Q/\partial L^2 < 0$, $\partial^2 Q/\partial K^2 < 0$

$Q = f(0,0) = 0$

In this relationship, $f(..)$ denotes the mode of producing Q by means of labour, L, and capital, K, in an appropriately chosen technology that yields optimal quantity of the output, Q. Furthermore:

Nominal wage, $W = MP_L.p$, where, $MP_L = \partial Q/\partial L$ is the marginal productivity of labour, and $p.MP_L$ denotes the nominal value of the marginal product.

Nominal rent, R, to capital is likewise given by, $R = MP_K.p$, with similar explanation for MP_K.

In a perfectly competitive economy, the total output is exhausted by payments to factors of production. This is also the direct implication of the circular flow of goods and services in the economy. Thus,

$Q = L.MP_L + K.MP_K$

Thereby, revenue, $Rv = p.Q = L.(p.MP_L) + K.(p.MP_K)$, and

Marginal revenue product of labour $= \partial Rv/\partial L = p.MP_L = W$

Marginal revenue product of capital $= \partial Rv/\partial K = p.MP_K = R$

Finally real returns to factors are,

$$w = W/P = MP_L,\ r = R/P = MP_K$$

From these relations we obtain the condition for optimal and efficient allocation of resources, that is allocation of the cost of production among factors of production. We must remember here that in the sense of economic growth, all such factors are taken up in their aggregate form as also the meaning of output is that of value of total goods and services produced by means of employing L and K. The number of factors can be expanded by including land, energy, human capital, entrepreneurship for instance, without loss of generality in the above types of relationships.

The optimal resource allocation relationship is thus,

$$MP_L/W = MP_K/R = 1/p$$

Furthermore, in a *perfectly competitive economy*, the price of the aggregate bundle of goods expressed as a suitable price index equals the marginal cost of production. The marginal cost in turn equates with marginal revenue, MRv. That is, $p = MC = MRv$. Hence,

$$W = MP_L.MRv,\ R = MP_K.MRv$$

These are alternative expressions for the marginal revenue product of labour and capital, respectively.

The above relationships between output and factor utilisation point out that the structure of growth, which here implicates the technological shift between factors to enable them to produce efficiently and optimally in a perfectly competitive sense, is based on the key notion of the marginal rate of substitution between these factors. It is indeed this single principle of neo-classical economics that is permanently entrenched in all economic theory at all levels. (Robinson, 1961). According to this principle, it matters little whether output is optimally produced by means of a capital-intensive (i.e. capital–labour ratio = K/L increasing over time) or a labour-intensive (i.e. labour–capital ratio = L/K increasing over time) technology.

Accordingly, there are shifts experienced between sectors that use one or the other factors more at different levels of intensity in the production of their outputs. In Figure 9.1, we bring out these factor-specific output relationships.

Figure 9.1 Neo-classical substitution principle explaining resource allocation and economic growth.

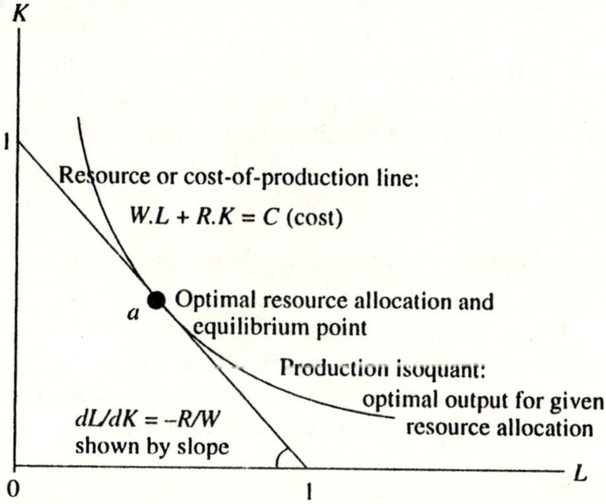

Keynesian Outlook on the Structure of Economic Growth

Keynes's general equilibrium system is seen to be in a perpetual state of underemployment equilibrium. This means that because prices of output and factors remain inflexible downwards, particularly due to institutional causes, it therefore becomes impossible for markets to clear at marginal productivity values. The full employment concept in the Keynesian system thus acquires a new meaning. Full employment output is realised when, given certain price stability, corresponding maximum levels of factors are employed for producing the output. This is equivalent to saying that a full employment output level is consistent with non-inflationary spending, enabling employment of the maximum quantity of factor inputs that can be so employed. In this spending, the most critical one in Keynes's general equilibrium system is government expenditure on goods and services (Samuelson, Nordhaus and McCallum, 1988).

The well-known national income identity for a general equilibrium system is,

$$Q = C + I + G + (X - M)$$

where, Q denotes GDP; C denotes consumption expenditure; I denotes investment expenditure; G denotes government expenditure; X denotes export revenue; M denotes import bill. Hence, $(X - M)$ denotes general trade surplus (> 0) or trade deficit (< 0). When capital flows are also considered in this, then $(X - M)$ denotes balance of payments surplus (> 0) or balance of payments deficit (< 0).

Now consider how economic growth is generated in the above equation. First, if a saving is affected in the above equation, then it is a withdrawal from consumption spending, which must subsequently enter investment accounting to yield a return and close the gap of consumption. We then write in functional form,

$$C = C(Q),\ S = I, \text{ but, } S = S(Q,i) = I(Q,r,i),\ G = G(Q),\ (X - M) = T = T(Q)$$

Hence, $Q = F(r,i)$, where, r denotes the rate of return on investment; i denotes the interest rate. $F(..)$ denotes a functional relationship of Q to r and i. This expression is further extended by including the marginal propensity to spend, MPS_p. MPS_p relates with and spending by means of the expression,

$$dQ = (dI + dG)/(1 - MPS_p)$$

But, $dI = (\partial I/\partial Q).dQ + (\partial I/\partial r).dr + (\partial I/\partial i).di$

$$dG = (\partial G/\partial Q).dQ$$

Hence, $dQ = [(\partial I/\partial r)dr + (\partial I/\partial i)di]/[1 - MPS_p - \partial/\partial Q)$ (Productive Spending)

$$= [(\partial I/\partial r)dr + (\partial I/\partial i)di]/[1 - MPC]$$

where MPC = marginal propensity to consume.

We can now see what causes economic growth to occur in the Keynesian system. The contributory factors are real returns, r and MPC. The negative factor is the rate of interest, since, $\partial I/\partial i < 0$.

The implication of all these relations is that the Keynesian form of economic growth is premised in productive spending alone, and in this, interest rate does not constitute a productive outlet as it is a deterrent to investment, and hence to output. Interest rate is thus also seen as a deterrent to marginal propensity to spend, since economic growth is seen here to depend on both productive returns and MPS_p.

The structure of economic growth in the Keynesian economic system is thus a study of a determined shift away from unproductive to productive spending. Very often, it is the private sector that undertakes productive spending under the informative guidance of sound governments and institutions. Hence, the same structure of growth in the Keynesian system implies a coordinated shift to the private sector with sound government and institutional guidance. When compared with the neo-classical prescription of growth, the Keynesian system docs not invoke choice of technology and marginal substitution principle in resource allocation.

In Figure 9.2 we bring out the various growth-related relationships showing the nature of structural components of economic growth in the Keynesian system. Quadrant 1 shows the equilibrating process between output and spending (aggregate demand, *AD*), establishing full employment output, Q^* at the spending level AD^*, and thus the full employment point, E^*. Movement towards E^* is gradual by means of equilibrating aggregate demand (*AD*) and aggregate supply (*AS*). In quadrant 2, E^* is shown to be associated with full employment of factors, *L* and *K*, along the productivity curve 0*T*. Thus, *L* and *K* must both be increasing in adaptive ways in this system, unlike in the neo-classical system. In quadrant 3,

Figure 9.2 Structure of economic growth in the Keynesian system

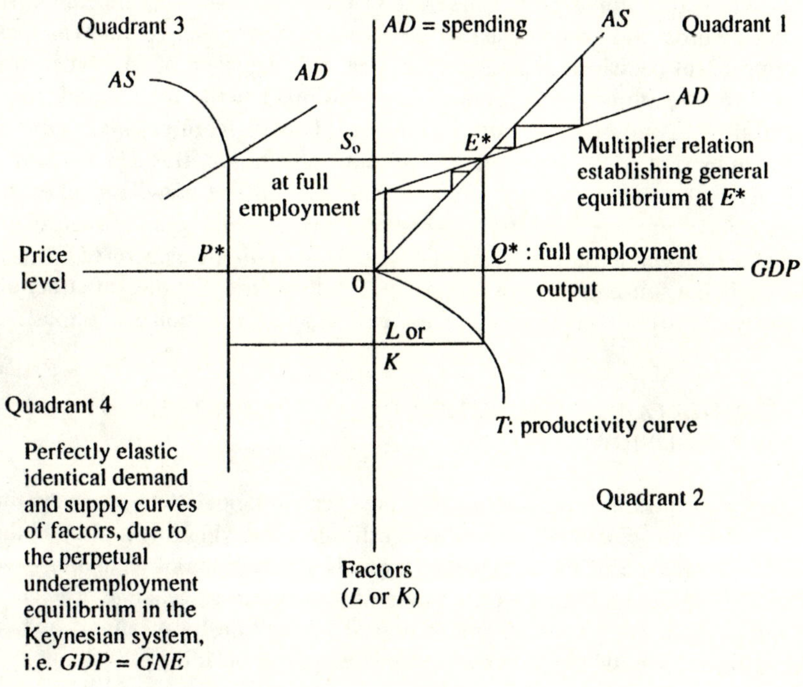

E^* is shown to be non-inflationary along the elastic part of the aggregate supply curve of output in the Keynesian system. This establishes a price level P^*. In quadrant 4, P^* is shown to fully employ the maximum possible labour at this non-inflationary level of output. Hence, the supply and demand curves of factors are together coincidental and perfectly elastic at P^*. This nature of identical demand and supply also points to the perpetual equilibrium, albeit underemployment equilibrium, that exists in the Keynesian system. For this reason *GDP* = Gross National Expenditure (GNE), everywhere along the aggregate supply curve.

The structure of economic growth is thus predominated by *AD* and *AS*. Within this spending cycle, factor markets attain their full employment levels and thus augment each other. For contrarily, if any one factor was to substitute another in a neo-classical sense in a state of imperfect competition, as is the case of Keynesian economy, then this would reduce the potential use of one of the factors below its full employment level. This would contradict the Keynesian definition of full employment.

Yet the problem of the Keynesian perspective on economic growth is that it is incapable of answering the intersectorial structure of economic growth and to influence the structure of prices and resource allocation. In other words, unlike neo-classical economics, Keynesian economics does not present decision-making possibilities. It is deprived of an ethical rule to direct resources into productive spending. On the other hand, neo-classical economics, in spite of having all these features, loses ethical worth by dint of the principle of marginal substitution. Besides, the structure of growth points to the study of sectorial shifts in neo-classical economics. It implies a shift between the private and public sectors in Keynesian economics in terms of where the spending is generated so as to establish a full employment output. In all, therefore, the idea of structure conveys different meanings in neo-classical and Keynesian economics.

TECHNOLOGICAL INDUCTION IN FACTOR AND OUTPUT RELATIONSHIPS

The next question to investigate is how technological change affects the nature of neo-classical marginalist substitution and what role it plays in the Keynesian type of the structure of growth. By the idea of technology we will mean here a choice of the mode of production to generate efficiency and productivity. Thus, augmentation of production by means of human capital and capital equipments is embodied in this meaning of technology.

Neo-classical Outlook

In Figure 9.3, we show that when technological induction appears in the aggregate production function, the productivity curve shifts upwards for the same quantity of inputs – labour or capital – remembering that because of the marginal rate of substitution implied in the production function, one of the inputs must remain fixed, once production ensues. This implication is independent of technological induction.

Next, in a two-commodities case, X_1, X_2, technological change in the production of these goods shows an outwards evolution of the production functions for the goods. Hence the production possibility surface, P_1P_1 shifts outwards to $P_1'P_1'$, etc. Three particular cases are shown of such a shift (Allen, 1970): (i) when there is a definite shift away from X_1 (say agriculture) to X_2 (manufacturing). Such a technological change is

Figure 9.3 Production possibility surfaces and output-factor relations in a neo-classical framework with technological change

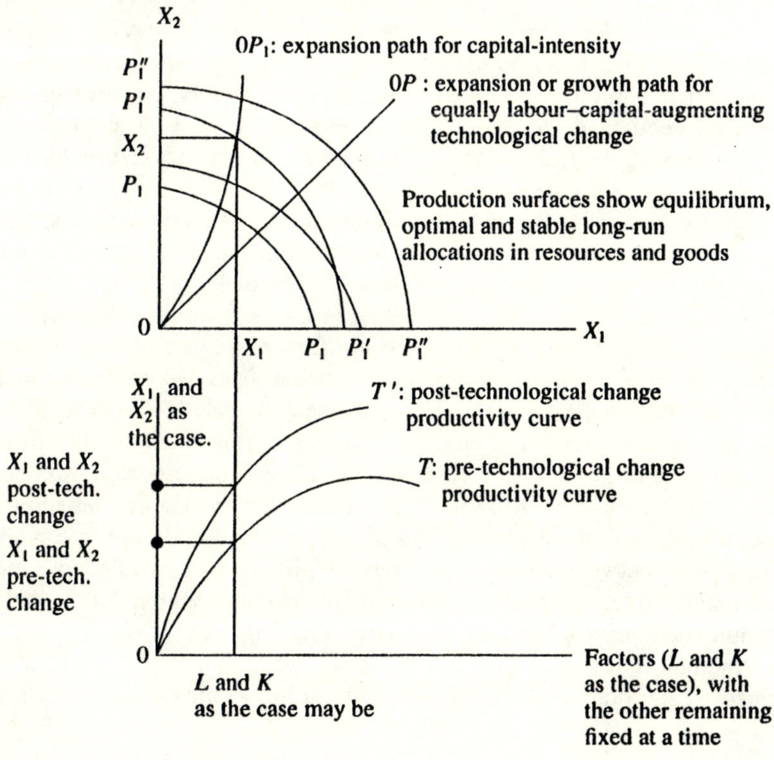

termed as capital-augmenting. (ii) When there is a definite shift towards X_1, the technological change is said to be labour-augmenting. (iii) when both X_1 and X_2 are simultaneously realised, technological change is said to be equally labour–capital-augmenting. In all such cases, the expansion paths of outputs, shown by $0P_1$, $0P$, etc., denote the technologically induced paths of economic growth. The slope at any point along this path gives the definite marginal shift between X_1 and X_2 that is taking place.

Most often, it is noted that the fear of long-run economic uncertainty, scarcity of human capital, and constraints of efficiency and productivity among entrepreneurs in the neo-classical production function, makes X_1, hence labour (assuming X_1 is labour intensive), more susceptible to replacement. In such a case, technological change is of the capital-augmenting type. The path of economic growth is then described along the technologically induced path, $0P_1$.

In each of the above cases, the output expansion paths are shown to be stable, efficiency generating, productivity generating, and equilibrium generating in the goods and factors markets. Consequently, every point along such a path provides two equivalent results: first, the relative prices of goods that indicate the direction of substitution between goods (hence factors) remain stable and fully observed in the market. Secondly, opportunity costs between goods and factors are fully determinate in order to define shifts. Thus, although the technologically induced expansion path shows that both of the goods, and consequently factors, are being utilised, yet the nature of substitution and opportunity cost remains unchanged all along the path. In other words, this implies that technological change occurs in the neo-classical system by way of substitution and opportunity cost.

Such a condition is often referred to in the literature as *structural adjustment* (Pratt, 1983). Its arguments are that in the face of low levels of economic growth, substitution to more efficient factors is necessary so as, subsequently, to generate output that can be reallocated to other factors in the long run. The same argument of structural adjustment applies to the substitution of goods and their replacement over the long run. Structural adjustment makes no allowance, except by means of a computation of social cost, as to the degree of dislocation between goods and factors that takes place between the short and long run. Many such cases of transition are known to have replaced goods and factors permanently. A case is that of automated unemployment caused by technological change.

Another example of the permanent cost of automation that has taken place by the determined shift from agriculture to manufacturing can be found in the history of economic thought. The school of physiocracy, which preceded the classical school, considered that agriculture was *the* productive sector to which all other sectors were linked for sustenance. Consequently, agricultural labour was considered to be *the* productive labour. GDP as national output was measured totally in terms of rents (*net product*). With the coming of the classical school and the advent of industrial revolution in Europe, the shift was towards manufacturing as *the* productive sector and of manufacturing labour as *the* productive labour. Ever since the industrial revolution, there has existed a dichotomy between the agricultural hinterland, mostly of the developing world, where low prices and easy access to primary resources prevailed, and the manufacturing heartland of the industrialised world. Even when shifts occurred within the agriculturally abundant economies, there has existed such a dichotomy within the developing nations.

Consequently, the process of economic growth, as understood by the classicists in terms of specialisation, division of labour and bits of individuated economic activities within the enterprise towards producing the final good, applied to the manufacturing sector alone. Economic growth and the formation of wealth (of nations) was thus associated with manufacturing activities. Capitalists and entrepreneurs thereby took to the regime of capital-centered orientation to economic growth for earning fast profits, ignoring the concerns of sustainability in the growth process.

Keynesian Outlook

Technological change as an explicit induction of economic growth, cannot be shown in the Keynesian system. This is because the national income accounting equation and those components associated with this subsume any technological effects within the investment expenditure variable. The returns in turn are captured by the real rate of return on investment. Thus the entire effect of technological change is shown by the shift of the aggregate demand and supply functions rightwards. These carry with them higher levels of full employment outputs and bring about greater utilisation of aggregate factors of production.

In Figure 9.4, we show the nature of technological induction of economic growth in the Keynesian system. By its very nature, the Keynesian system is aiming at a non-inflationary regime of economic growth. In this figure, as aggregate demand AD_1 shifts to AD_2; aggregate supply AS_1 shifts to AS_2, the original general equilibrium, E_1 cannot be sustained at the inflationary level, E'. E_1 must move to E_2 finally.

Figure 9.4 Treating sustainability and technological change in the Keynesian system

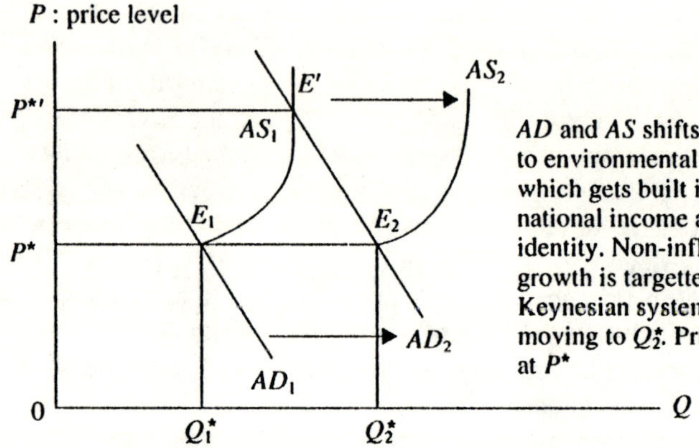

AD and *AS* shifts are due to environmental expenditure, which gets built into the national income and accounting identity. Non-inflationary growth is targetted in the Keynesian system, with Q_1^* moving to Q_2^*. Price stabilises at P^*

Consequently, the full employment output, Q_1^* shifts to the post-technologically induced level, Q_2^*. The price level stabilises around P^*, downward from $P^{*\prime}$.

The interesting point to note here is that while Q_2^* brings about the simultaneous utilisation of factors of production by technological induction, this does not necessitate a marginalist substitution and opportunity cost. Besides, since government expenditure variable, *G*, in national income accounting equation is instrumental in bringing about social productivity, therefore, the state of simultaneity between goods and factors must be realised by appropriate policy measures. In the Keynesian system, the well-known instruments to attain such conditions are fiscal, monetary and income policies. But the most important one for our case will be the use of a sustainable development policy with the focus being on sustainability. *Sustainability* here means the joint attainment of economic growth, price stability, economic welfare, distributive equity and economic efficiency, without having to take recourse to the neo-classical type of marginalist substitution between the goals of economic growth and distributive equity. The concept of sustainability is linked with the social structuring of economic growth and development. It addresses issues of social justice, employment, social welfare, and the treatment of the environment as commons for the benefit of mankind and future generations. Sustainability is thereby, not a mere study of environment as a target for preservation. Rather, environment is treated as an instrument to achieve human and natural well-being (Agius, 1990; Inglott, 1990).

THE ISLAMIC FRAMEWORK OF A THEORY OF ECONOMIC GROWTH AND DEVELOPMENT

The question of sustainability, its underlying idea of sustainable development, the ecological focus in this and the relevant issues of its measurement, bring us to the concept of *economic growth and development* in Islamic perspectives. We now have to go through the whole sequence of reconstructions on the theory of economic growth in an Islamic framework. This paradigm is posed here as the alternative to Third-World development, particularly applied to Malaysia.

We have seen that in the neo-classical framework the marginalist substitution, even in the technologically induced growth path, makes the goals of economic efficiency and distributive equity to be attainable in a trade-off. In the Keynesian macroeconomic general equilibrium system, the absence of decision-making leaves unanswered how the simultaneity between the goals of distributive equity and economic efficiency can be attained. Thus, the Keynesian system even with technological induction in it is seen to be ethically neutral.

ENVIRONMENT, SUSTAINABLE DEVELOPMENT AND ECONOMIC GROWTH

Neo-classical and Keynesian Treatments

All approaches to sustainable development treat environment as a capital good or a service. Nature and ecology become capital goods and objects of preservation. Consequently, such a good has a price that must define an underlying competing process for the use of resources. Now the environment as a good can be reproduced by means of capital and labour use. In the neo-classical framework, the focus on efficiency and productivity of these factors to attain targets of the environment makes them substitutable factors. The significant point to note here is that the target of sustainable development in the neo-classical environment-focused growth regime treats this very target as the objective function, no matter how the constraints of factor use enter the cost-of-production relation.

In the Keynesian sense, environment protection becomes an accounting entry in the national income accounting and expenditure equations. It is now important to identify environment either as a consumption good or as an investment good. If environment is treated as a consumption good, it enters the aggregate social welfare function. Subsequently, the social welfare function with environment in it, treats economic growth and the environment as competing substitutes. This reverts the treatment of sustainable development to the neo-classical picture.

When environment is treated as an investment good, it is linked with the conversion of current-consumption restraint (= saving) to investment intertemporally. Here too a substitution process is involved along an intertemporal production possibility curve. Future yields on environment become consumption benefits. These once again enter the social welfare function. The neo-classical implications are once again obvious (see Figure 9.5).

Alternatively, environmental investment may be treated in the *AD*- and *AS*-shifts in Figure 9.4. But in such a case, the nature of environment good is not attended to. There remains no particular relevance to the process of ecologically conscious treatment in the development process in Keynesian

Figure 9.5 Treatment of environment in intertemporal consumption and savings framework

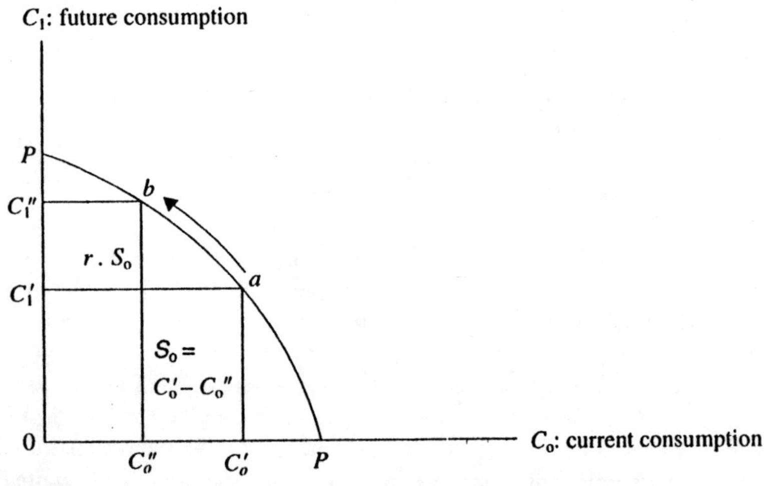

Saving, $S_o = C_o' - C_o''$, goes into intertemporal resource allocation. But total intergenerational consumption is not reduced. For this saving adds to future consumption by the return of $r.S_o$. Now a shifts to *b*, causing intergenerational consumption, C_I, to increase from C_I' to C_I'' for present consumption being restrained from C_o' to C_o''. Thus, neo-classical treatment of sustainable development is always based on consumption-based social welfare maximisation. This negates any meaningful treatment of sustainable development by an intertemporal restraint in consumption.

framework. Particularly in this is the unanswered question in this system to the following: is environmental investment a technological advancement in capital equipments to be environmentally friendly? Is investment both in human capital and equipments a sufficient cause for equally-capital–labour augmenting technological change? In all such cases, Keynesian economics cannot offer an answer, unless one goes through the neo-classical economic explanation of trade-offs and then formulates the marginal propensities in respect to various environmental treatments invoked here.

Islamic Treatment of Sustainability

In the *Islamic politico-economic framework*, sustainability as a *process of interactions* between the purely economic and social goals becomes the object of attainment. Development now proceeds by invoking the discursive process of applying specific *Shari'ah* (Islamic Law) rules emanating from polity to the ecological order. A subset of the ecological order is the market system, wherein the *Shari'ah* rules formed discursively in polity, aim at transforming consumptional, productive and distributional preferences of agents. In the case of environment consciousness as an instrument for bringing about such preference changes, the *Shari'ah* rules selected may be appropriate technological choices that can be readily used by available skills, so that from these first level technologies upgraded ones can be reproduced, as adaptation between available skills and appropriate technology proceeds. Such an idea liberates the environmental conscious development process from the notion of pushing low levels of human capital into high-level foreign technologies, to which available skills cannot readily adapt. Such misalignments between skills and technology cause immense amounts of costs, indebtedness and dislocation of labour. The results are capital-intensive choice of technology, unemployment, inequitable distribution of wealth, loss of self-reliance, resource depletion and a high cost of subsidising imitative development. The idea of sustainability is then lost.

FUNCTIONALISING THE ATTRIBUTES OF *SHARI'AH* IN DEVELOPMENT PARADIGM AS A *PROCESS*

The attributes of *Shari'ah* are premised in the *Qur'anic* precepts of just ends (balance = *Adl*), creativity (dynamics = *Khalq-in-Jadid*), felicity (*Falah* and *Tazkiyah*), purpose (*maqasid*) and certainty (*Haqq-ul-Yaqin*).

The totality of these by their cause–effect relations establishes the framework of the *process of development* in Islam. They at once also established the *socio-economic reality*. The interactions that take place heuristically between polity and the ecological order (subset as market), being premised on these attributes of *Shari'ah*, simultaneously bring about an internal transformation (*Hablum-min-Allah*) and a communitarian transformation (*Hablum-min-Annas*).

The *Shari'ah*-based transformation is premised in the simple assumption that truth must always be received by the greater generality of mankind and will ultimately overwhelm falsehood. As a result, any coercion is avoided in the discursive transformation process that agents in polity and markets enjoy. Coercion is totally replaced by knowledge formation as interactions proceed between polity-providing *Shari'ah* rules, and the ecological agents responding to these rules (*Ahqam*) by way of learning responses. The learning inputs from the ecological order to polity become new springs of knowledge formation and post-evaluation for polity. The ensuing interactive process thus becomes circular and continuous.

In the case of sustainability, an example of such an ongoing interactive process is provided by an extensively interlinked economic order that must exist in the Islamic political economy – intersectorially, across enterprises, various transactions and between polity and all the other agents. Social justice results from the realisation of appropriate technology, cooperative enterprises and transactions including those of the *mudarabah-musharakah* types (profit sharing, equity participation). Other development financing instruments are cofinancing, joint ventures and secondary financing instruments. All these aim at attaining product diversity, economic diversification and risk diversification, and public shareholding in enterprises. Well-coordinated decision-making between capitalists, workers, financiers and other worthy representatives of the community on matters of technological choices, appropriate goods to produce and consume, and wage–profit relations, exist in the grand interlinked framework in the Islamic political economy. Now such well-coordinated and cooperative enterprises in the Islamic political economy produce broadened ownership, thereby generating distributive equity. They also create simultaneously a sustainable development environment and congenial structure of economic growth by means of interlinkages and diversification, thereby generating economic efficiency and productivity. The discursions (interactions leading to knowledge formation) that proceed continuously among all agents unify the agent-specific preferences in the midst of the ongoing transformation process. Such a transformation is a *process* due to the continuous presence of the underlying discursions and is caused by *simultaneity* of polity-market preferences realised jointly through interactions.

The market order is thus transformed by means of the integration of *Shari'ah* rules (*Ahqam*) in socio-economic and political activities. The same process is intensified by continuity of the never-ending and emerging *interactive–integrative preference unification* among the agents, premised on the *Shari'ah* rules (Choudhury, 1995).

FORMALISING THE CONCEPT OF THE ISLAMIC DEVELOPMENT *PROCESS*: THE PROCESS MODEL OF DEVELOPMENT INVOKING *SHARI'AH* ATTRIBUTES

The Islamic development process as a simultaneous realisation of growth and distributive equity, with the environment as an instrument necessary for sustainability, can now be formalised as follows:

Let $S = (JB,P,F,C,Cr)$ denote the *Shari'ah* premise defined by the components, *JB*: just balance, *P*: purpose, *F*: felicity, *C*: certainty, *Cr*: creativity. From *S* arises a final policy rule that transforms behaviour in society at large. Let this policy rule be denoted by $\mathbb{P}(S)$. Since such a policy rule is discursed (interactive preferences) before it becomes integrated in the socio-economic transformation process, a sequence of *knowledge-forming processes* is therefore generated prior to the formation of policy (*Ahqam*). Let Θ_i (i = 1,2,...., denoting number of interactions) be these knowledge parameters that form $\mathbb{P}(S)$. Hence, $\{\mathbb{P}(S)[\Theta_i])\}$ denote the interactive *knowledge-forming parameters*, $i = 1,2,\ldots$, as interactions proceed by continuity and re-emergence of newer refinements of older consensus on various issues. An extended version of this sequence is obtained by incorporating socio-economic variables within it, as is the case of environment as a socio-economic variable. We also include the sustainability variables, x, to provide the much needed set of interlinkages among agents in this interactive order. Let $x = (E,g,d)$. Hence we now have $\{E,g,d,\mathbb{P}(S)[\Theta_i]\}$, where, E denotes a level of environment protection. Each of the variables depend upon a priomordial set of $\{\Theta_i\}$-values. The slight difference between S-attributes and $\{\Theta_i\}$-values is that the latter is a functional way of understanding the former in real life situations by the method of discursions that takes place between polity and the ecological agents. Thus, while $\{\Theta i\}$ are subject to revisions with $i = 1,2,..,n,\ldots$ S-attributes are not subject to change, as they remain axiomatically unifying foundations of the *Shari'ah* process model of development in our case, and in general for the Islamic political economy.

Furthermore, we note that there exist interlinkages among the knowledge-formation process and the socio-economic transformation process by means of feedbacks that define the continuous interactive-integrations. Hence the following circularity exists:

$$\{\mathbb{P}(S)[\Theta i]\} \rightarrow_{P1} \{x(\Theta i)\} \rightarrow_{P2} \{(x,\mathbb{P}(S))[\Theta_{i+1}]\} \rightarrow_{P3} \{x'(\Theta_{i+1})\} \rightarrow ..._{Pn}$$
etc.

where, x' denotes newer levels of socio-economic values that depend upon recursive $\{\Theta i\}$-values. *Pi* denote processes occurring by interactions, $i = 1,2,\ldots n,\ldots$

We now establish the social well-being function, $W(..)$ centred on environment in the relational concept of ecology and interactive transformation process of the Islamic concept of development:

$$\text{Simulate } \{\Theta i(\mathbb{P}(S))\}\ W = W(E,g,d)[\mathbb{P}(S)[\Theta i]]$$

subject to,

$$E = f_1(g,d)[\mathbb{P}(S)[\Theta i]]$$

$$g = f_2(E,d)[\mathbb{P}(S)[\Theta i]]$$

$$d = f_3(E,g)[\mathbb{P}(S)[\Theta i]]$$

$$\Theta_{i+1} = f_4(E,g,d,)[\mathbb{P}(S)][\Theta i]$$

The appearance of $\{\mathbb{P}(S)[\Theta i]\}$-values outside the functionals, f_j, $j = 1,2,..4$, means the continued dependence of the inner variables on this primordial source of *Shari'ah*, forming knowledge that leads to integration through interactions and further dynamic evolutions. The derived relations in circular forms shown by the f_j functionals point to the central importance of socio-economic interlinkages.

Now *simultaneity* between economic efficiency (growth variables = g) and distributive equity variable (d), is shown to be realised by a treatment of the environment variable as an instrument (E). Subsequently, E is itself reproduced by such a simultaneous relationship as shown. This is the *concept of sustainability* in which, by means of treating the environment in the framework of appropriate technology, coordinative and cooperative institutions and behavioural change, all premised on the attributes of S, the politico-economic activities are recreated. Circularity and interactions are thus established by cause–effect. The market system in this sense becomes *endogenised, that is embedded, by attributes of ethics derived from the S-source.*

Post-evaluation of the developmental process is signified by the measurement of the well-being function, $W(..)$, which must be a compound functional of all the variables. We then note how the *Shari'ah* attributes have become instrumental in defining the concept of sustainability as a simultaneity among economic and social goals. The attribute of just balance is treated as the combination of the normative and positive aspects of distribution and ownership. Purpose is treated as a reflection of stability and worth. Felicity is the well-being itself. Creativity is signified by the interactive and evolutionary process of knowledge formation in the process model given here. Certainty is reflected by the relationship between spiritual–material purpose and yield.

DIAGRAMMATIC EXPLANATION FOR THE *SHARI'AH*-BASED PROCESS MODEL OF DEVELOPMENT

In Figure 9.6, the flow of functional relations among variables with environment within it is circular. But we must note particularly the interactive box among the variables. In this box the social well-being function is shown to be the criterion of post-evaluation of past policies developed upon *Shari'ah* attributes. One then notes that the responses so derived for revision, affirmation and continuity of the learning process leads us not to change *S*. Rather such corrective learning processes commence from the stage of $\mathbb{P}(S)$ and are followed by recursive formation of $\{\mathbb{P}(S)[\Theta_i]\}$-values. Finally, one notes that while interactions lead to integration by means of convergence of the knowledge-formation process between polity, the ecological agents and its post-evaluation, such stages of integration or consensus are not terminal ones. New recursions emerge as the levels of learning and issues at hand evolve. The dynamics of the Islamic heuristic process are thus endless. This establishes the relevance of the simulative model defining the cause–effect relations of interlinkages (Choudhury, 1993).

Pricing and Resource Allocation Questions in the Process Model

We will now briefly examine how prices and resource allocations are determined in the above interactive order. Growth paths such as 0*P*, shown in Figure 9.3, are not any more equilibrating, optimal and stable, as in the *neoclassical sense*. That is because discursions in the *Shari'ah*-based process model cannot generate such fictitious notions of equilibrium, optimality and

Figure 9.6 The *Shari'ah* process model of development and sustainability: treating simultaneity between growth and distribution

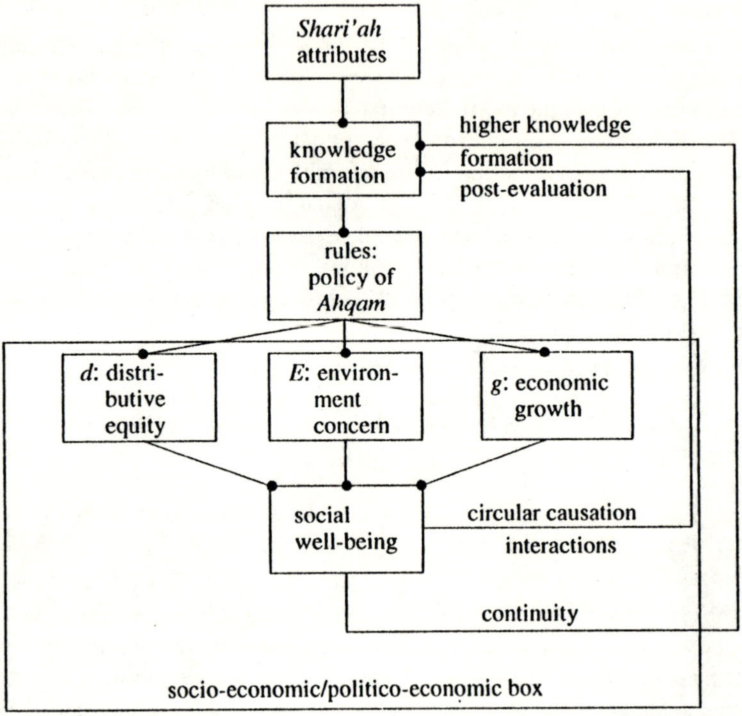

stability. Human and institutional behaviours are not predominated by economic rationality and rationalism in Islamic political economy. Rather the socio-economic and political worlds, through their interactions, are seen to generate dynamically evolutionary alternatives every time a discursion is on and a *process* is activated, or equivalently, knowledge is formed.

In this milieu, price is determined as in the classical economic framework, but now as a *notional* concept rather than as an exact concept (market prices). Price ceases to be utility-based demand-determined, as in neo-classical economics. The resource allocation according to relative prices is given by the condition of complementarity between feasible goods that enter Islamic markets. Now all that is bad is marginalised, with the long-run target of elimination. Hence, either by product discounting, high tax levies and phased in bans by policies, 'bads' are marginalised in the market exchange.

To formalise, let p_j denote the price of *i*th good, X_j, $j = 1,2$. p_j is determined by the knowledge-induced adaptive excess demand relationship,

$E[dEx(p_j)/d\Theta_i]\neq 0$, since $\{\Theta_i\}$ is evolutionary and never becomes static. Consequently, its knowledge-induced socio-economic variables, such as p_j here, cannot remain static. Here, E denotes expectation; Ex denotes excess demand function in p_j.

Resource allocation is determined by

$$dX_1/dX_2 = D_1(p_1)/D_2(p_2)$$

where D_j denotes the expected demand function for jth good, X_j, j = 1,2. Each of these values is knowledge-induced by means of $\{\Theta_i\}$-values. This result is the consequence of complementarity along the technologically induced growth path of the economy, as interactions by means of $\{\Theta_i\}$-values continue.

Hence *technology is defined in the Islamic sense* as knowledge induction of the *process* of discovering, developing, managing and delivering the socio-economic result of attaining well-being. Compare this to the neo-classical notion of technological as choices of production modes under conditions of full information, optimality, equilibrium, long-run stability and resource substitution among competing ends. Included in this is the unethical end of trade-off between economic growth and distributive equity.

The pricing relation as notional and shifting demand–supply conditions with incomplete information is shown in the upper portion of Figure 9.7. The shifting expectational equilibrium points, denoted by E_1, E_2, etc. along $0T$, define the moving equilibrium points. This conveys the idea of notional prices. In the lower portion of Figure 9.7, we show the resource allocation case, with the trajectory $0P$ of the nature of a fibre bundle due to the multiple nature of interactions that characterise decision-making in the Islamic political economy.

Note also that because of the circular causation nature of the sustainable development process described above, the well-being function must be simulated over interactively recursed values of $\{\Theta_i\}$. For those who may not be conversant with the formalisation given above, the same message is conveyed in Figure 9.6.

GENERALISING THE CONCEPT OF SUSTAINABILITY TO THE CONCEPT OF WEALTH IN THE ISLAMIC FRAMEWORK

What is true of environment as an instrument, is equally true of the *nature of wealth*, its generation and distribution in the Islamic political economy. Wealth is generated by shared ownership as a form of interlinkages. It is

Figure 9.7 Pricing and resource allocation in the Islamic interactive framework

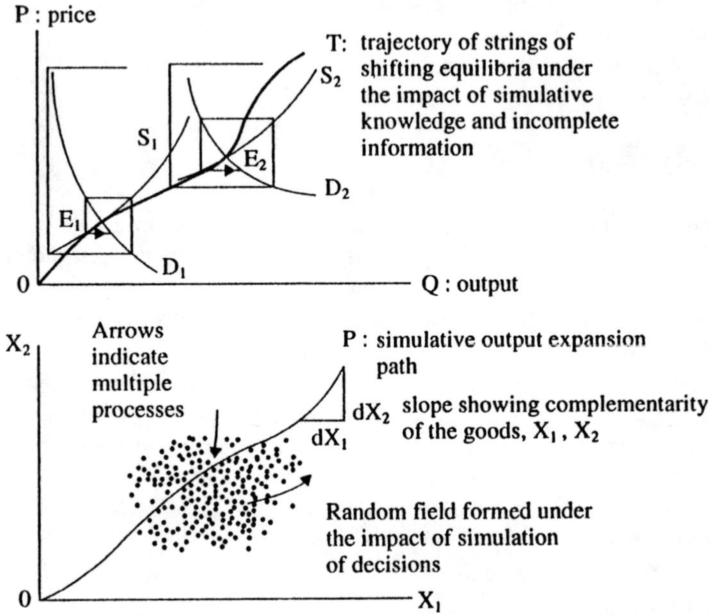

equitably distributed by means of the instruments that generate wealth according to the precept of ownership by means of sharing in the productive process. These are indeed the Madinite ideals of ownership during the times of the Muhajirin and Ansars (al Umari, 1991).

The instruments for generating interlinkages revolve around *mudarabah-musharakah* (profit sharing and equity participation). But an extended definition of these concepts is necessary. The precept of coordination and cooperation must be inherent in these instruments. We would then have such development financing instruments based on economic cooperation and coordination. Only in this way can universal interlinkages be generated and sustained. The cooperative objective in the midst of interlinkages premised in *Shari'ah* roots is a semblance of systemic unification in the Islamic order.

We note the distinct concept of wealth, its formation and distribution in the Islamic framework, from that in classical economics. In the latter case, wealth is produced out of an extensive range of individuated activities, each specialising for efficiency through a division of labour.

POLICY IMPLICATIONS OF A SUSTAINABLE DEVELOPMENT TREATMENT OF GROWTH REGIME

Neo-classical Policy Approaches Relating to Environment and Sustainable Development

The concept of sustainability as defined in the Islamic socio-economic framework brings to our attention the policy issues to realise such an ecologically balanced universe. We will again proceed on a comparative approach between neo-classical, Keynesian and Islamic frameworks. We will attend to these approaches by looking at the topic of control of pollutants (emissions) at source in an enterprise.

In the neo-classical approach, such an emission-controlling device is seen solely as an efficient device for reducing the cost of an enterprise towards meeting its social requirement for pollution control. The enterprise adopts the method as a substitution of its alternative more expensive methods of pollution control. The process towards adopting and developing such methods is internal to the firm, where managerial decision-making becomes embedded within the hierarchy of the enterprise itself. There is no need in such mechanical adoptions to consider social efficiency and linkages to develop and manage the technology. Hence the concept of total economic efficiency developed by meeting environmental requirements becomes an exercise simply in managerial efficiency. Neo-classical substitution occurs by replacing older methods of pollution controls by newer ones, without in the first place improving the older ones by means of upgrading intermediate technologies until they are phased in to yield newer technologies. In the substitutional case, factors, goods, sectors, skills, technologies, financing instruments and enterprises are all replaced, causing in its wake massive structural adjustment costs. Such costs are not seen to be internalised in the computation of managerial efficiency of pollution control at source. Thus the denial of interlinkages in technological change alienates the goal of attaining economic growth from the side of the social relevance of growth.

In recent times, the concept of environment–economic relations has taken up this neo-classical meaning for environment as a good competing with other goods/services. The pricing formula for such a treatment of environment in an efficiency framework is presented by incentives, subsidies and penalties. Consequently, such pricing measures enhance the same type of production relations internal to the firm.

Keynesian Policy Approaches Relating to Environment and Sustainable Development

When governments induce environmental consciousness, Keynesian policy induction would aim at increasing the marginal propensity to spend on environmentally friendly and pollution abating outlets. This measure is taken up along with investment expenditure to induce growth in the environment-related industry. In this way, the goal of pollution control at source is followed by investment in such devices and by the governmental subsidies to encourage production of such devices. Thereby, while the marginal propensity to spend in environmentally friendly outlets is promoted, there is no mechanism in the macroeconomic order to organise the desired linkages to steer away the narrow goal of production efficiency towards the socially interlinked ways. In other words, governments and the private sector do not spend under any well-directed ends to control environmental degradation through socio-economic linkages.

Fiscal expansion for environmental spending has no relationship with monetary policy. Consequently, interest rates increasing under the impact of fiscal expansion will cause a negative effect of interest rates on the income–investment multiplier. The production cost would increase and this would annul the effect of the marginal propensity to spend in environmentally friendly ways on the income multiplier.

Islamic Policy Approach in Relation to Environment and Sustainable Development

In the interactive development process with *Shari'ah* rules, the key policies to be looked at are of the microeconomic nature and those that generate interlinkages across the Islamic political economy. With regards to controlling environmental pollution at source in the Islamic firm, the technology is phased in by means of a coordinated decision-making between workers and management on the nature and quantity of goods to be produced and the upgraded kinds of intermediate technologies that are carried through for development into better technologies incrementally. Thus, the nature and quantity of goods along with the evolutionary nature of technology, establishes interlinkages. This reduces adjustment cost arising from replaced technology. Intersectorially, this provides uses of inputs across a variety of sectors in order to realise the upgrading of technology needed and its marketability through the service sector. Costs are thus reduced internally to the firm in terms of upgrading intermediate technologies into advanced ones. This reduces external indebtedness for the firm.

Human capital is advanced through the process of technological adaptation of available skills. External costs are minimised by means of diversification through product, technology and human capital linkages across sectors that all participate in the question of the nature of goods to be produced and the evolutionary nature of upgraded intermediate technologies to be developed. In the economy-wide sense, this also reduces the external debt costs that have increased phenomenally in Muslim countries due to their reliance on imported technologies and machine components.

Finally, there is the overarching social cost control from the political side. This occurs by way of increasing self-reliance and indigenous adaptation between available skills and technology, both taken up in an interactively dynamic form of advancement. Freedom from external indebtedness also enhances the Muslim countries' internal stability and togetherness. Much more as well, incremental advancement of intermediate technological brings about inter-country linkages in the Muslim world, causing internal markets to prosper. Along with all these comes political power to the Muslim countries and particularly to the microenterprises. The latter are to be viewed as the future carriers of politico-economic change through the kind of *Shari'ah*-based transformation process we have presented here.

The significant difference between the Islamic approach and the other approaches to growth and development in the midst of evironmental focus is the direct *cause–effect interrelationship of the principle of universal complementarity and ethical endogeneity (systemic) afforded by the unifying and interactive–integrative process model premised in Shari'ah.* In all other systems, behaviour, institutions and policies are methodologically embedded in their own *universal principle of substitution and generate ethical neutrality or ethical exogeneity in the market system.*

THE STRUCTURE OF GROWTH IN ISLAMIC PERSPECTIVES

The structure of growth in Islamic perspectives is described by the essence of all kinds of linkages in the economy–society-wide sense. Since such linkages give rise to complementarity and interactions, the other characteristics of the structure of growth is the institutional mode of endogenising ethics in markets and to premise all interactions in the unifying methodology, irrespective of differences in the issues and problems at hand. Such a methodology is afforded by *Shari'ah* according to its attributes mentioned earlier.

The structure of growth as so defined in the Islamic political economy carries with it complementary and interlinked relationships in factor markets. Thus, prices and resource allocation intersectorially are explained by interlinked changes in the *markets of complementary factors and goods*.

In all these, *population increase* is seen not as a deterrent but rather as a positive contributor to economic growth, when markets and appropriate consumption, production and distribution are realised by the transformation process. Population as a factor in the growth model, through the labour market and its complementarity with the capital market, becomes an informed matter of choice by the individual, when empowerment, ownership and participatory democracy as institutional forces enter the total transformation process in the political economy.

As we have shown in the measurement of growth in other systems, population increase is seen as a deterrent to growth. This is due to the substitutional nature of resources, goods and factors in the presence of an inflexible quantum of information, once it is maximised by assumption, although not by reality. Consequently, scarcity and competition, rather than cooperation and extensive policy coordination as afforded by Islamic political economy, build the development process.

COMPARATIVE EXAMINATION OF APPROACHES TO ECONOMIC GROWTH FOR MALAYSIA

Table 9.1 shows the sectorial trend and shares of GDP for Malaysia in recent years (Government of Malaysia, 1991). Table 9.2 shows the sectorial shares of employment for Malaysia and other demographic statistics for the same years. It is clearly seen that there is a pronounced shift in GDP and employment away from the agricultural sector to the manufacturing and service sectors. The fact that the growth rate of the population in Malaysia has remained low, between 2.4 and 2.5 per cent annually over the last two decades, whereas the labour force has grown by approximately 3 per cent during this time, indicates that the labour force participation rate remained fairly high. Yet the sectorial shifts from agriculture to manufacturing and services point out that labour force activity in the primary sector would have remained low. The expected sectorial labour force participation rates and employment shifts in such a case also point out that agricultural labour would have experienced low productivity growth. This in turn would have corresponded with their lower wages. We show the average labour productivity trends in Table 9.3.

These average labour productivity trends are coupled with the fact that employment in agriculture and forestry increased by a mere 0.9 per cent

Table 9.1 GDP trend and shares by sectors, Malaysia 1985–95

	1985		*1990*		*1995*	
	M$mill	*% shares*	*M$mill*	*% shares*	*M$mill*	*% shares*
Agriculture & forestry	11 854	20.8	14 829	18.7	17 580	15.5
Manufacturing	11 263	19.7	21 381	27.0	36 860	32.4
Wholesale & retail trade, hotels & restaurants	6 911	12.1	8 700	11.0	13 410	11.8
Finance, real estate & business services	5 121	9.0	7 650	9.7	12 070	10.6
Government services	6 957	12.2	8 459	10.7	10 440	9.2
Other services	1 301	2.3	1 656	2.1	2 430	2.1

Source: Government of Malaysia, *Sixth Malaysian Plan 1991–5* (Kuala Lumpur, 1991), table 1–2.

annually during the decade 1985–90, and declined by 0.2 per cent annually during the period 1990–5. In manufacturing, employment increased by 8.6 per cent annually during 1985–90 and by 5.7 per cent annually during 1990–5. In the service sector the respective period increases of employment were on the average, 5.6 per cent and 5.4 per cent annually, for these time periods, respectively.

Such trends can only mean that output in the agricultural sector was not being reinforced by linkages with the manufacturing and service sectors. This caused both output and employment to decline in the primary sector. With the small population base of Malaysia, this shift away from agricultural sector spells problem of sustainability of the agricultural sector once intersectorial linkages are removed.

The nature of sectorial delinking with displacement of labour in the face of unbalanced productivity increases between the primary and other sectors is found to be of the neo-classical origin. This socio-economic picture is reinforced by policies and market transformations that intensify in the face of neo-classical orientations to growth now taking place in

Table 9.2 Sectorial trends and shares of employment, Malaysia ('000)

				Increase ('000)		*Average annual growth rate (%)*	
	1985	*1990*	*1995*	*5MP*	*6MP*	*5MP*	*6MP*
Population ('000)	15 864.0	18 010.2	20 262.7	2 146.2	2 252.5	2.5	2.4
Labour force ('000)	6 039.1	7 046.5	8 114.0	1 007.4	1 067.5	3.1	2.9
Unemployment ('000)	414.5	425.5	361.7				
Unemployment rate[1] (%)	6.9	6.0	4.5				

							New jobs ('000)		*Average annual growth rate (%)*	
Sector	*('000)*	*(%)*	*('000)*	*(%)*	*('000)*	*(%)*	*5MP*	*6MP*	*5MP*	*6MP*
Agriculture & forestry	1 759.6	31.3	1 837.6	27.8	1 821.9	23.5	78.0	−15.7	0.9	−0.2
Mining & quarrying	44.4	0.8	39.1	0.6	40.7	0.5	−5.3	1.6	−2.5	0.8
Manufacturing	855.4	15.2	1 290.2	19.5	1 699.1	21.9	434.8	408.9	8.6	5.7
Construction	429.4	7.6	426.9	6.4	547.5	7.1	−2.5	120.6	−0.1	5.1
Non-government services[2]	1 716.3	30.5	2 177.0	32.9	2 770.9	35.7	460.7	593.9	4.9	4.9
Government services	819.5	14.6	850.2	12.8	872.2	11.3	30.7	22.0	0.7	0.5
Employment	5 624.6	100.0	6 621.0	100.0	7 752.3	100.0	996.4	1 131.3	3.3	3.2

Notes

[1]Estimates of unemployment in Malaysia follow the internationally accepted definition of unemployment and include all persons in the labour force who, during the reference period, were without any work although available for employment. The estimates cover those who were not actively looking for work and they accounted for about half of the total number of unemployed.

[2]Includes electricity, gas and water; transport, storage and communications; wholesale and retail trade, hotels and restaurants; finance, insurance, real estate and business services and other services.

Source: Government of Malayisa, *Sixth Malaysian Plan 1991–5* (Kuala Lumpur, 1991).

Malaysia. The deliberate policies of the industrial sector and urban growth in Malaysia are complementary activities. In the face of these trends by cause and effect, there appears to be a trade-off between government and private sector finances towards development. While government finances

Table 9.3 Average productivity of labour by sectors, Malaysia ($)

Average labour productivity: (M$GDP/employment)	*1985*	*1990*	*1995*
Agriculture & forestry	6.74	8.06	9.64
Manufacturing	13.17	16.57	21.69
Service	8.00	8.74	10.53

Source: As Tables 9.1 and 9.2.

are still oriented to help out rural development, private sector finances are geared overwhelmingly towards industrial development. In the total financing between 1986 and 1991, it was found that agriculture sometimes received declining amounts; the highest increase was 18.1 per cent in 1989 and it was 9.5 per cent in 1991. Contrarily, the manufacturing sector enjoyed increased amounts, increasing from 4.5 per cent in 1986 to 33.3 per cent in 1989 and 25.6 per cent in 1991 (Government of Malaysia, 1991).

As opposed to the neo-classical trade-off signalled by the sectorial shifts in output, employment and capital, an Islamic approach to development premised essentially in global socio-economic complementarity would signal just the opposite. The nature of goods in the primary and manufacturing sectors, being now graduated baskets of basic needs with varied categories and levels of refinements, must interlink the agricultural, manufacturing and service sectors for the resources, production and marketing of the final good. The circularity of output and factor use that exists now must show factor productivity to be moving under the force of growth in the real factors and outputs themselves. This conveys the idea of factor-augmented technological growth induction in the production menus.

As an illustrative case, if the sectorial labour productivity was to stabilise around the figure for the economy as a whole, this would be M$14.65. This is a crude indicator of interlinkages, as the implication of assuming equal economy-wide average labour productivity is that inter-sectorial linkages would be causing this figure of $14.65 to attain across the sectors. With this illustrative case, the resulting pattern of adjustment in sectorial growth of labour productivity needed to attain the overall economy-wide average labour productivity across sectors is shown in Table 9.4.

Table 9.4 Estimate of adjustments in the change of average labour productivity when uniform sectorial interlinkages exist, Malaysia

Adjustment in growth rate for average labour productivity = $(Q/E)/(Q_i/E_i)$ = M$14.65/$(Q_i/E_i)$ = $1+g_i$, with g_i as the growth rate of labour productivity by sectors *i*.

Adjustment in growth rates by sectors = g_i	*1995*
Agriculture	52 %
Manufacturing	–32 %
Services	39 %

Source: Tables 9.1 and 9.2.

The above scenario is not the only way of establishing productivity adjustments in the Malaysian economy through a process of intersectorial complementarity. For instance, if the target was to raise the sectorial labour productivities altogether, then a much greater adjustment would be required for the agricultural and services sectors.

In the case shown in Table 9.4, the inference is that the manufacturing sector has grown in an unsustainable way in the presence of overall sectorial trade-offs, as explained earlier. Thus, to remove the inherent weakness of the Malaysian economy that can come from the doors of manufacturing expansion with no primary sector linkages, and an overly debt-creating import reliance on manufacturing components and foreign direct investments, an overall sectorial reorganisation is projected here in the framework of the Islamic approach to socio-economic development with global complementarity within it.

The kinds of weaknesses that can come into the Malaysian economy from the existing tempo of industrial expansion are as follows: overdependence on foreign direct investment as liability (Ali, 1992), lack of skilled manpower, uncertainties of the export-led economy in the face of monetary policies abroad, and the external debt-propensity built upon the capital goods imports (SESRTCIC, 1993). In 1991, Malaysia was ranked at 26 in the risk ranking done by *Euromoney* (1991). Although this was the best among the members of the Organisation of Islamic Conferences it was a low standing internationally.

Thus a negative adjustment in growth of labour productivity for the manufacturing sector is explainable from the point of view of the intersectorial developmental adjustments that this will generate. This is a matter of restructuring growth in the Malaysian economy. A negative adjustment of labour productivity growth does not mean that either output or employment in the manufacturing sector needs to decline while other sectors are being expanded. For a negative adjustment in labour productivity growth can arise from the fact that the growth of employment in the manufacturing sector outstrips the rate of growth of output in this sector, although both employment and output would be increasing together. When this is the case, much of the employment would be gained in those manufacturing enterprises that are linked to the agricultural sector by forward and backward linkages.

The rapid growth of employment in the face of sectorial interlinkages implies that population increase must be targeted as a mandatory goal for Malaysia under the Islamic approach to socio-economic development. Otherwise, the shortage of labour cannot sustain such a goal. With the population relationship built into the total socio-economic relationships, the critical complementary factors are all incorporated in the Islamic socio-economic development scenario. These appear as complementary between population increase and labour force increase, feeding into labour-intensive sectorial interlinkages. Such interlinkages in turn would define the nature of adjustment and structural change required simultaneously to achieve high productivity changes in the Malaysian economy across all sectors.

A BRIEF NOTE ON THE RECONCILIATION PROBLEM BETWEEN MONETARY AND FISCAL POLICIES IN NEO-CLASSICAL, KEYNESIAN AND ISLAMIC FRAMEWORKS

Our last issue on the comparative approach to economic growth and development is that of the role of money in growth. This is a technical question in the light of how money is treated in the economic literature, that is, either as exogenous or endogenous aggregates.

Neo-classical Policy Orientation

In neo-classical economics, money as an aggregate is neutral to economic growth, as it does not enter the aggregate production function as a factor of production. Money as an aggregate simply plays the role of exchange and store of value. Thus, in the Quantity Equation, money is shown to be related to the actual system of exchange in the goods and securities markets. From the side of the goods markets, the quantity of money in circulation is shown to be a function of price level. Contrarily, an increase in price level is causally shown to affect the quantity of money. From the side of the securities market, the quantity of money is determined by interest rates. Contrarily, an increase in the interest rate increases the supply of money along the money supply curve. Thus, prices and quantity of money are not causally related in any determinate form. Furthermore, the types of money arising from the goods market (M1) and from the securities markets (higher than M1) have different responses to prices and interest rates. This too compounds the causality problem of money and prices in the Quantity Equation.

Keynesian and Monetarist Policy Orientations

In Keynesian economics, the supply of money is exogenously determined by the central bank. Demand for money is determined by the sum of transaction demand, precautionary demand and speculative demand components. These are disparate functional relations. Consequently, there is a great deal of uncertainty for monetary equilibrium to occur in the Keynesian general equilibrium system. Economic expectations belie a move to monetary equilibrium. To get over this problem, Keynesians have always favoured fiscal policy over monetary policies to stabilise the economy. Thus a non-inflationary growth-oriented policy moving the economy to full employment in the Keynesian system is enacted by recourse to fiscal policy (Sawyer, 1982).

However, the monetarists and new classicists advocate the supremacy of monetary policies for economic stabilisation. They play down the importance of fiscal policy for stabilisation purposes. In this way, the return of monetarism echoes the problems of the Quantity Equation we have discussed above. Consequently, in this debate, the Keynesian process to a full employment equilibrium is fraught with uncertainties according to the monetarists while vice versa it is valid for the Keynesians.

Between the two schools of thought, we conclude that monetary and fiscal policies remain extremely unstable in the determination of full employment output and the potential level of economic growth. Consequently, both the monetary sector and the expenditure sector continue to give signals that are abortive of each other.

Islamic Policy Orientation

In the Islamic political economy, the intrinsic nature of interlinkages for any purposeful activity to be qualified as the functional effectiveness of

Shari'ah in the socio-economic order means a return to microeconomic foundations of policy development. Thus macroeconomic relations and policies take the form of an economy-wide effect of microeconomic activities and policies.

Money in Islamic markets is truly currency carrying the token value of goods that are actually exchanged in real and not promissory markets. The secondary market for securities thus devolves into actual transactions taking place between demand and supply of goods where money as currency becomes a medium of store of value, not of exchange. Money does not change hands; hence there is no velocity of money in circulation. Goods change hands by invoking the dissimilar and valuational medium of money as currency. *Money is not held as liquidity, as in Keynesian economics. Rather money is held as currency to value good in exchange* (Choudhury, 1992).

Since money has no role of exchange, therefore it fetches no price. Only the real markets determine prices and currency value of money as its store of value. At the end of these relations, money as currency in Islamic markets has a definite relationship to price level. Now an increase in money as currency does not increase prices, for there is no relationship from the side of quantity of money to prices in real markets. Contrarily, a change in price levels determined by the pure medium of exchange in real markets determines the quantity of currency to be transacted for meeting the ensuing exhange. This remains universally true across both goods and securities markets, for in every case the reference is to real markets and not to promissory ones.

Thus, the Islamic role of money in economic growth is realised through the use of money as currency to value real goods and services in exchange. There is, therefore, a positive relationship between the quantity of currency in circulation and the level of economic growth, for the latter determines the former. On the other hand, the more viscuous is the exchange in real markets, the more the currency demand. Hence there is a circular relationship between exhange (i.e. markets) and currency value. *Money as currency thus becomes a productive factor in Islamic markets.*

Consequently, policies developed around such an endogenous money result in stability attained by the minimisation of uncertain expectations (Desai, 1989). Such expectations we have shown besieges the Keynesian system and monetarism (new classicism). It also transforms money as currency value into a factor of production, unlike the neutrality of money as a productive factor in the neo-classical system. *Money as currency value thus acquires a well-definition of money as a stable aggregate.* There is no concept now of excess or shortage of monetary aggregates causing price and growth instabilities, as in the case of the Keynesian and monetarist schools.

The immediate policy implication of such a nature of money is the need for Islamic financial institutions and enterprises to promote market-oriented activities using *Shari'ah* instruments. But since such markets cannot presently be opened up in the presence of interest rates, therefore, the precondition is to institutionalise and endogenise the role of *Shari'ah* in the Islamic transformation process. Islamic banks and central banks in Muslim countries should keep this point of view in mind. They could develop tradable bills carrying asset values as prices. Bullion can then be supplied by the central bank in accordance with the value of the tradable certificates. The Muslim world has always been aware of the goods-denominated *numeraire* value of a mandatory poor due called *Sadaqatul Fitr*.

CONCLUSION

We have presented in this chapter an overview of a comparative theory of economic growth in neo-classical, Keynesian and Islamic socio-economic systems. In this way we have shown that the most crucial focus of economic growth as a developmental *process* is to bring about sustainability that would be embedded (endogenous) in the socio-economic order. This is the idea of ethical endogeneity. The theory of economic growth taken up in such a *concept of sustainability as a process* invokes an altogether new approach to theorising and policy analysis, in the midst of complementarity across sectors, markets, goods, skills, communities and nations. Such a universal sway of interlinkages and diversifications of economic activities invokes the principle of unification as premised in *Shari'ah* in terms of its attributes of just balance, purpose, felicity, creativity and certainty. This essentially is the foundation of the interactive–integrative process of continuity and causation that generates growth, distribution, stability and well-being in the Islamic political economy simultaneously. We have termed this principle of universal interactions, complementarity and interlinkages as the *Principle of Universal Complementarity*.

In all other systems only the polar view is upheld. That is, neo-classical economics is embedded inescapably in its own principle of marginalist substitution. This endogenises the neo-classical markets with the same substitution conditions by cause and effect of its own. Keynesian economics is ethically neutral as there exist no decision-makers in macroeconomics. What happens to government expenditure and structural change in the economy is left totally to market forces in which, by reversion, neoclassical preferences prevail. This alienates the process of sustainability.

At the end of the study we have shown that in regard to fiscal and monetary policy matters and their relations with real markets, only the Islamic system provides definite and stable consequences. This is a methodological result on an alternative perspective of Third-World development with an illustrative application to Malaysian economy.

References

Agius, E. (1990) 'Towards a Relational Theory of Intergenerational Ethics', in Busuttil, S., Agius, E. Inglott, P.S. and Macelli, T. (eds) *Our Responsibilities Towards Future Generations* (Malta: Foundation for International Studies), pp. 73–93.

al Umari, A.D. (1991) *Madina Society at the Time of the Prophet, Vol. 1* (Herndon, VA: International Institute of Islamic Thought).

Ali, A. (1992) 'Technology Transfer in Manufacturing Industries via Direct Foreign Investment', *Journal of Economic Cooperation Among Islamic Countries*, 13(3–4), July/October, pp. 137–59.

Allen, R.G.D. (1970), *Macroeconomic Theory: A Mathematical Treatment* (London: Macmillan).

Burmeister, E. and Dobell, A.R. (1970) *Mathematical Theories of Economic Growth* (New York: Macmillan).

Choudhury, M.A. (1992) 'The Endogenous Theory of Money and Islamic Capital Markets', *Journal of Economic Cooperation Among Islamic Countries*, 13(2–3).

Choudhury, M.A. (1993) *Comparative Development Studies: In Search of the World View* (London: Macmillan; New York: St Martin's Press).

Choudhury, M.A. (1994) 'Theory and Practice of Islamic Political Economy', paper presented at the International Workshop on Islamic Political Economy in the Midst of Capitalist Globalisation, Science University of Malaysia Penang, Malaysia, 20–22 December. Now in *Hamdard Islamicus*, Vol. XVIII, No. 4, Jan. 1996.

Desai, M. (1989) 'Endogenous and Exogenous Money', in Eatwell, J., Milgate, M. and Newman, P. (eds) *New Palgrave: Money* (New York: W.W. Norton).

Euromoney quoted in SESRTCIC document (see below).

Government of Malaysia (1991) *Sixth Malaysia Plan, 1991–1995* (Kuala Lumpur: Government Printer).

Inglott, P.S. (1990) 'The Common Heritage and the Rights of Future Generations', in Agius, E. *Our Responsibilities Towards Future Generations* (Malta: Foundation for International Studies), pp. 67–72.

Ministry of Finance (1992) *Economic Report, 1992/93* (Kuala Lumpur: Government Printer).

Pratt, R.C. (1983) 'The Global Impact of the World Bank', in Torrie, J. (ed.) *Banking on Poverty, the Global Impact of the IMF and the World Bank* (Toronto: Between the Lines).

Robinson, J. (1961) 'Prelude to a Critique of Economic Theory', *Oxford Economic Papers*, 13.

Samuelson, P.A., Nordhaus, W.D. and McCallum, J. (1988) *Macroeconomics* (Toronto: McGraw-Hill Ryerson).

Sawyer, M.C. (1982) *Macroeconomics in Question, The Keynesian–Monetarist Orthodoxies and the Kaleckian Alternative* (Armonk, NY: M.E. Sharpe).

SESRTCIC (Statistical, Economic and Social Research and Training Centre for Islamic Countries) (1993) *Documents Presented by SESRTCIC: Twenty-First Conference of Foreign Ministers*, Ankara, Turkey, 24–29, April pp. 28–32.

10 Structural Adjustment within Malaysian Agriculture in Response to Rapid Industrialisation

Haji Mohammad Alias and
Masudul A. Choudhury

OBJECTIVES

The principal objectives of this chapter are to identify and analyse the various sectorial substitutions and their consequences that are taking place between agriculture and industry in the Malaysian promotion of industrialisation. Within the industrial sector we will focus on manufacturing. The chapter falls into three parts to realise this objective.

First, a brief coverage will be provided on a comparative trend in agricultural and industrial development by virtue of the prevalent Malaysian agricultural and industrial policy frameworks. This will present the perspective of the problem that we will be analysing in regard to this comparative sectorial development.

Secondly, we will put these trends in an analytical framework to investigate the question whether allocative efficiency and stability are to be gained from the intersectorial substitutions that are taking place, or do such substitutions lead to instability and delinked development? In this section we will explore the dynamics of the process of structural change within agriculture. We will also examine the role of agricultural and industrial policies towards stabilising adjustment costs and realising linkages between these sectors.

Thirdly, we will extrapolate on the position and prospects of agriculture in a rapidly industrialising economy. The effectiveness of the various agricultural strategies and programmes to strengthen the commercialisation of the sector, especially among the smallholders, will be examined, as will the role of agriculture in supporting the agro-based industry. An assessment of future growth performance of agriculture will take into account production constraints, such as shortages of labour, productivity trends, financial and technical efficiency problems as well as low levels of investment in agriculture.

HISTORICAL TRENDS IN COMPARATIVE EVOLUTION OF AGRICULTURE AND INDUSTRIALISATION IN THE LIGHT OF MALAYSIAN DEVELOPMENT POLICIES

The Malaysian economy has achieved sustainable growth and structural transformation since independence in 1957. In the 1960s, the economy was mainly based on primary commodities. Agriculture and mining, primarily tin, contributed 46 per cent to the Gross Domestic Product (GDP) while the manufacturing sector contributed less than 10 per cent. The growth of the economy depended on the export performance of a few commodities, namely, rubber, tin and timber. In 1961, these contributed 70.7 per cent to total export earnings with rubber alone accounting for 48.4 per cent. Exports of manufactured goods contributed a meagre 4.5 per cent to total export earnings (see Table 10.1).

Several considerations required appropriate policy responses from the state. First, being a trade-oriented economy with commodity prices deter-

Table 10.1 Structure of commodity exports

Commodity	*Unit*	*1961*	*1970*	*1980*	*1990*
Value					
1. Rubber	$M	1 567	1 724	4 617	3 027
2. Tin	$M	533	1 013	2 505	902
3. Crude petroleum	$M	107	202	6 709	10 639
4. Timber	$M	188	842	3 799	7 108
5. Palm oil	$M	61	264	2 515	4 399
6. Manufactured goods[a]	$M	146	333	7 839	43 978
7. Other exports	$M	636	784	188	9 593
Total	$M	3 238	5 162	28 172	79 646
Structure					
1. Rubber	%	48.4	33.4	16.4	3.8
2. Tin	%	16.5	19.6	8.9	1.1
3. Crude petroleum	%	3.3	3.9	23.8	13.4
4. Timber	%	5.8	16.3	13.5	8.9
5. Palm oil	%	1.9	5.1	8.9	5.5
6. Manufactured goods[a]	%	4.5	6.5	27.8	55.2
7. Other exports	%	19.6	15.2	1.7	12.0
Total		100.0	100.0	100.0	100.0

[a]SITC groups 5–8
Source: Malaysia Department of Statistics.

mined in the world markets, the economy was subjected to the adverse effects of terms of trade changes. Secondly, the economy was characterised by a substantial degree of dualism (Stern, 1987, p. 37). Within the agriculture sector there existed a modern estate sector, characterised by high productivity, and a traditional smallholder sector, characterised by low productivity and low incomes.

The state implemented deliberate policy measures in the 1960s and 1970s primarily to diversify the export base. Varying degrees of effect from industrial diversification were experienced in the agricultural and mining sectors. Agricultural production grew by about 6 per cent per annum in the 1960s, mainly attributable to the rubber subsector. However, real income from rubber growing fell in the 1960s because of the steady decline in natural rubber prices in the face of strong competition from synthetics. The estate sector was also affected by this decline in prices. But estates were able to produce rubber profitably because of substantial increases in yields through the use of high yielding planting materials and improved management and planting techniques.

Agricultural diversification began in earnest from late 1960s and into the 1970s. New crops such as oil palm and cocoa were planted on a large scale, mainly for export. Favourable prices relative to natural rubber were instrumental in fostering the switch from rubber cultivation to these crops. In the case of oil palm, a combination of favourable endowment, both in physical and human resources, a growing demand for palm oil and palm oil products in the international markets and supportive government policies helped to explain the rapid growth of this industry. Smallholders were encouraged to plant the new crops through replanting schemes and subsidised inputs such as fertilisers and high yielding planting materials. The state established research institutes such as the Malaysian Agricultural Research and Development Institute (MARDI) and the Palm Oil Research Institute of Malaysia (PORIM) to help develop better planting materials and transfer technologies to farmers.

In the 1970s, agricultural production grew at a remarkable 5.1 per cent per year. Rubber and oil palm accounted for more than half of total agricultural output. While rubber exports continued to increase in value terms from (US)$1724 million in 1970 to $4617 million in 1980, the increase in the value of palm oil exports has been phenomenal, from $264 million in 1970 to $2515 million in 1980.

Structural change also occurred within the mining sector. The significant discovery of major oil fields in the mid-1970s contributed significantly to petroleum exports. Crude petroleum exports contributed $202 million in 1970, increasing to $6709 million in 1980.

The diversification within the agricultural sector and the mining sector has reduced the initial overreliance on rubber and tin for export earnings.

Industrialisation to diversify the economy has gone through three stages. In stage one, starting from the early 1960s, industries were geared towards the domestic market, primarily for import substitution. In stage two, starting from early 1970s, the industrialisation strategy focused on the export markets. Growth in manufacturing received an impetus from the development of resource-based processing industries and labour intensive industries, producing mainly for export. Industries producing electrical goods, textiles and footwear were important components of the manufacturing sector. The development of labour intensive manufacturing industries was motivated by the policy concern to tackle the high rate of unemployment, especially among rural youth, in the early 1970s. The agricultural sector was not able to generate enough employment. The government introduced direct measures, including fiscal incentives, to attract foreign direct investment (FDI) into manufacturing activities. Tax concessions and 'pioneer status' were given under the Pioneer Industries Ordinance introduced after Independence. The new Investment Incentives Act of 1968 was followed by the Free Trade Zone Act of 1971 to promote the development of export processing zones. The export zones were dominated by FDI from the United States and Japan. The investments were able to generate employment opportunities through the setting up of labour intensive manufacturing industries, namely, textiles and electronics sub-sectors.

In stage three, beginning from the early 1980s, the state initiated a heavy industrialisation programme. This entailed the establishment of capital intensive and skill intensive manufacturing industries. The drive into heavy manufacturing is motivated by the concern that domestic industries should not be technologically left behind in a rapidly changing world. Government involvement is justified because of the inability of the private sector to provide the industrial thrust in this area. A number of public enterprises were established, the principal one being the Heavy Industries Corporation of Malaysia (HICOM) in 1980.

The combination of rapid economic growth, 5.0 to 5.4 per cent per year in the 1960s, 8.1 per cent in the 1970s, and 6.7 per cent during the First Outline Perspective Plan (1971–90), and the diversification of the economic base, has led to a structural shift in the economy. The share of the agriculture (forestry and fishing) sector in total GDP declined from 29.0 per cent in 1970 to 18.7 per cent in 1990. During the same period, the manufacturing sector's contribution increased from 13.9 per cent to 27.0 per cent (Table 10.2). By 1987, manufacturing had surpassed the agricul-

Table 10.2 Composition of the Gross Domestic Product (GDP) by industry of origin and average growth rate[1]

	1970[2]	1975	1985	1990	*Average growth rate 1971–90 %*
Agriculture, forestry and fishing	29.0	27.7	20.8	18.7	4.4
Mining and quarrying	13.7	4.6	10.5	9.7	4.9
Manufacturing	13.9	16.4	19.7	27.0	10.3
Construction	3.8	3.8	4.8	3.5	6.4
Services	39.6	47.5	44.2	41.1	7.6

[1]GDP is measured at 1978 prices.
[2]Adjusted to 1978 prices.
Source: Government of Malaysia, *The Second Outline Perspective Plan*, 1991–2000 (Kuala Lumpur: National Printing Department, 1991).

ture sector for the first time as the leading sector. The economy has transformed from an agriculture-based economy at Independence to one which is manufacturing based. The path for Malaysia to become an industrialised economy has already been put in place.

The structural shift in the economy is reflected in the export structure, which is more diversified with less reliance on primary commodity exports. By 1990 the share of manufactured exports in total export earnings had risen to 55.2 per cent compared to 27.8 per cent in 1980. During the same period the share of primary commodity exports (including crude petroleum) in total export earnings declined from 71.5 per cent to 32.7 per cent. The major contributors in 1990 were crude petroleum (13.4 per cent), timber (8.9 per cent), palm oil (5.5 per cent) and rubber (3.8 per cent). The decline in the relative contribution of rubber has been significant – 48.4 per cent in 1961, 33.4 per cent (1970) and a meagre 3.8 per cent in 1990.

RECENT TRENDS IN AGRICULTURAL DEVELOPMENT

Table 10.3 shows the percentage distributions of GDP, employment in the agricultural and manufacturing sectors, and in the major occupations. We also show the shares of production value in agricultural related manufacturing products in comparison to those in primary agricultural products;

Table 10.3 Comparison among some critical indicators in agriculture, total manufacturing and agro-based manufacturing, Malaysia 1984–92 (percentages)

	1986	*1987*	*1988*	*1989*	*1990*	*1991*	*1992*	*1993*
Shares of GDP by industry in 1978 constant prices								
Agriculture	21	22	21	20	16	17	16	15
Manufacturing	21	23	24	25	27	28	29	31
Shares of employment by industry								
Agriculture	32	32	31	29	28	27	26	25
Manufacturing*	15	16	17	18	19	20	21	21

Employment by occupation (shares)	*1985*	*1990*	*1992*
Professional and technical	7.5	7.9	9.1
Administrative and managerial	2.3	2.5	2.6
Clerical	9.7	8.8	9.8
Sales	11.1	11.6	12.0
Services	11.4	11.3	11.8
Production	27.3	27.6	28.4
Agriculture	30.6	30.2	26.3

Producer price index 1978 = 100	*1988*	*1989*	*1990*	*1991*	*1992*
Food and live animals	154.3	163.8	174.8	195.8	198.9
Beverages and tobacco	177.9	182.7	184.3	197.1	204.4
Animal and vegetable oils and fats	98.3	88.5	67.2	77.8	88.9
Manufactured goods*	122.1	132.0	128.5	128.9	128.4
Export:					
Textile	139.8	118.0	127.9	132.6	137.1
Wood related	132.4	116.7	133.4	139.3	145.8
Rubber related	232.6	104.8	113.9	123.5	136.1
Domestic-oriented:					
Food beverages and tobacco	115.2	112.1	119.7	116.8	116.3

Consumer price index 1990 = 100 (inflation rate)	*1988*	*1989*	*1990*	*1991*	*1992*
	94.4	97.0	100.0	104.4	108.6
	(2.5)	(2.8)	(3.1)	(4.4)	(4.6)

Table 10.3 *Continued*

Commodity balance of trade as percent of GDP	*1986*	*1987*	*1988*	*1989*	*1990*	*1991*	*1992*
Food, beverages and tobacco	−1.9	−1.1	−1.7	−2.4	−1.7	−2.0	−1.1
Animal and vegetable oils and fats	6.1	6.5	8.3	8.2	6.9	6.8	3.9
Manufactured goods*	−2.5	−2.0	−4.0	−5.8	−7.6	−10.0	−4.8
Total balance	12.8	21.8	16.5	9.6	0.7	−7.3	−1.6

Total government expenditure by areas = operating + development as percentage of total federal govt. expenditure	*1988*	*1989*	*1990*	*1991*	*1992*	*1993*
Agriculture and rural development	7.0	6.3	6.2	5.6	5.3	5.7
Trade and industry*	4.7	4.3	8.8	3.5	4.2	3.1

Shares of commercial bank advances and loans by industry	*1986*	*1987*	*1988*	*1989*	*1990*	*1991*
Agriculture	6.1	5.9	5.4	5.4	5.2	4.8
Manufacturing*	17.1	17.4	19.7	20.9	23.2	24.2
General commerce	17.4	17.2	16.9	15.7	14.4	13.2

*includes items such as scientific equipments, leather goods, furniture, plastic goods, machinery and related goods.
Computations done on the basis of data derived from the source: Ministry of Finance *Economic Report, 1992/93* (Kuala Lumpur, 1992).

the volume of bank lending to agriculture in comparison to manufacturing and general commerce; total government expenditure (operating + development) in agriculture and trade and industry; export value of agro-based manufacturing; the trade balance in agro-based manufacturing and total manufactured goods; foreign investment in agro-based manufacturing; producer prices for agro-based manufacturing and manufacturing of materials. The purpose here is to show the nature of substitution taking place between the agricultural and manufacturing sectors in terms of factor use, labour productivity and incentives towards production. We then deduce the nature of allocative efficiency and intersectorial linkages that can be expected from these percentage distributions.

We note from Table 10.3 that since agricultural shares of output and employment are both declining, therefore,

$$(d/dt)(Q_{ag}/Q) < 0; \ (d/dt)(L_{ag}/L) < 0 \tag{10.1}$$

That is, $g + g_{ag} < 0$; $n + n_{ag} < 0$. In either case, since the Malaysian economy is not seen to show signs of negative overall growth of output and labour as exemplified by her experience of high growth rates and low unemployment rates, therefore, in the long run, $g_{ag} < 0$ and $n_{ag} < 0$.

This result implies a discomforting trend towards long-run substitution of labour and output from the agricultural sector by those in the industrial sector, unless such trends are arrested by appropriate agricultural policies. This scenario of negative long-run growth in the agricultural sector is a sign of the Dutch disease problem in this sector and is initiated on the supply side. As growth slows down, this carries along with it a slowdown in the derived demand for agricultural labour.

Noting that

$$q_{ag}{}^{L} = Q_{ag}/L_{ag} \tag{10.2}$$

which yields, $dq_{ag}{}^{L}/q_{ag}{}^{L} = [dQ_{ag}/Q_{ag} - dL_{ag}/L_{ag}]$, computations will show that the right-hand side expression is positive for Malaysia. Hence, based on the agricultural sector alone, without studying intersectorial linkages, we find that rates of change of labour productivity are still positive in the agricultural sector. This result holds because the rate of growth of agriculture is higher than the negative rate of change in agricultural employment. Current estimates (1991–3) of $dq_{ag}{}^{L}/q_{ag}{}^{L}$ are marginally above 1 per cent, a low figure indeed.

Now the question remains as to how the productivity of labour moves in agriculture in the perspective of intersectorial linkages. To investigate this question we proceed as follows:

Let $q_{ag}{}^{L} = Q_{ag}/L_{ag}$. Then, $dq_{ag}{}^{L} = d[\{(Q_{ag}/Q)/(L_{ag}/L)\}(Q/L)] = d[(s_{ag}{}^{Q}/s_{ag}{}^{L})(q_L)]$, where, $s_{ag}{}^{Q} = Q_{ag}/Q$, $s_{ag}{}^{L} = L_{ag}/L$, $q_L = Q/L$

$$dq_{ag}{}^{L} = q_L.(s_{ag}{}^{Q}/s_{ag}{}^{L})[dq_L/q_L + (ds_{ag}{}^{Q}/s_{ag}{}^{Q} - ds_{ag}{}^{L}/s_{ag}{}^{L}) \tag{10.3}$$

From the data, rates of change in the shares of agricultural output and employment remain fairly constant. Hence, $ds_{ag}{}^{Q} = 0 = ds_{ag}{}^{L}$.

Therefore,

$$dq_{ag}{}^{L} = q_L.(s_{ag}{}^{Q}/s_{ag}{}^{L}).dq_L/q_L = (s_{ag}{}^{Q}/s_{ag}{}^{L})dq_L \tag{10.4}$$

That is, finally, $dq_{ag}{}^{L} = dq_L$; or, $q_{ag}{}^{L} = \alpha + \beta q_L$, or written in inverted form, $q_L = A + Bq_{ag}{}^{L}$. The result shows that the total labour productivity is directly linked to agricultural productivity. Conversely, the agricultural sector should be so linked as to make the productivity of total labour depend upon the productivity of agricultural labour. In other words, this means that labour productivity depends upon the intersectorial linkages that can be generated (Rahman, 1992).

Furthermore, by writing,

$$q_L = A + B.q_{ag}{}^{L} \tag{10.5}$$

as

$$(Q_{ag} + Q_M)/L = A + B.q_{ag}{}^{L}$$

we obtain

$$s_{ag}{}^{L}.q_{ag}{}^{L} + s_M{}^{L}.q_M{}^{L} = A + B.q_{ag}{}^{L}$$

That is,

$$q_M{}^{L} = a(s_M{}^{L}) + b(s_{ag}{}^{L},s_M{}^{L}).q_{ag}{}^{L} \tag{10.6}$$

where

$$a(s_M{}^{L}) = A/s_M{}^{L},\ b(s_{ag}{}^{L},s_M{}^{L}) = (B - s_{ag}{}^{L})/s_M{}^{L} \tag{10.7}$$

The expression here shows that productivities of the agricultural and other industrial sectors and their rates of change are interrelated. But according to the trends in GDP and employment shares given in Table 10.3, the interrelationship is shown to be based on non-constant coefficients. This result will be extended later (Pindyck and Rubinfeld, 1976).

TRENDS IN THE INDUSTRIAL SECTOR (MANUFACTURING)

Sectorial Productivity

As for the agricultural sector, we apply the same methods to study the nature of economic evolution in the manufacturing sector. In reference to Table 10.3 we note that,

$$(d/dt)(Q_M/Q) > 0, (d/dt)(L_M/L) > 0 \quad (10.8)$$

Hence, $g + g_M > 0$, $n + n_M > 0$, implying that, $g_M > 0$, $n_M > 0$, in the long run. But now, $g_{ag}/g_M < 0$, $n_{ag}/n_M < 0$, although $g > 0$, $n > 0$, implying that a long-run substitution would exist between the agricultural and manufacturing sectors in Malaysia if the present sectorial trends continue.

Recent estimates (1991–3) of dq_M^L/q_M^L are found to be quite uncertain, ranging between 10.7 per cent in 1991, 7.6 per cent in 1992 and 2.1 per cent in 1993 (Ministry of Finance, 1993). One can then deduce that relative rates of change in agricultural productivity to manufacturing productivity happens to remain well below unity. This again is a sign of long-run substitution of economic efficiency that is taking place in the agricultural sector in Malaysia. What is all the more alarming is that with the high but rapidly declining concentration of labour in the agricultural profession as shown in Table 10.1, the long-run adjustment cost of such sectorial substitution is expected to be high in terms of productivity transformation, production efficiency and sustainability in sectorial linkages. Government intervention in protecting transfers to the agricultural sector will itself be a costly one, particularly in the face of Malaysian privatisation now picking up momentum in the midst of a combination of issues such as structural adjustment, and income and investment multipliers generated by acquiescence to global export orientation (Bienen and Waterbury, 1992).

Value added, as another indicator of productivity, shows that between the period 1990 and 2000 agricultural sector value added (in constant 1978 US dollars) will increase by a mere 3.1 per cent annually. In the list, oil palms will contribute a mere 2.8 per cent, rubber 1.4 per cent, and woods 4.0 per cent. Manufacturing value-added growth has been 15.7 per cent in 1990, 13.9 per cent in 1991, and 10.5 per cent in 1992 (Jomo, 1992; Rahman, 1992).

Sectorial Wage Differentials

Wage rate differentials between the agricultural and manufacturing sectors in Malaysia are high. The rapid shift of shares in employment and GDP from the agricultural to the manufacturing sector, but with a large concentration of labour still in the agricultural sector, requires that human resource development must be extremely fast and effective; the structural shift and change must be innovatively organised; and a fair degree of government presence in the industrial sector will have to be sustained in the short run to absorb labour reallocated from the agricultural sector. On the supply side of the labour market, high sectorial wage differentials are causing rural to urban migration. But this is driving up prices as signified by increasing inflation rates (rate of change in CPI in Table 10.1) in recent years.

To examine the relation of productivity movements to wage differentials we proceed as follows:

Let $\Delta w = w_{ag} - w_M$, denote the wage differential, with w's being wage variables in the sectors shown. We are assuming that Δw is a function, $f(q_L)$, of total labour productivity, q_L. Then,

$$d\Delta w/dq_L = (\partial\Delta w/\partial q_{ag})dq_{ag} + (\partial\Delta w/\partial q_M)dq_M \tag{10.9}$$

$d\Delta w/dq_L$ will be positive if and only if, $|\partial\Delta w/\partial q_{ag}| < |\partial\Delta w/\partial q_M|$. That is, $\partial q_M/\partial q_{ag}| < 1$, which is not the case for Malaysia as we have seen. Hence the other case is for $d\Delta w/dq_L < 0$. That is, $|\partial\Delta w/\partial q_{ag}| > |\partial\Delta q_M|$, meaning that variations in the wage differentials are affected much more by changes in agricultural productivity as a target than changes in manufacturing productivity, which appears to be high. Now, $\partial q_M/\partial q_{ag} > 1$, and this is acceptable from our earlier observations. There is now a definite complementary relationship between the labour productivities in the agricultural and the manufacturing sector if wage differentials have to be reduced on the basis of productivity change. Such a complementarity we have seen earlier to exist. Presently, productivity change has been related with movements in wage differentials.

Substitutions between the agricultural and manufacturing sectors will not prove such complementarities to exist, but complementarities will be much desired both from the side of long-run adjustment between the two sectors and the growth of wages in the sectors on grounds of growth in labour productivity. In the short run, productivity complementarities have existed between the agricultural and manufacturing sectors. Also, household incomes have increased for the Bumiputeras, who happen to be in the majority in the agricultural sector. Monthly household income for Bumiputeras increased from M$339 in 1976 to M$928 in 1990. These constitute 67 per cent and 80 per cent of overall average income level in Malaysia in 1976 and 1990, respectively (Government of Malaysia, 1991). Hence, a good deal of wage convergence was in fact realised. Similar perspectives on wage increases, labour productivity and comparative advantage are pointed out by Hoey (1992).

Occupational Consequences of Sectorial Productivity Change

The structure of manufacturing related occupations also appears to point to a scarcity of trained manpower to man the process of structural shifts.

Furthermore, this percentage being low, the agricultural sector appears to be doubly affected by even lower percentages of such occupations that would exist in agricultural related activities either in resource-based or primary-based activities (e.g. production related). Hence, if such is the nature of occupational structure, the wage differentials are also expected to remain low in the short run. In the long run, the convergence of wages will depend upon the effective application of human resource development overall.

Scarcity of total labour will be a constraint in this regard, unless enterprises become labour-saving. This symptom is seen in the agricultural sector, where employment is declining. Although scarcity here is expected to drive up agricultural wages and thus generate smaller wage differentials, yet labour saving technology would require trained manpower tied to such technology. In the face of scarcity here, efficiency will suffer, resulting in a weaker relationship between the productivity changes in the two sectors. If substitution is allowed for with labour-saving technology, then the previous result on linear relationship between q_{ag} and q_M would imply declining long-run productivities in both sectors.

Therefore, with labour-saving techniques, resulting in increasing wages in agriculture converging with manufacturing wages but with long-run substitution between labour productivities, the overall economic efficiency will decline in the long run. The random nature of productivity variations can be seen from the following trends: in 1971, the measured output–capital ratio was 4.86; 2.09 in 1981; and 2.75 in 1991. The capital–labour ratio was 1.31 in 1971; 3.29 in 1981; and 4.53 in 1991. Hence, the output–labour ratio, that is measured average productivity of labour must have remained unstable during this period of time (Choudhury, 1995).

PRICE RELATED EFFECTS OF STRUCTURAL SHIFTS

Referring back to Table 10.3 we note that producer prices have increased consistently throughout the period 1988–92. But the directly agricultural related primary goods or manufactured goods, for example, food, beverages and tobacco, have performed much better than animals, oils and fats. High and increasing producer indices in the face of much lower consumer price indices show that the agricultural producer had an incentive to be attached to the agricultural sector. Also the agro-based manufacturer had an incentive to increase output in these goods. This provides a further possibility for wage adjustment between the agricultural and manufacturing sectors, and to retain labour in agricultural primary production or in agro-based manufactures.

This is evidence that supports the view that wage and cost adjustment can occur without massive dislocation of labour intersectorially.

How does this explain the negative growth of labour and the low yet positive labour productivity of labour in the agricultural sector? The answer can be afforded by the fact that production here has become labour saving; human resource development has remained low; and the direction of sectorial linkage between the agricultural and manufacturing sectors has been from the former to the latter and not in the reverse direction as well. We have pointed out earlier evidences in regards to labour-saving technology, low human resource development and low agricultural productivity characteristics. To examine the issue of sectorial interlinkages, we note that labour-saving technology in agriculture, low labour productivity and increasing wages in the face of increasing price incentives towards agricultural production, were running up the cost of agricultural production and thus causing production inefficiencies in this sector. The wage increase in the agricultural sector was thus mainly due to causes internal to this sector.

On the other hand, labour productivity being high, with employment increasing along with production in manufacturing, this shows that labour and productivity substitutions are taking place between agriculture and manufacturing. Therefore, technological change in manufacturing is not generating the desired complementarity with the agricultural sector in this direction.

TRADE RELATED CONSEQUENCES OF STRUCTURAL SHIFT IN AGRICULTURE

Trade Balances and Sectorial Growth

The next issue to investigate in relation to producer incentive in agriculture and agro-based industries is the role of foreign trade in these goods on structural shift. This aspect is important because of the significantly open feature of the Malaysian economy. In Table 10.3 we note that producer prices in export-oriented agro-based sectors, such as wood-related products and rubber, are the highest, whereas food, beverages and animal products have maintained a domestic demand with lower and steady producer prices. This indicates that export-oriented agro-based manufactures were having an incentive effect in the production of such goods.

We have thus noted that labour-saving technological change in agriculture and the consequential increasing wage levels are followed by a mismatching of such wage increases with low productivity gains and associated production inefficiencies. This implies that export-orientation in primary agricultural and agro-based goods is not having an efficient impact. One of the consequences of productivity and efficiency gains in any export-oriented sector is to increase the contribution of trade balances of that sector to GDP, the former being a critical part of economic growth in a predominantly open economy. When we refer to Table 10.1 we note that except for animals, oils and fats as commodities, producer prices being low, provided an incentive for export. The food and beverages commodities and the manufacturing sector showed overall trade deficits. Hence the contributions of these deficits to GDP was negative too.

The conclusion one derives from the above-mentioned trend is that structural shift in agriculture has not been efficient in terms of its relations with productivity, cost of production and now export-orientation. Even if the trade deficits were eventually turned into surpluses, that will appear from the side of agro-based industry, since the difference will be felt here. The animals, oils and fats having low producer prices, can generate surplus only at the cost of lower terms of trade. But terms of trade are exogenously determined in the world market. Hence, their negative effect on agro-based manufactures as shown in Table 10.1 cannot be resolved simply by a pursuit of export-oriented structural shift. Thus, in terms of production efficiency, lower terms of trade result in lower unit values of export. Such a change in trade deficits in agro-based commodities will, therefore, not resolve the inefficiency problem of the agricultural sector in the absence of a complementary interlinkage with the manufacturing sector. A further explanation of this point will be given later and in the technical appendix.

Impact of Foreign Investment on Sectorial Structural Shift

Further insight in the trade components of structural change can be obtained by observing the foreign investment data by selected sectors in agro-based industry. Foreign investment in all agro-based activities shown in Table 10.3 appears to be uncertain, with no particular trend emerging. But almost everywhere a declining trend in shares is noted. This may explain a jitteriness in investors in the agro-based sector in view of the inherent inefficiencies and low productivity experienced in the agricultural sector and their effect on agro-based production.

Thus, in all cases we find that there is a withdrawal of investments from agriculture and agro-based industries but towards other manufacturing industries. In the face of ongoing privatisation, this trend has the danger of creating substitution and delinking between these sectors. The result could then be an immiserising growth in both of these related sectors, by virtue of the fact that the change in labour productivity in these sectors happens to be low.

Structural Shift in the Light of Privatisation

A way of tackling the problems of low productivity and financial as well as technical inefficiencies in agriculture is to leave structural transformation to the private sector. In this way, pricing, wages, technical change and trade-orientation are expected to be brought in line with desired productivity and efficiency growth. Increased wages in the agricultural sector have been greatly contributed to by government transfers and protection of the marginalised entrepreneurs under the Malaysian New Economic Policy and continues on in the New Development Policy. This approach is necessary to maintain growth (economic efficiency) along with distributive equity.

The intensifying process of privatisation in Malaysia seems to be reflected in the decreasing Federal Government expenditure as a percentage of total expenditure. This trend is seen to occur both in the agricultural and manufacturing sectors. Thus, the financial and technical inefficiencies associated with structural change between the agricultural and manufacturing sectors appear to be noted by investors. In the private sector, too, we find this point to be further reflected in accordance with government perspectives. Thus, loans and advances from commercial banks to the agricultural sector appear to be declining, while those to the manufacturing sector appear to be increasing. Even the fact that the share of commercial loans and advances to general commerce is lower than that to manufacturing intensifies this focus on manufacturing. Such mobilisation of financial resources thus appears to be deliberate and in accordance with the Malaysian Government's outlook in industrialisation to the year 2000 and beyond.

Privatisation and Export-Orientation in Structural Shift

Privatisation is taking place from three routes. First, there is a deliberate withdrawal of financial resources by the Malaysian Government from all kinds of production related activities. Secondly, commercial banks are allocating funds increasingly into manufacturing and away from agriculture. Thirdly, foreign investments are proving to be lumpy in non-agro-based manufacturing. These trends prove that in the short run a substantial degree of displacement in employment, intersectorial delinking, and loss of financial and technical efficiency caused by lack of complementarity between sectors, are expected to mark the regime of structural shift from agricultural and agro-based manufacturing to other types of manufacturing.

In this milieu of change, there is danger to stable economic growth in the long run, if such trends continue. Malaysia could be sacrificing her opportunity to build upon the dynamic and complementary comparative advantages available in the agricultural and agro-based manufacturing by shifting into other forms of manufacturing activities. Besides, in the absence of this linkage, a shift to other manufacturing industries by virtue of lumpy foreign investments in these sectors would mean increased vulnerability to the external sector. Malaysia would thus be made to continue as price taker in such a vulnerable export-oriented trend but with structural problems remaining in agriculture and agro-based industries. This point has been recognised in the literature (Ali, 1992).

Sectorial Complementarity Using Joint Production Technology

The relationship among structural shift from agriculture to manufacturing, the underlying productivity and efficiency arguments and the process of privatisation, revolve around the concern with factor substitutions by the choice of labour-saving technology. Instead, to generate production complementarities among sectors, joint production technology can be adopted. A joint production function is contrary to neo-classical production function characterising the sectorial substitution approach.

Long-run factor and output substitutions are the means of bringing about adjustment of costs, wages and technological change between the sectors in the neo-classical case. But from our earlier formalisation, we have found in the case of Malaysia that if long-run efficiency and productivity are to be attained, there must be complementarity among the sectors in regards to attaining targets in these goals. Thus, the joint production menu and the neo-classical one contradict each other in regard to the long-run perspectives for Malaysia. The production menu found to be taking place at present reflects deliberate substitution, contraction and withdrawal of financial, physical and human resources from agriculture and agro-based manufacturing. This is the consequence of a neo-classical production menu. Indeed, the contraction in employment, loss of financial and technical efficiency and low productivity in agriculture may very well be due to the feedback effects of this contractionary mode of change.

In the joint production case between agriculture and manufacturing for Malaysia, we would consider the following production function. Being induced by evolving economy–institution–society interactions, it is not based on the opportunity cost concept, and hence does not reflect neoclassical type factor and resource substitutions (Rhoads, 1985):

$$Q = F(Q_{ag}, Q_M, \theta) \tag{10.10}$$

where, Q denotes total output of joint production; Q_{ag} denotes output of the agricultural sector; Q_M denotes output of the manufacturing sector; θ denotes a set of policy variables that help to interconnect Q_{ag} and Q_M in the production of Q.

The associated conditions of the joint production are,

$$Q_{ag} = f(Q_M, \theta);\ \theta = \theta(t) \tag{10.11}$$

We then have a simulation objective function:

$$\text{Simulate } \{\theta\}\ Q = F(Q_{ag}, Q_M, \theta) \tag{10.12}$$

$$\text{subject to, } Q_{ag} = f(Q_M, \theta) \tag{10.13}$$

$$\theta = \theta(t) \tag{10.14}$$

This joint production function can then be extended to the factor markets, wherein the factors between the sectors will also be interrelated via the policy vector, $\{\theta\}$. Hence, simulational type derived relationships are extended to the factors' markets through the simulation of the intersectorial production menus.

SECTORIAL STRUCTURAL SHIFTS AND MALAYSIAN DEVELOPMENT POLICIES: EXAMINATION BY MEANS OF THE JOINT PRODUCTION MENU

In the case of Malaysian Agricultural Policy, the

> overriding objective of the Policy is the maximisation of income through optimal utilisation of resources. Its specific aims include the achievement of a balanced development between the agricultural and manufacturing sectors, enhancement of the integration of the sector with the rest of the economy and in particular,,the manufacturing sector and the achievement of a higher level and greater depth of food industry

development. Agricultural development efforts will be implemented on the basis of sustainability. (Ministry of Agriculture, 1993)

$$\text{Now } \{\theta\} = \{G_{ag}/G_M, Ln_{ag}/Ln_M, H_{ag}/H_M, \tau) \quad (10.15)$$

where, G_{ag}/G_M denotes the ratio of government expenditure between agriculture and manufacturing (Table 10.3); Ln_{ag}/Ln_M denotes the ratio of loans and advances between agriculture and manufacturing (Table 10.3); τ denotes technological choice (labour-augmenting); H_{ag}/H_M denotes ratio of human resource investment between agriculture and manufacturing.

In the case of Malaysian industrial development policies, the overriding focus is placed on (Ministry of International Trade and Industry, 1993): (i) promotion of high-tech and high value added industries; (ii) identification and promotion of new sources of growth in resource-based manufacturing (e.g. wood-based, rubber, oleochemicals, mineral-based and non-metallic mineral-based); (iii) promotion and development of small and medium size industries to reduce dependence on imported parts and components.

Thus between the two sectors, the stated policy objectives aim at interlinking the two. In Figure 10.1 we show that while the government would look after a joint increase in G_{ag} and G_M, they would mobilise these towards attaining H_{ag} and H_M. On the other hand, the commercial banks would increase Ln_{ag} and Ln_M towards attaining appropriate labour-augmenting technical change, τ. But since appropriate τ would be linked with human resource development, therefore, private sector policies conform with government policies in the agricultural and agro-based manufacturing sector. Thus by the complementarity of these policy packages, the two sectoral productions are linked to each other. If this is not the case, then a disproportionate resource allocation between agriculture and manufacturing will defeat the purpose of attaining labour-augmenting technical change. The objectives of the Agricultural and Industrial Policies would contradictory each other.

In Figure 10.1 we show that there must be policy alignment in any direction, that is, from Ln_{ag}/Ln_M (at point A_0) to H_{ag}/H_M (B_0), from Ln_{ag}/Ln_M to τ (D_0) (shown by dotted arrow), both affecting in this way, the level of Q (C_0) (e.g. Q_1 as starting level) in the combination of Q_{ag} and Q_M space, along $0C_0C_1C_2T$. Through one complete revolution of such relationship either along the bold or dotted lines in the direction of the arrows shown, increasing levels of output (e.g. Q_1, Q_2, Q_3, etc.) are formed. Thus feedbacks between policies and between Qs and policies in evolving cycles of interrelations are established.

Figure 10.1 Simulation in a joint production menu with agriculture and manufacturing complementarity

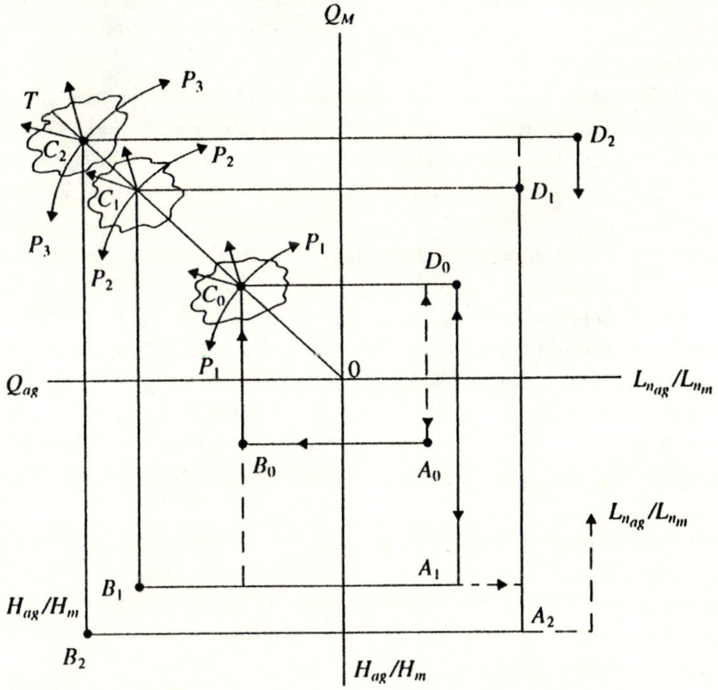

It is important to note that $0T$ denotes the locus of simulated values of $Q = F(Q_{ag}, Q_M, \theta)$ under the feedbacks, $Q_{ag} = f(Q_M, \theta)$, $\theta = \theta(t)$. This is shown to take place here by interactions among policy and output variables. Hence, if such policies are based on complementarity, then the result will be complementarity also between Q_{ag}, Q_M. Contrarily, if policies are conflicting or they reinforce substitutions between agricultural and manufacturing sectors, then the Q values will lie on a neo-classical type production possibility curve of Q_{ag}, Q_M values as shown by P_1P_1, P_2P_2, P_3P_3, etc.

Complementarity exists because each Q-value becomes a sensitive point of interactive decision-making among participants from the agricultural and manufacturing sectors, private entrepreneurs and the government at large. Thus there exists a dynamic field of possibilities around Q-values that makes these evolve outwards. This phenomenon is indicated by the region of possibilities around the points C_0, C_1, C_2, etc. Arrows coming out of these regions indicate various possibilities. Similar regions of possibilities exist around the points $A_0 \ldots D_2 \ldots$ (not shown). In such a case, the production possibility curves do not exist. There are only possibilities determined by economy–institution–society interactions available along the positively evolving $0C_0C_1C_2T$ curve.

At the present time, short-run substitutions between the agricultural and manufacturing sectors in the midst of structural shift and privatisation make such evolutionary output trajectories impossible. However, the policy perspectives of the Malaysian Development Plan and Agricultural and Industrial Development aim at such sectorial interlinkages and policy coordination that generate a good degree of complementarity.

Our statistical examination in this chapter shows, that there is indeed a contradiction between the goals and the approach. In a privatisation framework, government withdrawal of resources appears to apply to both the agricultural and manufacturing sectors. But commercial bank loans and advances are found to be biased towards manufacturing. Consequently, technological change in the agricultural sector appears to be labour saving instead of labour augmenting. Consequently, the impact of human resource development in the agricultural sector is minimised. This explains our earlier inference, that misalignment among neo-classical type substitution-oriented policies may be adversely affecting Q_{ag} and Q_M and their consequences on low agricultural labour productivity, loss of efficiency and labour market contraction in the agricultural sector.

CONCLUSION

From our above mentioned empirical evidence and formalisation, we noted the following issues relating to structural shift in agriculture and industrialisation.

First, we found that productivity of labour remains positive but low in the agricultural sector and significant in the manufacturing sector. Thus, there is a sign of complementarity in labour productivity, but it is of the immiserising type (Kenen, 1985) and is found to be caused rather by contraction of employment of labour in the agricultural sector than due to real sector growth. The low measured labour productivity along with increasing wages (as signified by the household income of Bumiputeras) in the agricultural sector point to loss of financial and technical efficiency in this sector. Thus, a significant sign of delinked growth appears to exist between the agricultural and manufacturing sectors.

Secondly, we found a reinforcement of the above observation by taking recourse to price, trade and foreign investment statistics for the agricultural related commodities. In this case too we found that the contribution of terms of trade (implied) of agro-based commodities to real GDP and enhancement of these sectors by foreign investment, turn to be negative and low, respectively. Thus, a feedback is implicated to exist by cause and effect between inefficient production, low returns (as indicated by unchanging levels of producer prices) and investments. There also appears to exist a fair degree of uncertainty to the agricultural and agro-based sector from the side of foreign trade in the goods of these sectors.

Thirdly, the same conclusion of cause and effect between production, efficiency and financing is found to exist in regard to government and commercial bank prospects for supporting the agricultural sector. Here the implication made is that in the short run, privatisation and programmes towards rapid industrialisation are drawing away resources from agricultural sector activities. This point is also brought out by the rather low growth of value added in agro-based goods compared to those in manufacturing as a whole.

Fourthly, we found that because of low productivity of labour and inefficiencies in agricultural sector production, labour-saving technology was being implemented here. Thus, wage increases in the agricultural sector are found to come about not because of a neo-classical type of sectorial mobility of labour, but rather because of scarcity of labour and the resulting labour saving technology. Here limitations in human resource development is pointed out in the light of the skilled occupational structure and its smallness in the agricultural sector, where the share of production labour is the highest, although fast declining.

Fifthly, we deduced that a combination of these types of trends in the agricultural and agro-based sectors is proving to be sectorially delinking in the short run. This is found to be contrary to the goals of the Malaysian Government's policies in the areas of agricultural and manufacturing development and under the objective of attaining jointly economic efficiency and distributive equity goals during the period of the Malaysian New Development Plan to the year 2000 and beyond.

Finally, in light of the formalisation carried out and the various Malaysian policies referred to in this chapter, we found that the sound prescriptions of structural shift and industrialisation rest on developing interlinkages between the agricultural and agro-based manufacturing sectors. This option is argued to be the way to break the uncertainties caused by a shortfall in productivity in the agricultural sector, displacement of labour and inefficiencies of production (Rahman *et al.*, 1991).

Technical Appendix: Complementarity and Substitution in Structural Shifts

THE CASE OF COMPLEMENTARITY IN SECTORIAL STRUCTURAL SHIFT

In this appendix our objective is to derive the conditions prevalent on the side of socio-economic and policy variables under which the problem of complementarity and substitution between the agricultural and manufacturing sectors can be addressed. We will use an extension of the joint production function between the agricultural and manufacturing sectors that we have invoked in the text of this chapter. We will also use the list of socio-economic and policy variables in relation to Table 10.3.

The joint production function is,

$$Q = F(Q_{ag}, Q_M, \theta) \qquad \text{(A.1)}$$

with,

$$Q_{ag} = f_1(Q_M, \theta) \qquad \text{(A.2)}$$

$$Q_M = f_2(\mathbf{h}, \mathbf{P}) \qquad \text{(A.3)}$$

That is, $Q_{ag} = f_2 o f_1(\mathbf{h}, \theta) = f_3(\mathbf{h}, \theta)$ (A.4)

where

$$\mathbf{h} = (h_1, h_2, h_3, h_4, h_5, h_6, h_7, h_8, h_9) \qquad \text{(A.5)}$$

$$\theta = (\theta_1, \theta_2, \theta_3, \theta_4, \theta_5, \theta_6) \qquad \text{(A.6)}$$

with

h_1 denotes measured productivity of labour in agriculture (also value added);
h_2 denotes measured productivity of labour in manufacturing (also value added);
h_3 denotes wage rate in agriculture;
h_4 denotes wage rate in manufacturing;
h_5 denotes producer price index in agriculture;
h_6 denotes producer price index in agro-based manufacturing;
h_7 denotes trade balance in agro-based manufacturing;
h_8 denotes employment in agriculture;
h_9 denotes employment in manufacturing;
θ_1 denotes government expenditure in agriculture;

θ_2 denotes government expenditure in manufacturing;
θ_3 denotes commercial bank loans and advances in agriculture;
θ_4 denotes commercial bank loans and advances in manufacturing;
θ_5 denotes technological change;
θ_6 denotes foreign investment in agro-based manufacturing.

Note that human resource development expenditure is taken up with θ_1 and θ_2. We take θ as a relation among the θ_i-components by the general expression, $\theta = \theta(\theta_1, \theta_2,\ldots,\theta_6)$.
Now consider the following deductions:

$$dQ = (\partial F/\partial Q_{ag})dQ_{ag} + (\partial F/\partial Q_M)dQ_M + (\partial F/\partial)d\theta \tag{A.7}$$

$$dQ_{ag} = \Sigma_{i=1}{}^9(\partial f_3/\partial h_i)dh_i + (\partial f_3/\partial\theta)d\theta \tag{A.8}$$

$$dQ_M = \Sigma_{i=1}{}^9(\partial f_2/\partial h_i)dh_i + (\partial f_2/\partial\theta)d\theta \tag{A.9}$$

$$d\theta = \Sigma_{j=1}{}^6(\partial\theta/\partial\theta_j)d\theta_j \tag{A.10}$$

From these equations by substitution we obtain,

$$\begin{aligned} dQ = {} & (\partial F/\partial Q_{ag})\ [\Sigma_{i=1}{}^9(\partial f_3/\partial h_i)dh_i + (\partial f_3/\partial\theta)(\Sigma_{j=1}{}^6(\partial\theta/\partial\theta_j).d\theta_j] \\ & + (\partial F/\partial Q_M)\ [\Sigma_{i=1}{}^9(\partial f_2/\partial h_i)dh_i + (\partial f_2/\partial\theta)(\Sigma_{j=1}{}^6(\partial\theta/\partial\theta_i).d\theta_j] \\ & + (\partial F/\partial\theta)\ [\Sigma_{j=1}{}^6(\partial\theta/\partial\theta_j)d\theta_j] \end{aligned} \tag{A.11}$$

By rearranging the terms we obtain,

$$\begin{aligned} & \Sigma_{i=1}{}^9[(\partial F/\partial Q_{ag})(\partial f_3/\partial h_i) + (\partial F/\partial Q_M)(\partial f_2/\partial h_i)]dh_i + \\ & \Sigma_{j=1}{}^6[(\partial F/\partial Q_{ag})(\partial f_3/\partial\theta)(\partial\theta/\partial\theta_j) + (\partial F/\partial Q_M)(\partial f_2/\partial\theta)(\partial\theta/\partial\theta_j) + \\ & (\partial F/\partial\theta)(\partial\theta/\partial\theta_j)]d\theta_j = dQ > 0 \end{aligned} \tag{A.12}$$

In the case of complementarity, each h_i and θ_j contributes positively to dQ. Hence for each $i = 1,2\ldots9$; $j = 1,2,..,6$.

$$\begin{aligned} & [(\partial F/\partial Q_{ag})(\partial f_3/\partial h_i) + (\partial F/\partial Q_M)(\partial f_2/\partial h_i)]dh_i + \\ & [(\partial F/\partial Q_{ag})(\partial f_3/\partial\theta)(\partial\theta/\partial\theta_j) + (\partial F/\partial Q_M)(\partial f_2/\partial\theta)(\partial\theta/\partial\theta_j) + \\ & (\partial F/\partial\theta)(\partial\theta/\partial\theta_j)]d\theta_j = A > 0 \end{aligned} \tag{A.13}$$

Thereby, to maintain complementarity we must have,

$$dh_i/d\theta_j =$$

$$A - [(\partial F/\partial Q_{ag})(\partial f_3/\partial\theta)(\partial\theta/\partial\theta_j) + (\partial F/\partial Q_M)(\partial f_2/\partial\theta)(\partial\theta/\partial\theta_j) + (\partial F/\theta)(\partial\theta/\partial\theta_j)]/$$

$$[(\partial F/\partial Q_{ag})(\partial f_3/\partial h_i) + (\partial F/\partial Q_M)(\partial f_2/\partial h_i)]$$

$$= B > 0 \qquad \text{(A.14)}$$

That is,

$$A - [(\partial F/\partial Q_{ag})(\partial f_3/\partial \theta)(\partial \theta/\partial \theta_j) + (\partial F/\partial Q_M)(\partial f_2/\partial \theta)(\partial \theta/\partial \theta_j) + (\partial F/\partial \theta)(\partial \theta/\partial \theta_j)]$$

$$= B[(\partial F/\partial Q_{ag})(\partial f_3/\partial h_i) + (\partial F/\partial Q_M)(\partial f_2/\partial h_i)] \qquad \text{(A.15)}$$

Once again by rearranging this equation we obtain,

$$(\partial F/Q_{ag})[B.(\partial f_3/\partial h_i) + (\partial f_3/\partial \theta)(\partial \theta/\partial \theta_j)] +$$

$$(\partial F/\partial Q_M)[B.(\partial f_2/\partial h_i) + (\partial f_2/\partial \theta)(\partial \theta/\partial \theta_j)] = C > 0 \qquad \text{(A.16)}$$

with, $B.(\partial F/\partial \theta)(\partial \theta/\partial \theta_j) = \alpha > 0$, because of positive contributions made by each of the policy variables in the case of complementarity. This condition was also shown in Figure 10.1.

By observing complementarity once again, we must have positive effects from the agricultural and manufacturing output and policy contributions to total output, Q. Hence,

$$(\partial F/\partial Q_{ag})/(\partial F/\partial Q_M) =$$

$$C - [B(\partial f_2/\partial h_i) + (\partial f_2/\partial \theta)(\partial \theta/\partial \theta_j)]/[B(\partial f_3/\partial h_i) + (\partial f_3/\partial \theta)(\partial \theta/\partial \theta_j) = D > 0 \qquad \text{(A.17)}$$

That is,

$$(C - D) = [B(\partial f_2/\partial h_i) + (\partial f_2/\partial \theta)(\partial \theta/\partial \theta_j)]/[B(\partial f_3/\partial h_i) + (\partial f_3/\partial \theta)(\partial \theta/\partial \theta_j)]$$

$$(C - D)[B(\partial f_3/\partial h_i) + (\partial f_3/\partial \theta)(\partial \theta/\partial \theta_j)] = B(\partial f_2/\partial h_i) + (\partial f_2/\partial \theta)(\partial \theta/\partial \theta_j)$$

Again by the condition of complementarity,

$(\partial \theta/\partial \theta_j)[(C - D)(\partial f_3/\partial \theta) - B(\partial f_2/\partial \theta] = B(\partial f_2/\partial h_i) - B(C - D)(\partial f_3/\partial h_i)$, means

$$(\partial \theta/\partial \theta_j) = [B(\partial f_2/\partial h_i) - B(C - D)(\partial f_3/\partial h_i)]/[(C - D)(\partial f_3/\partial \theta) - B(\partial f_2/\partial \theta)]$$

$$= E > 0 \qquad \text{(A.18)}$$

That is, the existence of complementarity requires:

$$(\partial/\partial h_i)[Bf_2 - B(C - D)f_3] = (\partial/\partial \theta)[E(C - D)f_3 - BEf_2] \qquad \text{(A.19)}$$

This condition shows that there is a one-to-one relationship by feedbacks of cause and effect between changes in socio-economic variables and policy variables that are promoted for attaining sectorial complementarity. We therefore note that the two sides of equation (A.19) must have the same sign, and changes in socio-economic variables, h, and policy variables, θ, will transmit the same directional effects on the agricultural and manufacturing production functions, f_2 and f_3. It can be seen that only the case $C > D$ is applicable, for only in this case the positive sign of both the sides of (A.19) will yield $f_2/f_3 > 0$, only if $C > D$. Otherwise, a negative sign would result for f_2/f_3, which is absurd.

THE CASE OF SUBSTITUTION IN SECTORIAL STRUCTURAL SHIFT

Problems appear to enter the equations for the case of substitution from (A.14), for now this equation would not hold for each $i = 1,2,..,9$; $j = 1,2,..,6$. For example, substitution of labour in agriculture (L_{ag}/L_M) will be inconsistent with the continuing low labour productivity in agriculture as a socio-economic variable and with low financial expenditure in agriculture and agro-based industries as a policy variable. Likewise, continuing low financial expenditure in these industries as a policy variable is in conflict with the choice of labour-saving (i.e. capital intensive) technology as another policy variable. High producer price indices in agricultural and agro-based commodities as a socio-economic variable are in conflict with low growth in this sector as another socio-economic variable. In this way, a full system of conflicts between and among socio-economic and policy variables appear in the general equilibrium sense. Thus, long-run substitutions in the agricultural sector will not turn up $dh_i/d\theta_j > 0$, for any or all combinations of variables in the long-run general equilibrium.

Furthermore, we note by a repetition of the argument on signs of the two sides of equation (A.19), that if both sides are positive, then,

$$f_2/f_3 > 1/(C - D) > 0, \text{ implies } (C - D) > 0$$

but, also $f_3/f_2 > B/(C - D) > 0$, implies $B > 0$, hence a contradiction to the negative sign of B as it must be in the case of substitution among socio-economic and policy variables in the general equilibrium case.

This result points out that there is no clear indication as to the evolution of the economy in the long run in the presence of sectorial substitutions and sectorial delinkage. A joint production menu cannot be applied to the neo-classical case of substitution that we observe in the short run for Malaysia.

According to the above results, the case of short-run substitutions between agriculture and manufacturing becomes a source of production instability and is found to be contradictory to the agricultural and industrial policy goals. Measures should therefore be taken up immediately to use the goals of these policies to realise long-run complementarities in the structural shift that is now taking place in Malaysia.

THE EQUILIBRIUM RESULT BY MEANS OF INDUCTION OF SOCIO-ECONOMIC AND POLICY VARIABLES IN COMPLEMENTARY INTERSECTORIAL RELATIONS

In Figure 10.2 we showed that as relations between Q_{ag} and Q_M evolve, interactions among variables (h,θ), help to drive the economy along the trajectory

$OC_1C_2..T$. For points a, a' etc. there are points like b, b', but these points are not equilibrium points on the Q-surface. Only policy-market interactive points, such as, C_1, C_2, etc. are equilibrium points. These in turn yield the equilibrium points P_1, P_2, etc of Q-values, respectively. Thus, while all of the above points can yield increasingly positive values of Q ($dQ > 0$), only interactively determined equilibrium points can yield higher Q-values, P_1,P_2, etc. than the corresponding suboptimal ones, b, b', etc., respectively.

Three other points need to be noted here: first, points such as a, a', etc. belong to the neo-classical production possibility surface. The above result shows that neo-classical production relations, being policy neutral, do not yield to equilibrium sectorial linkages. Second, because the above type of equilibrium holds for each h_i and θ_i in the case of sectorial complementarity, therefore, the final equilibrating process and the (h,θ)-induced trajectory, $OC_1C_2..T$, is the final aggregation of all such individual trajectories that interrelate through a labyrinth of interactions. Only participatory dynamics of economy–institution–society interactions can determine such extensive processes. Third, we note that the coefficients of all the above equations, in which interrelations are developed and explained, are variable in themselves. This gives rise to the case often encountered in simulation models with regards to coefficients with probability distributions, this is the expected feature of coefficients in all interactive models.

Figure A10.1 Polity-market induced complementarity in sectorial structural shift

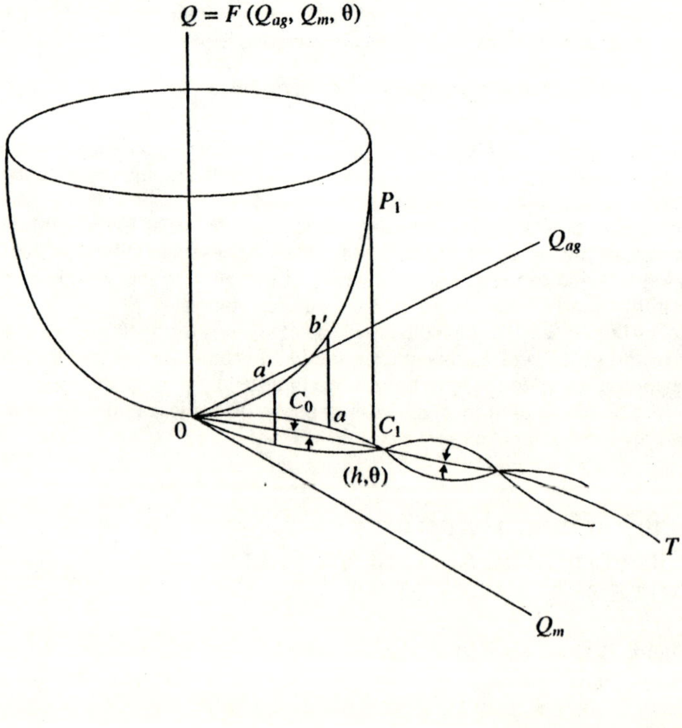

The simulation model of sectorial complementarity invoked in this chapter can generate a limited number of such cases. The neo-classical model is totally disabled in this area of economy–institution–society interface. The interactive type of joint production menu generating sectorial complementarity is proposed here as the alternative for Malaysian structural shift.

References

Ali, A. (1992) 'Technology Transfer in Manufacturing Industries via Direct Foreign Investment', *Journal of Economic Cooperation Among Islamic Countries*, 13(3–4).

Bienen, H. and Waterbury, J. (1992) 'The Political Economy of Privatization in Developing Countries', in Wilber, C.K. and Jameson, K.P. (eds) *The Political Economy of Development and Under-development* (New York, N.Y.: McGraw-Hill).

Choudhury, M.A. (1995) 'A Systems Model of the Malaysian Macroeconomy' *International Journal of Systems and Cybernetics*, vol. 24, no. 7.

Government of Malaysia (1991) *The Second Outline Perspective Plan, 1991–2000* (Kuala Lumpur: Government Printer).

Hoey, T.S. (1992) 'Labour Shortage, Comparative Advantage and the Future of Malaysian Agriculture', paper presented at the Workshop on Revitalising Agriculture in Malaysia's Industrial Economy, Kuala Lumpur, Malaysia, 14–15 September.

Jomo, K.S. (1992) 'Manufacturing Growth and Employment', *Journal of Economic Cooperation among Islamic Countries*, 13(3–4).

Kenen, P.B. (1985) *The International Economy* (Englewoods Cliffs NJ: Prentice-Hall), chapter 6.

Ministry of Agriculture (1993) *The National Agricultural Policy (1992–2010)* (Kuala Lumpur: Government Printer).

Ministry of Finance (1992) *Economic Report 1992/93* (Kuala Lumpur: Government Printer).

Ministry of International Trade and Industry Malaysia (1993) *International Trade and Industry Report 1993* (Kuala Lumpur: Government Printer).

Pindyck, R.S. and Rubinfeld, D.L. (1976) *Econometric Models and Economic Forecasts* (New York: McGraw-Hill), chapter 11.

Rahman, A.Z.A. (1992) 'Agricultural Development in Malaysia: Retrospect and Prospect', *Journal of Economic Cooperation among Islamic Countries*, 13(3–4).

Rahman, A.Z.A., Alias, M. Hj. and Mansor, J. (1991) 'Whither the Malaysian Agricultural Primary Commodities', paper presented at the National Seminar on Agricultural Primary Commodities, Kuala Lumpur, Malaysia, 3–4 June.

Rhoads, S.E. (1993) 'Kind Hearts and Opportunity Costs', in Cole, D. (ed.), *Microeconomics* (Sluice Dock, Guilford, CON: Dushkin Publishing).

Stern, J.S. (1991) *Malaysia: Growth and Structural Change* (Kuala Lumpur: ISIS).

11 Human Development Through Poverty Alleviation

Chamhuri Siwar

INTRODUCTION

An analysis of recent development experience indicates that there is a growing concern to link economic and human development. In the past, emphasis on attaining national income and GNP growth has resulted in countries not giving sufficient attention to redistributive measures, providing basic needs and extending the benefits of development to a large section of the population. Poverty still prevails in a significant proportion in the developing countries, causing debilitating effects on human development.

This chapter discusses the issues and processes of human development through poverty alleviation. The concept and definition of human development and how human development could be accelerated through poverty alleviation are discussed.

HUMAN DEVELOPMENT

The concern of human development is that people must be the centre of all development efforts. The central theme of the human dimension of development is to establish links between economic growth and human development, to investigate whether economic growth translates or fails to translate into human development.

UNDP (United Nations Development Programme) (1990) defines human development as a process of enlarging people's choice, including, to live a long and healthy life, to be educated and to have access to resources needed for a decent standard of living. As people are the real wealth of nations, the basic objective of development is to create an environment for people to enjoy productive and healthy lives, not just the accumulation of wealth and incomes.

The premise of this approach is that people are the beneficiaries of development. Although generally people want higher incomes, it is not the sum total of human life. Similarly, national income and economic growth are not automatically translated into the betterment of life, in terms of better nutrition, improved access to health, education, knowledge, and access to services and resources to secure improved living conditions.

Various countries' experiences demonstrate that there is no automatic link between economic growth and human development. Higher economic growth is no guarantee of human progress. There are cases of low human development levels associated with high incomes and conversely high human development levels associated with low or moderate incomes.

Generally, there are two sides to the process of human development: first, the formation of human capabilities such as improved health, knowledge and skills; and second, how people make use of these capablities for work or leisure. The focus of development is on people, on how they benefit from development. The expansion of income and wealth is only one objective of development. Income may be considered as a means, not an end. The attainment of high levels of incomes in itself is not important. What is more important is how income is spent to benefit people.

In an attempt to measure and monitor human development, UNDP constructed a human development index, incorporating a wide range of indicators, focusing on three essential elements of human life longevity, knowledge and decent living standards.

Life expectancy at birth is used as an indicator of longevity, which is closely associated with adequate nutrition, good health and education. In the absence of comprehensive data on health and nutrition, life expectancy is an important indicator of human development.

Measures of literacy are also important indicators of human development. Literacy figures provide a reflection on access to education, levels of education and human development.

Another key component of human development is access to land, credit, income and other resources. Since per capita income is the most readily available, it is often used to reflect command over resources needed for a decent standard of living.

The UNDP constructed a composite human development index to measure the level of human development. It has a value of between zero to one and incorporates attainment of overall human development and shortfalls from the desired target. It is realised that this composite index may not fully satisfy all measures of human development. It incorporates three essential components – longevity and knowledge which capture the formation of human capabilities and income as a proxy for access to resources needed for a decent standard of living and as a means for enlarging people's choice.

Why Human Development?

Human development differs from the conventional human capital, human resource development and human welfare approach. Human capital formation or human resource development captures only one aspect of human development, that is affecting the human resource or potential of a human being as an instrument for increasing capabilities for producing goods and services. In this sense, human beings are seen as a means of production, not an end of a development process. Human resources development attempts to affect the supply side of human beings.

On the other hand, the human welfare approach emphasises distributive policies rather than the production process. This approach puts people as the beneficiaries rather than participants of the development process. The basic needs approach focuses on the provision of basic goods and services such as food, shelter, clothing, health care, electricity and water supply, especially for the deprived groups. This approach focuses on the provision of goods and services and not on expanding people's choice.

In contrast, human development is not only concerned with human welfare and basic needs but also with the dynamics and processes of human development. This approach brings together the production and distribution of goods and services and also the processes of expanding people's choice. In this sense, human development is a more wide-ranging and holistic approach towards sustainable human development.

HUMAN DEVELOPMENT THROUGH POVERTY ALLEVIATION

Progress in Human Development

Table 11.1 shows selected human development indicators for Malaysia, displaying human development progress through various indicators such as income, expenditure, human development indicies and employment. UNDP's *Human Development Report* (1994a) rates that Malaysia made the most human development progress over a 32-year span. The report highlights the positive experience of Malaysia in overcoming disparities among its ethnic groups after the racial riots of 1969. The report praises Malaysia's remarkable success in social integration through the New Economic Policy (NEP, 1970–90), which successfully increased human

Table 11.1 Malaysia: human development indicators

Indicators	*Earlier years*	*Later years*
Population (million)	15.3 (1984)	181. (1992)
Land Area ('000 km)	—	330.0
Income		
GDP (bil. US$)	—	47.0
GNP per capita (US$)	1 819 (1987)	2 330 (1990)
Real GDP per capita (PPP $)	3 848 (1987)	6 140 (1990)
Income distribution and poverty		
Income share of lowest 40%	11.0 (1975)	13.9 (1989)
Ratio of highest 20% to lowest 20%	14.4 (1975)	11.1 (1989)
Gini Coefficient	0.50 (1970)	0.48 (1988)
Absolute poverty (%)		
Total	49.3 (1970)	17.1 (1991)
Urban	21.3 (1970)	7.5 (1991)
Rural	58.7 (1970)	21.8 (1991)
Public expenditure as % GNP		
Education	2.9 (1960)	7.9 (1986)
Health	1.1 (1960)	1.6 (1990)
Social security		0.5 (1990)
Percentage of total expenditure		
Defence	18.5 (1972)	
Education	23.4 (1972)	
Health	6.8 (1972)	
Amenities/social welfare	4.4 (1972)	10.5 (1983)
Economic services	14.2 (1972)	
Human development indices		
Human development index	0.800 (1987)	0.790 (1990)
Life expectancy (%)	70.0 (1987)	70.1 (1990)
Adult literacy rate (%)	60.0 (1970)	78.4 (1990)
Male	71.0 (1970)	87.0 (1990)
Female	48.0 (1970)	70.0 (1990)
Literacy index	0.3 (1985)	0.75 (1990)
Access to health services (%)		88.0 (1990)
Access to safe water (%)	34.0 (1975)	88.0 (1990)
Access to sanitation (%)	76.0 (1985)	94.0 (1990)
Daily calorie supply as % of requirement	101.0 (1964)	120.0 (1990)
Primary school intake (%)		100.0 (1988)
Completing primary education (%)		96.0 (1988)
Human development group	medium (1990)	medium (1994)

Table 11.1 *Continued*

Indicators	*Earlier years*	*Later years*
Employment		
Labour force as % of population		40.5 (1988)
Women labour force as % of total labour force		35.0 (1988)
% of labour force in agriculture	59.0 (1965)	31.0 (1991)
% of labour force in industry	13.0 (1965)	27.0 (1991)
% of labour force in services	29.0 (1965)	42.0 (1991)

Source: UNDP (1990–4) *Economic Report* (New York) (various years).

development levels of all classes of society, with the human development index (HDI) of the lagging ethnic Malays increasing one and a half times as fast as that of the ethnic Chinese. The report asserts that between 1960 and 1992 Malaysia has made the most progress in human development, starting from low HDI levels it has managed to increase the HDI by about 80 per cent.

In 1960, Malaysia was a middle income country with moderate human development and a reasonable income distribution. In the 1960s its per capita GDP grew by about 3 per cent, increased to about 5 per cent in the 1970s and decreased to about 2 per cent during the recession of the 1980s. After the recession, its economy grew tremendously, maintaining over 8 per cent during the past seven years (1988–94).

National income growth seems to have benefited a large segment of the population. Overall absolute poverty has been reduced from 49.3 per cent in 1970 to 17.1 per cent in 1991 with a significant reduction in both rural and urban poverty. However, income distribution remains quite inequitable, although the Gini Coefficient shows a reduction from 0.50 in 1970 to 0.48 in 1988. Nevertheless, a trend towards reduction in inequality is showing with an increasing income share for the lowest 40 per cent (from 14 per cent in 1975 to 13.9 per cent in 1989) and a reduction in the ratio of the highest 20 per cent to the lowest 20 per cent from 14.4 in 1975 to 11.1 in 1989.

UNDP's *Human Development Report* (1990) states that Malaysia experienced steady and sustained improvements in human development along with improvements and steady growth with equitable income distribution This was possible due to effective and well-structured across-the-board mesopolicies which were distributed equitably. This was notable in the NEP's emphasis on growth with redistribution as strongly laid down in its two-pronged objectives of poverty eradication irrespective of race and the restructuring of society. In addition, public spending in the social sector like health, amenities, social security and especially education are substantially high and benefit all segments of society, with special emphasis on rural areas where the incidence of poverty is greater.

In terms of human development, Malaysia is grouped among nations with a medium HDI of 0.8 per cent, with high rates of life expectancy, literacy, school enrolments and access to health, water and sanitation services. Generally, there have been improvements in most of the human development indicies as a result of sustained efforts at meeting basic needs, infrastructural development and various poverty eradication and restructuring strategies.

Poverty Alleviation and Human Development

Poverty has debilitating effects on human development. Shortfalls in income have often led to underachievement in education, health and nutrition. Alleviation of poverty will no doubt contribute significantly towards human development. With increased incomes and improvements in basic needs, people's access to better educational, nutritional and health services will increase and contribute significantly towards human development. Reductions in poverty are expected to contribute positively towards improving health, education, population growth and economic performance.

The sustainability of development is much broader than the concern and protection for the environment and natural resources. It includes also the potection of future human development and limiting the debt of human neglect.

Poverty often threathens the environment, and environmental degradation also reinforces poverty, as in the case of deforestation, salination, poor sanitation, and polluted and unsafe water. Programmes to alleviate poverty must also include plans for environmental improvements which are conducive for better living conditions, essential for human development.

The relationship between human development and poverty alleviation is captured in the statement: 'poverty is both a cause and a consequence of deficiencies in human development' (UNDP, 1991b). With poverty alleviation still at the top of the development agenda among nations, a serious assault on poverty will no doubt bring human beings into focus as the major beneficiaries of development.

Investigations into the phenomena of poverty have identified several of its causes that are related to human development: first, lack of intrinsic human development as in poor health, poor nourishment, lack of intellectual and manual skills and lack of motivation for self-improvement; secondly, people–resource imbalance or widening access of the poor to productive assets such as land, credit and other natural resources, exacerbated by population growth and natural or man-made disasters; thirdly, factors inhibiting the participation of the poor in development such as structural adjustment, legal framework and macro policies such as taxation, public spending exchange rate and pricing policies which may unintentionally adversely affect the poor. These factors act as constraints on the poor and their ability to improve their skills and to market their labour. These further inhibit the participation of the poor in the development process. Poverty alleviation which removes the constraints and redress imbalances of any unintentional adverse effects on the poor will certainly enhance human development.

Poverty alleviation is not just simply the delivering of benefits. It is about empowerment and involving people directly in the process of development. This may require 'bottom-up' measures where the beneficiaries have a say in the choice and design of projects intended to benefit them. Past experiences indicate that poverty alleviation strategies need to place heavy reliance on employment generation and not merely on income growth. Increased public spending on aspects of human development is more likely to have a greater impact on poverty reduction and, at the same time, in improving human development.

Some of the poverty alleviation programmes that are likely to affect human development include:

1. Macroeconomic policies which are likely to impact on the poor, including:
   (a) pricing, exchange rate, taxes, public spending policies;
   (b) food production, distribution and pricing policies;
   (c) environment and resources policies;
   (d) labour and employment policies.
2. Delivery of basic services include primary and secondary education, preventive and primary health care, communal water supply, sanitation (rural and urban) and housing programme for the poor.
3. Employment and income generation programmes include public work, human resources and skills development, generation of self-employment and small-farm productivity improvement though technology, credit and irrigation.

POVERTY ALLEVIATION

Poverty is a reflection of shortfalls and deprivation in various indicators of human development, such as life expectancy, educational and nutritional levels, per capita income and access to various goods and services. Poverty also signifies lack of progress in human development, inadequacy and underattainment in the desired levels of human development indicators and shortfalls in the attainment of human development.

Poverty Situation in Malaysia

In Malaysia, the higher incidence of poverty in the rural sector makes it a predominantly rural phenomenon. The magnitude of the poverty problem can be gauged by the number of poor households, the number of hardcore poor and the incidence of poverty (Tables 11.2 and 11.3).

Nationally, there has been a significant reduction in the number of poor households and in the incidence of poverty. The latter has declined from 49.3 per cent in 1970 to 17.1 per cent in 1990 and 13.5 per cent in 1993, and is projected to be reduced further to 8.8 per cent in 1995. However, the problem of poverty is more acute for Sabah (34.4 per cent) and Sarawak (21 per cent) compared to Peninsular Malaysia (15 per cent). Comparatively, the incidence of poverty in 1990 is still high for the rural sector, at 19.3 per cent, 39.1 per cent, 24.7 per cent and 21.8 per cent, respectively, for Peninsular Malaysia, Sabah, Sarawak and Malaysia.

While rural poverty has been significantly reduced, the problem of poverty among peasant farmers and fishermen remains acute. In 1990, the incidence of poverty among paddy farmers (30 per cent), rubber smallholders (24 per cent), coconut smallholders (27 per cent) and fishermen (39 per cent) remained high.

As for rural poverty, generally, the smallholding subsector was not able to offer an acceptable level of living without organisational support and heavy subsidisation. Smallholder agricultural enterprises are becoming less attractive, causing youth to be reluctant to be employed in agriculture in pursuit of better opportunities in urban-industrial areas.

Poverty is seen as a vicious circle of low productivity, malnutrition, low incomes, unemployment embedded in structural defects, reinforced by imperfect competition (middlemen monopoly-monopsony) and the relative neglect of the rural economy (Ungku Aziz, 1964). Early efforts to eradicate poverty through community development and infrastructural programmes were less effective in improving the well-being of rural communities. Efforts to organise self-help and self-reliance among them

Table 11.2 Peninsular Malaysia, incidence of poverty, 1970, 1976, 1984, 1987, 1990

	1970		*1976*		*1984*		*1987*		*1990*
	Total poor house-holds ('000)	*Incidence of poverty (%)*	*Total poor house-holds ('000)*	*Incidence of poverty (%)*	*Total poor house-holds ('000)*	*Incidence of poverty (%)*	*Total poor house-holds ('000)*	*Incidence of poverty (%)*	*Incidence of poverty (%)*
Rural	705.9	58.7	666.9	47.8	402.0	24.7	408.2	22.4	19.3
Rubber small-holders	226.4	64.7	73.8	58.2	67.3	43.4	83.1	40.0	24.0
Paddy farmers	123.4	88.1	150.9	80.3	67.3	57.7	54.4	50.2	30.0
Estate workers	59.4	40.0	—	—	16.0	19.7	11.7	15.0	29.0
Fishermen	28.1	73.2	17.6	62.7	9.5	27.7	10.7	24.5	39.0
Coconut small-holders	16.9	52.9	12.4	64.0	6.6	46.9	4.9	39.2	27.0
Other agriculture	128.2	89.0	274.4	52.1	158.8	10.0	—	—	—
Other industries	123.5	35.2	139.5	27.3	76.5	10.0	—	—	—
Urban	85.9	21.3	94.9	17.9	81.3	8.2	81.3	8.2	7.3

Source: Various Malaysian Development Plans.

Table 11.3 Incidence of poverty and number of poor households, 1985–95

		1985			*1990*			*1995*[1]		
		Total	*Urban*	*Rural*	*Total*	*Urban*	*Rural*	*Total*	*Urban*	*Rural*
Peninsular Malaysia										
Incidence of poverty	(%)	18.4	8.2	24.7	15.0	7.3	19.3	9.1	4.1	14.1
Number of households	('000)	483.3	81.3	402.0	448.9	77.5	371.4	329.5	73.3	256.2
Incidence of hardcore poverty	(%)	6.3	2.4	8.7	3.6	1.4	4.8	1.7	0.6	2.8
Number of hardcore poor	('000)	165.6	23.8	141.8	107.3	14.9	92.4	61.3	10.6	50.7
Total households	('000)	2 621.1	991.7	1 629.4	2 986.4	1 062.2	1 924.2	3 627.9	1 804.9	1 823.0
Sabah										
Incidence of poverty	(%)	33.1	14.3	14.3	38.6	34.3	14.7	25.6	8.5	33.0
Number of households	('000)	70.0	7.5	98.5	96.6	8.5	91.1	91.1	9.1	82.0
Incidence of hardcore poverty	(%)	9.7	2.9	11.7	8.5	1.7	10.1	5.5	1.3	7.2
Number of hardcore poor	('000)	22.3	1.5	20.8	24.7	1.0	23.7	19.4	1.4	18.0
Total households	('000)	229.8	52.4	177.4	290.8	57.7	233.1	356.0	107.3	248.7

Table 11.3 *Continued*

		1985			*1990*			*1995*[1]		
		Total	*Urban*	*Rural*	*Total*	*Urban*	*Rural*	*Total*	*Urban*	*Rural*
Sarawak										
Incidence of poverty	(%)	31.9	8.2	37.3	21.0	4.9	24.7	16.0	2.1	20.1
Number of households	('000)	90.1	4.2	85.9	70.9	3.1	67.8	64.9	1.9	63.0
Incidence of hardcore poverty	(%)	10.0	1.7	11.9	3.3	0.6	3.9	2.0	0.3	2.5
Number of hardcore poor	('000)	28.2	0.9	27.3	11.1	0.4	10.7	8.1	0.3	7.8
Total households	('000)	282.4	51.2	231.2	337.4	62.8	274.6	405.3	91.4	313.9
Malaysia										
Incidence of poverty	(%)	20.7	8.5	27.3	17.1	7.5	21.8	11.1	4.2	16.8
Number of households	('000)	649.4	93.0	556.4	619.4	89.1	530.3	485.5	84.3	401.2
Incidence of hardcore poverty	(%)	6.9	2.4	9.3	4.0	1.4	5.2	2.0	0.6	3.2
Number of hardcore poor	('000)	261.1	26.2	89.9	143.1	16.3	126.8	88.8	12.3	76.5
Total households	('000)	3 133.3	1 095.3	2 038.0	3 614.6	1 182.7	2 431.9	4 389.2	2 003.6	2 385.6

[1]Estimates.
Source: Governmnet of Malaysia (1991).

were unsatisfactory and cooperative schemes were not very successful. The need for institutional reform to remove fundamental obstacles and structural constraints to poverty alleviation was emphasised (ibid., 1964).

Review of Poverty Alleviation Strategies

Generally, poverty alleviation strategies have been implemented through various rural development programmes, whose goal is to improve the well-being of the rural population, especially the rural poor. Traditionally, this has been done through policies and strategies designed to increase productivity and incomes, creating greater employment opportunities, providing greater access to goods and services and extending the benefits of development to the rural population (Chamhuri Siwar, 1994a).

Since the majority of the poor live in backward and often remote rural villages, the alleviation of poverty often involves transforming traditional into modern villages with adequate basic amenities and infrastructures.

Rural development involves a multisectoral approach which includes agricultural development, rural industrialisation, infrastructural development and welfare programmes. However, since about 80 per cent of the rural population are engaged in agriculture-related employment and activities, agricultural and land development typically forms the crux of rural development programmes. This comes in the form of agricultural income and productivity-related programmes in attempts to transform traditional agriculture into modern agriculture, with the infusion of modern technology along with the provision of technical assistance, subsidies and basic amenities. Technological change and agrarian reform may complement agricultural development to yield greater impact. The main objectives of these programmes are to increase productivity and incomes, and ultimately to reduce poverty among rural households.

It is generally agreed that rural and agricultural development alone cannot be relied on significantly to reduce rural poverty. Strategies of rural industrialisation, sponsored rural out-migration, creation of non-farm employment, population control programmes, and community development and rural urbanisation form the non-agricultural components of poverty alleviation programmes. Together with the provision of infrastructure, basic needs and welfare programmes serve to improve the quality of life and well-being of the rural population and to bring about greater integration between the rural sector and the national economy.

Early efforts at poverty alleviation were incorporated into the National Rural Development Plan aimed at reorganising and mobilising institutions and efforts towards modernising and developing the rural sector. The

Ministry of Rural Development planned and coordinated the activities of all agencies related to rural development. At the district or local level, the District Rural Development Committees implemented, monitored and reviewed all rural development projects in what was known as the Rural Economic Development (RED BOOK) Plan located in District Operations Rooms, which recorded the progress and attainment of rural development projects at district level.

The emphasis of the RED Projects was on building infrastructure and institutions. The infrastructural approach was intended to provide linkages to the rural economy, provide rural employment and raise productivity and incomes of the rural peasants. The provision of a social and economic infrastructure providing rural roads, drainage and irrigation facilities, basic amenities providing rural electricity, water, schools, health-care, community and religious centres, etc., the creation of functional rural institutions to facilitate production and marketing functions, and the credit needs of the rural peasant were expected to generate rural employment besides raising productivity, incomes, human development and the socio-economic status of the rural population.

A more effective poverty alleviation measure was needed in the form of a structurally oriented programme that could absorb part of the underemployed rural population in the overcrowded agricultural sector. Large and expensive land development schemes under the Federal Land Development Authority (FELDA) became a catalyst for rapid rural development and has had great impact on poverty eradication and raising the socio-economic well-being of the rural population.

Rural industrialisation forms another strategy to increase employment, productivity and incomes of the rural population. The origin of this can be traced to the formation of RIDA (Rural Industrial Development Authority) to improve the well-being of rural communities by setting up rural or cottage industries. Later, RIDA was expanded into MARA (abbreviation stands for Council of Trust for Indigenous People), whose role has included provisions for training and educational facilities for the Malays to further their education and to increase their involvement in the urban industrial sector. This strategy was later given more emphasis in the New Economic Policy (NEP), implemented during the Second to the Fifth Malaysia Plan covering the period 1970–90.

To improve the effectiveness of poverty alleviation strategies, it was felt that a more integrated approach to rural development programmes was needed. Since rural poverty is mainly concentrated in some identifiable areas or regions of the country, such programmes are expected to achieve greater impact if they are targeted at certain areas or groups. In these 'areas' or 'regions', an integrated 'package' of programmes known as the Integrated Agricultural Development Programmes (IADPs) were to be implemented and coordinated to achieve better results (Chamhuri Siwar and Nik Hashim, 1988).

In the 1980s, income maximisation, rural poverty eradication and equity objectives were spelt out more clearly in rural and agricultural development programmes. The National Agricultural Policy places income maximisation from agricultural production as its prime objective in planning and implementing future agricultural development programmes (Ministry of Agriculture, 1984, 1992). Poverty alleviation policies and programmes to improve the socio-economic well-being are seen not as ends in themselves, but as means of preparing the rural population for intersectoral mobility and for making interim improvements in the lives and incomes of those who remain in the rural areas despite rural structural change.

In 1987, a 'new' approach to rural development was implemented with the launching of BUKU MERAH DUA (Red Book II) which attempted to revive the legacy of the RED BOOK plan of the 1960s. The 'new' approach emphasises the role of the district in spearheading rural development in a more integrated manner, using group farming, rural industries, cooperatives, rural urbanisation, regrouping and restructuring of traditional villages and commercialisation of agriculture.

In the 1990s, with significant reduction in the incidence of absolute poverty the strategy of poverty alleviation in the Second Outline Perspective Plan (SOPP) (1990–2010) will be reoriented towards the eradication of hardcore poverty, defined as those with household incomes of half the poverty line income (PLI). In 1990, the number of hardcore poor for the whole country was about 143 100 or 4 per cent of total poor households. The target is to eradicate hardcore poverty by the year 2000 through economic and non-economic assistance, human development, attitudinal change and self-reliance programmes. To ensure efficient implementation and to ensure all targets are reached, a specialised delivery mechanism is designed, including encouraging the participation of non-govermental organisations and the private sector (Harun, 1990; Government of Malaysia, 1991).

Another strategy is to reduce relative poverty, focusing on improving the socio-economic conditions of the bottom 40 per cent of the population. Basically, the strategy aims at reducing the income gap between the poor and the non-poor, reducing intersectoral, interethnic and interregional inequality. It is hoped that the growth process along with economic development and structural transformation will bring about more equality among the various strata of the population. The strategy of growth with redistribution will be the guiding principle necessary to bring about a more balanced growth among sectors, regions and states, and a greater equity in the distribution of benefits of growth.

Basically, poverty alleviation strategy adopted for the SOPP period relied on the growth process to solve the general problem of poverty, in addition to the more targeted strategy, education and training, more job opportunities in the non-agricultural sectors and structural changes in the economy, resulting in more non-farm income sources, are expected to alleviate poverty among the poor households.

An official assessment regarding anti-poverty programmes implemented since the 1960s and 1970s concluded that the 'have probably reached the limits of their effectiveness' and recommended that the broad-based approach be reoriented to focus on the more critical aspects of poverty eradication. This included assistance to the poorest households towards meeting their specific needs and focusing development programmes to underserved regions and less developed states to improve access to basic services and facilities (Government of Malaysia, 1991).

Since 1990, with the ending of the NEP, poverty alleviation programmes are aimed mainly at the hardcore poor through the Special Development Programme for the very poor and less developed states for better access to improved basic services. The concept of human development and self-reliance will be emphasised in poverty alleviation programmes.

A critical look at the special development programmes for the poorest shows that the components of the programme are not much different from those implemented under the broad-based approach. They include programmes directed towards heads of households consisting of priority in new land development and idle land schemes, land consolidation and rehabilitation programme, livestock rearing (chickens, goats, cattle), fishery programmes, rural sanitation and community water supply, special cash crops (e.g. honey and mushrooms), marketing and credit, cottage industry and handicrafts, infrastructure for depressed areas and housing assistance, and rehabilitation programmes. For the children, mothers and the elderly the special programme includes rehabilitation for malnourished cases, supplementary feeding, de-worming, rural libraries, supplementary feeding for kindergartens, textbook loans and scholarships for students, and housing for the elderly.

The special development programme for the poorest essentially consists of economic and non-economic 'handouts' which may defeat the self-reliance programme that the government is supporting through the benevolent loan scheme (Ikhtiar Project) currently implemented through the Amanah Ikhtiar Malaysia (AIM). The Ikhtiar project which has proved to be successful (Gibbons and Sukor, 1990; Chamhuri Siwar, 1991) is based on a benevolent loan programme where the *sahabat* (borrowers) are required to pay back the loan and also to attend centre meetings, motivational courses and study tours. Stringent means tests are conducted to determine their eligibility to the programme. By comparison, although the registry of the poorest is conducted to select beneficiaries to the special development programme for the poorest, the exercise itself is not free from political and administrative interference and hence may cause 'leakages' in the programme.

Although the poverty incidence at the macro level has declined significantly, at the micro and village levels, poverty problems remain acute, especially in remote areas isolated from mainstream economic activities and in areas inaccessible to infrastructures and not receiving the benefits of development. A recent survey (Chamhuri Siwar, 1994b) showed that the incidences of poverty are still high in the districts of Perlis (49.1 per cent), Padang Terap (63.8 per cent), Pendang (68 per cent), Kerian (64.1 per cent), Kuala Pilah (36.4 per cent), Besut (51.2 per cent), Hulu Trengganu (57.3 per cent), Kemaman (41 per cent), Bachok (52.8 per cent) and Kota Bharu (32.9 per cent).

The high incidence of poverty at the micro and village level suggests that the broad-based rural development approach implemented in the past may results in 'pockets of areas' not benefiting from the development process and inacessible to basic infrastructures and services. The reliance on the process of growth to resolve the poverty problem in the SOPP period may mean that some areas may still be bypassed by the development process, and the 'trickling down' process may not reach the poorest of the poor. In this sense, sustained human development programmes may contribute significantly towards poverty alleviation in the long run.

CONCLUSION AND POLICY ALTERNATIVES

UNDP (1994) identifies several causes for the weaknesses of many national poverty alleviation programmes in the Asia–Pacific region. They include the capacity constraints of central and state governments to implement programmes to ensure their sustainability, a top–down blueprint approach in project design and management, and administrative and organisational weaknesses and lack of adequate gender analysis.

Suggestions for improving the performance of poverty alleviation programmes basically hinges on strengthening the human development component, including improving governance by assisting government and NGOs in building up their capacities and in promoting empowerment of the poor to overcome various constraints to development (UNDP, 1994). Empowerment of the poor is a multifaceted and multidimensional process, consisting of socio-economic, educational and cultural empowerment. It involves the mobilisation of resources and people's capacities to facilitate initiatives by the poor, to take responsibility for their own development, to provide the poor with information, skills, knowledge and channels of communication, recognition of poor people's knowledge and value systems, provide the basis for developing appropriate technologies that could enhance labour productivity, increase income-earning potential and increase dignity, self-respect and well-being.

Concrete measures for improving the performance of poverty alleviation programmes include creating a condusive policy environment, improving project design through a community-based approach, strengthening management capacity, poverty responsive governance, integrating women into poverty alleviation programmes and developing an affective data base. Poverty alleviation is a mammoth task. Heterogeneity of poverty characteristics, differences in approaches towards poverty alleviation make the task more difficult.

Despite the above differences, there seems to be some agreement on the positive role of sustainable economic growth in poverty alleviation. Improved income distribution helps to eliminate poverty, harness the resources of the poor through bottom-up processes, and assists the poor to help themselves. In addition, governments need to facilitate anti-poverty programmes, account for differences among the poor and types of measures to alleviate them, avoid mistakes or failures in past programmes by learning from previous mistakes. Poverty is a result of deprivation of both physical and human assets like land, credit, technology, education, skills and health. Sustained human development could go a long way towards alleviating poverty.

There is also a need for the private sector to design activities to supplement and complement government, community and NGO interventions. Poverty alleviation and sustainable human development should be a national concern and hence the need for the private sector to assist national planners and community-based groups to benefit from sharing experiences from poverty alleviation programmes. There is wide scope for the replication of several successful programmes like the Ikhtiar project, macro and sectoral policies to provide credits and promote microenterprise that will greatly influence human development.

A review of poverty alleviation programmes raises several issues. These could subsequently be examined to make corrective actions to improve the effectiveness of projects.

The Number and Size of Projects are Too Many with a Relatively High Cost

The large number of projects implemented by many agencies may create coordination problems and are seen not to be conducive for networking at regional and district levels. They may also create linkage problems at project levels. This may not be conducive for optimal programming and implies the need for coordination and concentrating resources on specific themes and areas or regions.

Lack of Focus on Human Development

Poverty alleviation generally follows a target group approach, targeted at specific groups like padi farmers, rubber smallholders, estate workers, fishermen, and coconut smallholders. Most projects are aimed at increasing productivity and incomes of the target groups through technology and production oriented programmes, lacking focus on self-reliance. This may seem to dilute the focus on the issues of human development and poverty alleviation.

Lack of Targeting of the Poor

Initially, most of the projects were not targeted specifically to the poor in the subsectors. Various impact studies show that poverty still abounds and demonstrate only in direct impacts or benefits in terms of improvements in the quality of life of the poor (Sukor *et al.*, 1993).

Learning from the weaknesses and also taking into consideration various changes that have taken place in the country, recent poverty alleviation programmes are packaged differently and are strongly thematic, are oriented more towards the very poor, stressing the programme approach, encouraging involvement of NGOs parallel financing and more direct involvement of the private sector.

Programmes categorised under Human Development are thought to have a direct impact on human development and poverty alleviation. They have tried to tackle basic problems and shortfalls in human development, such as lack of sanitation and water supply, basic education programmes, health management, nutrition and population planning, household food security, life skills, vocational training, entrepreneurial development, credit for the poor, income generation, microenterprise development, and integrated strategies for poverty eradication, rural improvement and sustainable human development.

References

Chamhuri Siwar (1991) 'Credit Programme for Rural Development and Poverty Alleviation in Malaysia', *Asia Pacific Journal of Rural Development*, 1 (2) December.

Chamhuri Siwar (1992) 'Rural Development and Poverty Alleviation: The Impact of Integrated Agricultural Development Projects (IADPs)', in Johari, Mohd. Yaakub (ed.) *Regional Development in Malaysia: Issues and Challenges* (Kota Kinabalu, Sabah, Malaysia: Institute for Development Studies (Sabah)).

Chamhur Siwar (1994a) 'Rural Development, Poverty Alleviation and Rural Transformation', in INTAN, Malaysia Development Experience (Kuala Lumpur: National Institute of Public Administration (INTAN)).

Chamhuri Siwar (1994b) 'Poverty Profile in Malaysia: Findings from 10 Districts in Peninsular Malaysia', in Ariffin, Jamilah (ed.), *Poverty Amidst Plenty* (Petaling Jaya, Malaysia: Pelanduk Publications).

Chamhuri Siwar and Nik Hashim, Mustapha (1989) *Integrated Rural Development in Malaysia: An Assessment.* Monograph No. 4 (Bangi: Fakulti Ekonomi, Universiti Kebangsaan Malaysia).

Gibbons, D.S and Sukor Kassim (1990) *Banking on the Rural Poor* (Penang: Amanah Ikhtiar Malaysia and Universiti Sains Malaysia).

Harun Hashim (1990) 'Alleviating Rural-Poverty: The Malaysian Experience with Special Emphasis on Self-Reliance Programmes', paper presented at the Second Southeast Asian Roundtable on Economic Development, ISIS, Kuala Lumpur, Malaysia, December.

Government of Malaysia (1991) *The Second Outline Perspective Plan (1991–2000)* (Kuala Lumpur: National Printing Department).

Mahbub ul Haq (1991) 'Human Development in Asia and the Pacific', in Naya, S. and Browne, S. (eds), *Development Challenge in Asia and the Pacific in the 1990s* (Honolulu, Hawaii: UNDP and East–West Center).

Ministry of Agriculture (1984) *National Agricultural Policy* (Kuala Lumpur: Government Printer).

Ministry of Agriculture (1992) *National Agricultural Policy* (Kuala Lumpur: Government Printer).

Naya, S. and Browne, S. (eds) (1991) *Development Challenges in Asia and the Pacific in the 1990s* (Honolulu, Hawaii: UNDP and East–West Center).

Sukor Kassim *et al.* (1983) *Study of Strategy, Impact and Future Development of Integrated Agricultural Development Projects* (Penang: Centre for Policy Research, Universiti Sains Malaysia).

UNDP (1990) *Human Development Report, 1990* (New York: Oxford University Press).

UNDP (1991a) *Human Development Report, 1991* (New York: Oxford University Press).

UNDP (1991b), *Poverty Alleviation Asia and the Pacific: The UNDP Response,* Report of a Regional Workshop, Kuala Lumpur, 26–28 May.

UNDP (1992a) *Human Development Report, 1992* (New York: Oxford University Press).

UNDP (1992b) 'Fifth Inter-country Programme for Asia and the Pacific 1992–1996', MAC 5 Meeting of AID Coordinators in Asia and the Pacific Manila.

UNDP (1993a) *Human Development Report 1993* (New York: Oxford University Press).
UNDP (1993b) 'Inter-country Programme for Asia and the Pacific Progress Report' (New York: United Nations).
UNDP (1994a) *Human Development Report, 1994* (New York: Oxford University Press).
UNDP (1994b) 'Regional Poverty Alleviation Programme for Asia and The Pacific' (mimeograph).
Ungku Aziz (1964) 'Poverty and Rural Development in Malaysia', *Kajian Ekonomi Malaysia*, 1 (1), June.
Ungku Aziz (1969) 'Fundamental Obstacle to Rural Development with Special Reference to Institutional Reform' (mimeograph).

12 Instruments of Participatory Enterprise for Grassroots Development

Masudul A. Choudhury

Since the advent of the Bretton Woods institutions, the following episodes in the rise of capitalism, the demise of socialism and the rise of the multilateral trade organisation, the world today still faces a grim prospect of 3 billion abject poor (United Nations, 1991), acute disparity between the North and the South and increasingly de-equalizing external deficits for the poor countries. These conditions are found to aggravate the difficulties of the developing countries in addressing their social and economic problems. While the North is today advancing towards a postmodern era of its own, the developing countries and their poor find themselves deeper in the grips of hopelessness. Inequality and deprivation rule the cause and effect of the social and economic relations between nation states and within nations, be these the industrialised or the developing ones.

What is more troubling is that the history of global socio-economic evolution, gaining prominence in an integrating and trading world, is an incessant record of the poor being alienated in this development process. The question to ask is whether trade, development and the globalisation process in this post-cold war era are meaningful for human development (UNDP, several issues). The subsequent question to that above is whether, in the continuing scene of the Western arrangement of socio-economic, institutional and political relations, a postmodern age will be any different from the one that has passed since the advent of Western colonialism? (Abdallah, 1993). Are modern states able to devise appropriate grassroots arrangements by means of financial instruments linking development and trade in an empowering, equalising and entitling mould?

OBJECTIVES

In this chapter we intend to examine these questions. First, we will proceed by inquiring about the problems with the existing financial instruments and socio-economic variables in terms of development at the grassroots. Secondly, we will look at the picture of globalisation and trade to tie in with the issue of development in the light of such instruments. Thirdly, we will proffer a rationale for and features of alternative financial instruments for realising entitlement, empowerment, distribution, economic growth and self-reliance at the grassroots.

CONCEPT OF THE GRASSROOTS

The terminology of grassroots we are using here means that hierarchical segment of society comprising the poor, marginalised groups, microenterprises, intellectuals and other interest groups, all of whom collectively share in the common goal of enhancing each other by complementarity of interests. Thus through this collective interest there finally emerges the uniquely shared preferences among the groups. Sacrificing this common goal would result in a deprivation of the collective as a whole. Self-interests of the cooperating agents of the grassroots become transformed by cause and effect into mutually enhancing benefits. At the end, the concept of grassroots is an idea prevailing in overall development.

In this context, the goal of the grassroots is to attain a feasible level of collective well-being as an index of various types of entitlement, empowerment and socio-economic variables, including a factor in it that sustains the well-being. The idea of well-being here is then a complementary function of all such variables, interactively related to each other and resulting in a simultaneity of the goals of economic efficiency and distributive equity.

The constraints of the goal of attaining well-being are the costs of attaining a basic needs regime of development and the mechanism of establishing complementarity among the agents of the grassroots. A similar constraint exists among the science, technology, human resources, human development and organisational levels promoting grassroots development. All these constraints are however, fairly low-cost relations as it is costless to improve the lot of the poor (Sen, 1975); to promote a basic needs regime of development (ILO, 1976); and to bring these about by a participation of the poor in their own collective interests. All of these constraints include financial variables, development and trade-related variables that promote entitlement, empowerment, distributive equity and economic efficiency in a complementary mode.

Since complementarity is a function of interactions among the agents, socio-economic variables, mechanisms and processes in question, and because interactions also generate by cause and effect a flow of knowledge in these factors, both the index of well-being and the constraints as cost of attaining interactive relations therefore become uniquely augmented by the knowledge values (caused by interactions) generated in these systems. Extensive global interactions emerge as a result.

CRITICAL SOCIO-ECONOMIC AND FINANCIAL VARIABLES IN GRASSROOTS DEVELOPMENT

The principal socio-economic variables in the above relations can be enumerated as follows. Some of these apply strictly to the mainstream approach to grassroots development. Hence their analysis will differ between such an approach and the authentically grassroots approach that we will take up in this chapter.

For generating entitlement it is seen to be necessary to generate employment, wages, transfer incomes and exchange entitlement variables consisting of price level, human capital, assets and tradability, all taken up in the midst of a private ownership economy (Sen, 1986).

For generating empowerment, some of the socio-economic conditions required are work, productivity and efficiency, all adopted in the midst of a market economy. For realising income distribution, subsidy and social expenditures are activated by governments using general tax revenues, while taxing corporations and capital gains at much lower rates. Besides the socio-economic variables, empowerment requires political power shift from the established hegemony of public authority to the grassroots.

The principal financial instruments used to realise entitlement, empowerment, distribution and economic growth are as follows. For generating entitlement, bonds are floated for developing and financing assets at the grassroots. Low interest rate loans are provided. Empowerment is financed by a participatory share in a common fund at the grassroots. Such a fund by the name of Earth Fund, was proposed by the NGOs at the Rio Earth Summit (Network, 1992). Distribution is targeted by the financial instrument of tax relief and subsidies realised by general revenues.

Trade-related variables conventionally used are as follows: protection of infant industries at the grassroots to establish entitlement in the midst of a market-driven economy; comparative advantage to empower grassroots, particularly in the agricultural sector; wage-related incentives to allocate labour between the agricultural and manufacturing sectors according to comparative advantage and relative total productivity gains.

RELATIONSHIP OF SOCIO-ECONOMIC AND FINANCIAL VARIABLES IN ATTAINING ENTITLEMENT AND EMPOWERMENT: A CRITIQUE

We will now bring together all the above-mentioned variables and instruments in a socio-economic criterion function for attaining entitlement, empowerment, distributive equity and economic efficiency or factor productivity. We note that in received socio-economic models it is impossible to attain both distributive equity and economic efficiency or productivity together (Phelps, 1989). Any one of these goals substitutes the other in the sense of neo-classical marginalist trade-offs. Consequently, variables such as transfer income (oriented to targets of entitlement and distribution) and economic growth (oriented to empowerment and economic efficiency) appear as gross substitutes. Likewise, the financial instruments of subsidy and soft loans, serving distributional objectives, appear in a marginalist trade-off with general tax revenue and profit-sharing instruments as efficiency oriented financial instruments. In the trade sector, foreign direct investments generate marginalist conflict between the industrial and agricultural sectors. Consequently, either foreign trade is pursued by optimising the export of commodities, which by the nature of their low terms of trade cause lower economic growth or indebtedness, or else commodities are substituted by a focus on capital goods, albeit not with reduction of external indebtedness and liabilities. Thus developing economies experience structural shifts from agriculture and agro-based sectorial activities to secondary sectorial and heavy industrial activities. Linkages are ignored (Hirschman, 1989).

The net result of such neo-classical type marginalist substitutions as the inherent perspective of existing approaches to grassroots development, to be found in the structural adjustment model of privatisation, has been the perennial problem of leaving out the poor and the societal interface in developmental planning. Nation states formulate development planning in isolation of the need for participation by and at the grassroots, in the sense of this concept defined ealier. International development organisations, be they the World Bank, the International Monetary Fund and regional development organisations or new trading blocs mushrooming around the world, pursue policies towards complementarity between structural adjustment and IMF conditionalities (Helleiner, 1983; Pratt, 1983). Social spending and its focus on generating appropriate financial instruments that would support grassroots development are marginalised. We find, therefore, that in the world scene the problem of poverty remains the most outstanding social issue with three billion of the poor subsisting in spite of four decades of structural development policy. External debt continues to fall on the back of the poor in spite of the IMF's pursuit of its conditionalities.

These observations further point out that during the post-Uruguay Round advances towards globalisation, nation states in particular and the world as a whole are deepening the application of a neo-classical gross substituting approach of the poor in favour of privatisation, trade and economic growth. National economies in the midst of severe competition and outward orientation to be competitive, themselves orientate their development plans in the midst of the neo-classical-type market-dominated models. The grassroots as the fundamental target group of developing nations are thus left out and alienated in the present globalisation process (Choudhury, 1993a).

ORGANISATIONAL FEATURES OF MICROENTERPRISE IN RECEIVED ECONOMIC ARRANGEMENTS

The organisational features of a microenterprise in the neo-classical marginalist substitution model of structural adjustment can now be seen. A microenterprise specialises in marginal sector activities, which in most cases involve agricultural commodities, small-scale agro-based oriented and small-scale trade and service oriented activities at best. In a competitive model of survival and profit optimisation involving the privatisation process, such microenterprises become individuated enterprises, not cooperative ones. Consequently, they remain as price takers and suppliers of low value-added goods in the otherwise oligopolistic market environment confronting microenterprises. Besides, the feature of price-taking by microenterprises subjects them to limiting pricing conditions set by predatory oligopolies. The adverse profit levels in such a case for microenterprises finally drive them out of markets or cause them to be integrated horizontally by dominant suppliers (Martin, 1988). This is one of the reasons for a high bankruptcy rate of microenterprises.

In the neo-classical model and organisational behaviour, the competing nature of microenterprises taken within themselves causes their profits to remain low. This makes expansion difficult. Thus the grassroots enterprise in its individuated form remains bereft of power to change its fate in the face of market forces acting against it. This results in deprivation of entitlement, empowerment and growth in the midst of a private-ownership economy. Examples of the latter are markets experiencing privatisation and globalisation.

Microenterprises cannot therefore form an organisation of their own. An organisation is treated here as a solidarity of mutually cooperating microenterprises with the objective of deciding collectively on issues of production, technology, inputs and pricing, leading to an acquisition of viable forms of market shares. The activities of the organisation thus involve collective but regimented decision-making, the raising of investment and share capital by a mix of financial instruments, and serving the common benefit of both the shareholders and management (Simon, 1960; Williamson, 1981).

In the absence of such organisational features, microenterprises cannot influence political regimes to orientate economic evolutions, development planning and foreign trade in their favour. Decisions on transfer technology, inflows of foreign direct investments and commodity pricing are done by national governments under the force of globalisation, in the absence of any interface with the grassroots and their microenterprises. Entitlement, empowerment and distribution cannot thereby coexist with the government's targets on economic growth.

In the case of producer associations as organisations serving the interests of microenterprises, the absence of strong unions at this level and the low initiation fees generated from these marginalised enterprises make production associations ineffective in promoting the well-being of the grassroots.

An example here is the inability of NGOs to instrumentalise production associations at the grassroots levels in accord with the commercial and business focus of the Rio Earth Summit on sustainable development (Keating, 1993). Another example is the inability of production associations for the Bumiputeras in Malaysia to push the Malaysian Government towards forming the much talked about Bumiputera Commercial and Industrial Complex (Government of Malaysia, 1991). The Malaysian Government has prevailed unilaterally with its own decision in this matter. Where the grassroots financing organisation in Malaysia by the name Amanah Ikhtiar has been active, this was made possible by finances from the Malaysian Government and other financial institutions to provide for the grassroots as transfer incomes for start-up businesses (Gibbons and Kasim, 1991). Thus once again the predominant decision is trickled down to the grassroots, without the latter being able actively to determine its own needs through microenterprise–government enterprise.

Amanah Ikhtiar operates on the framework of the Grameen Bank model of Bangladesh. The latter, too, is found to be limited in its capacity towards expanding the level of operations of microenterprises. The second and subsequent loans made out by the Grameen Bank to its microenterprises are found to be riskier than the first loan, which is a mere 5000 Bangladesh Taka. Likewise, Grameen operations are not oriented towards politically empowering the grassroots (Choudhury, 1993). The existence of production associations is unheard of between the Grameen Bank and microenterprises.

The nature of marginalist substitution and power benignity of grassroots in their microenterprises is equally true when technological cahnge is induced at the grassroots in the neo-classical sense. Technological induction of production and inputs of production are then generated from the viewpoint of economic needs necessary for profitability and productivity. On the other hand, only such preconditions of economic growth are assumed to lead to investments generating output, and in turn output is recycled towards a further technological induction of production. Development and trade are both treated as instruments in such a relationship between technology and economic growth. Hence, the nature of a relationship between the power benign grassroots and the dominance of the socio-political establishment perpetuates in the midst of a directed technological change by the establishment. This is the neo-classical of technological change and its consequencies at the grassroots levels.

THE QUESTION OF COST AND TECHNOLOGY IN THE NEO-CLASSICAL MODEL RELATING TO THE GRASSROOTS

Technological induction of economic growth brings about human and resource mobilisation at the grassroots at a cost. In the neo-classical model, this is the opportunity cost of substituting growth for distribution. Now when wages in the agricultural sector relative to the industrial composite wages increase, such increases are brought about not by gains in factor productivity in the agricultural sector, for technologically is not agriculture biased. Hence, relative wage increases cause inflationary pressures and increased opportunity cost to potential investors, with labour productivity remaining lower than wage rate. Investments are consequently reversed from agricultural activity into manufacturing activity. This case is particularly true of Bangladesh and Malaysia (Government of Bangladesh, 1990; Ministry of Finance, 1993). Thus a marginalist substitution model always causes an impoverising low-level equilibrium trap for grassroots development even, in the midst of technological change (Enke, 1962).

The question of neutrality of technological change to grassroots development renders the concept of appropriate technology open to criticism in a neo-classical model of resource allocation. The fact of the matter is, that a direction of technology to agricultural activity in the face of an opportunity cost of capital surmised in this sector by the neo-classical model means a costly way of using resources. Thus, both by way of reversion of investment back to manufacturing and by way of the substituting nature of resources between agriculture and manufacturing, technology will predominantly be of secondary manufacturing and service sector types. Any appropriate technology with both cost-saving and social features thereby becomes subject to market consequentialism in the neo-classical model of growth, employment and technological induction.

Policy content in the midst of market models of growth, development and technological change causes market distortion. Such distortions cannot revert suboptimal points of entitlement, empowerment, distribution and economic growth, called 'starvation points' (Sen, 1986), to the optimal production possibility curve. The reason behind this is that an induction of entitlement bundle by policy measure will cause a displacement of some of the growth and economic efficiency. In this way, yet another component of the entitlement–empowerment bundle, namely exchange entitlement, is adversely affected in a private-ownership economy. Likewise, if income distribution is to be generated using general revenues, then production must be encouraged. Whereas, taxation and production exist in conflict with each other in the competing private-ownership economy. This causes further substitutions between taxation (subsidy = tranfer incomes) and growth (= development in neo-classical sense). The social entitlement (social security) and exchange entitlement bundles thus exist in perpetual conflict in the marginalist substitution model, causing suboptimal resource allocation points ('starvation points') under policy induction, never to reach optimality without a large opportunity cost as perceived in the neo-classical model of growth, entitlement, empowerment and distribution (Choudhury, 1993a).

A SUMMARY OF THE ABOVE SECTIONS

The nature of individuation of the microenterprises in a model of national and global neo-classicism makes any organisational feature economically and politically non-viable overall. The organisation of economic cooperation among such enterprises cannot arise in the neo-classical model of markets, privatisation and competition. Entitlement, empowerment, distribution and economic growth as complementary forces in a developmental model of grassroots amelioration cannot be attained in the neo-classical model of marginalist substitution.

COOPERATIVE FRAMEWORK USING COMPLEMENTARITY AND WORKPLACE DEMOCRACY

We next turn to the cooperative type of grassroots development and once again go through the nature of the alternative socio-economic model and the nature of financial instruments that must now be linked with the new outlook on trade and development. Thereby, the concept of organisation at the grassroots is invoked.

We return here to the nature of global complementarity among activities and variables entering the index of grassroots well-being. The principal complementarity to address here is one of simultaneity between the goals of economic growth and distributive equity. We must examine in this regard the role of financial and development instruments, the nature of technological change and organisation at the grassroots.

A cooperative at the grassroots level is conceptualised here as an organised association of microenterprises interacted with each other within the framework of workplace democracy. Here a list of financial instruments along with organisational features can be noted.

One case is that of the Employee Share Ownership Plan (ESOP) (Wisman, 1991). It operates by virtue of the employees contributing a portion of their wages towards a common fund run as an investment fund by the employer. The employer takes up shares in the investment returns from such a fund. In this way, a mutual benefit is generated between the employer and the employee who share the returns on the common fund investment. The employer is then effectively paying discounted wages. This enables the employer to control the cost of operation. Saving on cost and share capital together augment the existing investment portfolio of the enterprise. On the side of the employees, they have the option as a group of buying back the company in the extreme situation of plant closure, by using the accumulated fund of share capital. Employment is then maintained and production continued during adverse economic circumstances, to the mutual benefit of employers and employees. Employers can now develop cooperative ventures with employees to salvage the enterprise. Such a cooperative workplace democracy has been found to work particularly effectively during recessionary times by saving employment and increasing efficiency, and reducing the cost of operations with the input of the above-mentioned type of wage discounts (Weitzman, 1984).

The more universal form of ESOP is the USOP (Universal Share Ownership Plan) model of workplace democracy (Ellerman, 1991). In the USOP model employees are able to establish an internal financial basis for looking after their pooled funds and to cooperate more universally with other ESOPs. The internal financial institution of USOP is a banking system spread across all cooperating ESOPs, thus forming a viable financial basis of the USOP system. With the expansion of both the USOP system and, thereby, of its financial system, liquidity and investment opportunities are established (Vanek, 1975). The limiting investment opportunities are the enterprises themselves. Hence, an overall general equilibrium system interconnecting the enterprise, its financial system and its internal labour market is sustained. At the same time, such a financial system, by insulating its capital market to the internal market of its own, reduces the vulnerability of USOP to recessionary consequences of the economic environment.

APPLYING WORKPLACE DEMOCRACY MODEL TO GRASSROOTS DEVELOPMENT: REPLACING THE NEO-CLASSICAL MARGINALIST SUBSTITUTION PARADIGM

The above-mentioned types of workplace democracy models can be extended to grassroots microenterprises in terms of developing producer associations and organisations of microenterprises in the framework of the USOP model. In Malaysia, there is a special focus placed today on promoting Bumiputera shares and ownership in various enterprises. At the grassroots level, agricultural and agro-based enterprise shares are promoted in two ways. First, there can be self-generated integrated enterprises of producer associations established within the enterprises themselves. Secondly, the broad concept of grassroots across all sectors in the economy, motivated by the common interest of promoting the common good, makes it possible to extend cooperative enterpises among varying levels of enterprises and sectors, each motivated by the same principle and programme of mobilising self-reliant shares and expanding the emergent economic and financial base. The total transformation in these fronts is thus brought about by marginalising the linkages of grassroots development from the economic environment based on marginalist substitution.

The internalising nature of such emergent grassroots cooperative organisations and enterprises, both of economic and financial activities, causes dual sectors of economic activity in the total economy. One of the sectors is guided by cooperations of grassroots microenterprises and the other by the establishment of enterprises based on the neo-classical marginalist principle. Grassroots microenterprises now grow in the midst of non-competition with other enterprises. Resource transfers are not received from the economic establishment. In this way, the groundwork of productivity gains and efficiency gains are established in the midst of the cooperative organisation to advance common well-being at the grassroots.

Productivity gains are realised by adapting emergent technological change to progressively developing skills, rather than having lower skilled labour cope with a target of such a technology that remains foreign to labour at the grassroots. The use of capital in an adaptive manner generates alignment between technological change and factor productivity. This reduces the cost of operations. Entitlement is then generated by the function of productivity gains through adaptive technology (Choudhury, 1981).

The nature of such a technological adapation can be explained as follows. We consider three categories of labour – skilled, semi-skilled and unskilled. We assume that education, human resource development and technological diffusion in a cooperatively integrated model are interactively developed. Hence they are used as the common good enhancing the next rounds of skill formation and its cause–effect relationship with technological adaptation. Factor productivity is thus realised by interactive forces operating in the workplace. First, a costless way of initial adaptation of technology to available skills, and not the reverse way, is established in the the formal workplace. In the second round, this productivity is enhanced by diffusion of human resource development in the workplace. Thirdly, a progressive adaptation of technological change to skill formation is realised. Fourthly, there is externality caused by informal interrelationship between all kinds of labour in the workplace, causing further advancement in knowledge transmission across the system.

Wage–employee relationship is now addressed. Technological adaptation in the above type of cooperative workplace environment means growth of wages in line with productivity gains. Consequently, the problem of inefficiency of production is also overcome. By the extensive nature of a variety of complementing enterprises in our concept of the grassroots, the growth of productivity is enhanced. In each of these categories, the internal labour market allocates labour in a complementing way. Thus, as the cycle of progressively transformed output of skilled labour proceeds, they are reallocated across a variety of enterprises. The dual or segmented labour market characteristics of a marginalist outlook are thus broken down as knowledge is diffused, interactions proceed and wages increase by productivity gains and resource allocation across the internal labour market of the grassroots enterprises.

FINANCIAL INSTRUMENTS FOR DEVELOPING A COOPERATIVE GRASSROOTS ENTERPRISE

The financial instruments of joint venture, equity financing, cofinancing, profit-sharing, trade financing and diversifying of shares in this portfolio of investments become the backbone of development. Entitlement, distribution and economic growth are now formed by the monotonically positive relationships between wages, investment returns, ownership, human resource development and its consistency with productivity gains. Joint ventures act across a variety of enterprises. Cofinancing acts between the internal financial base, the higher level enterprises and the marginal enterprises. Equity financing acts across capital-using enterprises at the grassroots in terms of its broad definition provided in this chapter. Profit-sharing acts in mobilising all categories of labour and capital in the form of a USOP model. Trade financing acts across all sectors encompassing the grassroots.

These financial instruments cannot substitute among themselves, because of the intrinsic nature of cooperative decision-making in such a grassroots organisation. This is guided by information, monitoring and sharing of benefits that come about from the exercise of these instruments. Likewise, there cannot be substitution among socio-economic variables, such as wages and profit shares attained by participation at all levels; productivity gains keeping in tune with wage changes; economic efficiency caused by the absence of opportunity cost; and technological change adapting to progressive skill formation. If the contrary was true even in a limited sense, a global substitution would occur. Hence, it is the organisational responsibility to maintain strict sustainability of the complementary type of relationships among the activities and variables mentioned here. In this way, the process of grassroots transformation brought about by the exercise of the financial instruments is premised in the underlying Principle of Universal Complementarity, a concept that applies here to interlinkages across all activities (Choudhury, 1994).

DELINKING THE GRASSROOTS ENTERPRISE FROM THE NEO-CLASSICAL ECONOMIC ENVIRONMENT

The delinking of cooperative grassroots level participatory enterprises from the neo-classical economic order is necessary in order to preserve the complementary nature of interrelationships at the grassroots. Linking the grassroots with the neo-classical environment in financial instruments and organisational behaviour would displace the complementary relationship among the socio-economic variables. This in turn would upset the complementary relationship among the financial instruments as well. It is therefore not to the interest of the grassroots to link up with the neo-classical socio-economic environment and thus to lose its self-reliant power, and face the high cost of marginalist substitution, with the final prospect of extinction of this interest group in a sweep of market consequentialism caused by the dominant neo-classical socio-economic order (Sen, 1985).

The grassroots interest to delink itself from the neo-classical socio-economic environment is also caused by its own prospect for expansion and gaining political power at large. The organisational structure must thus educate the grassroots agents by pervasiveness of education and information on the point that the neo-classical environment is out there to replace them by the very nature of its domineering socio-economic relations, institutional behaviour and self-interest (Dyke, 1981).

From the shift in socio-economic relations towards cooperation and the emergent political power, grassroots enterprises are capable of forming collective organisations such as consumer and producer associations. Empowerment is thus established and the momentum of global transformation towards complementary forms of activities and socio-economic relations is gained. The hegemony of power by national governments and the global order is neutralised by the growth of cooperating hierarchies of grassroots enterprises, small to large in size, each complementing the other.

CREATIVE SUSTAINABILITY AT THE GRASSROOTS

Creative sustainability of the grassroots can now be defined as its method of survival and expansion across nation states and then the global order by increasing levels of integration across hierarchies of interacting enterprises and organisations. This involves the simultaneous attainment of entitlement, empowerment, distribution and economic growth by virtue of the complementary nature of organisational relations, socio-economic goals and variables. The productive, efficient and social foundations of the grassroots enterprises as the preconditions of their survival and expansion must reinforce each other by cause and effect. In this way, the premise that well defines the sustainability of the grassroots is the Principle of Universal Complementarity. This principle implies global interlinkages amongst all agents and activities, which can only be possible by purposeful interactions among these entities.

This idea of creative sustainability stems from the nature of interactive integration and its cause–effect continuity that exists in the cooperative and complementary model of the grassroots. The same cannot be identified in the individuated, discontinuous and alienated model of neo-classical marginalist substitutional order.

We bring together in Figure 12.1 the idea of creative sustainability in the interactive-integrative model of the grassroots. In this diagram we also show the essentially discontinuous nature of neo-classical relations, that grounds the individuated and alienated nature of its relations.

Figure 12.1 The interactive–integrative model of the grassroots and the discontinuous nature of the neo-classical model

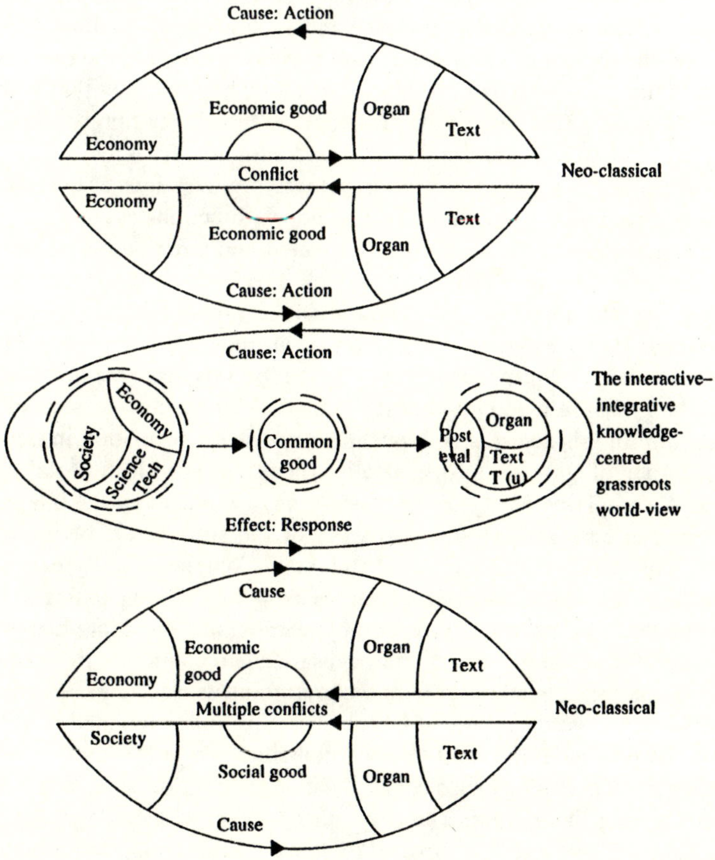

The grassroots organisation is shown to comprise, first, a principal system of its textual relationships ($T(\Theta)$) from which it derives its world-view. This is where the knowledge of creative sustainability premised on the Principle of Universal Complementarity as its integrating epistemology is embedded. From it is derived primordially the laws and operational aspects of the grassroots organisation (Organ). The third part of organisational behaviour at the grassroots is its capability to post-evaluate its previous actions and learn from changes or affirmation of these actions (Post-eval).

Internal interactions proceed among the agents of the grassroots enterprises, who are elected democratically and in a decentralised manner, because of the variety of enterprises that comprise the grassroots. These interactions develop a policy package as directions and guidance to the total social order facing the grassroots enterprises. Thus an arrow of cause/action carries this policy impact to the total social order. The total social order comprises Economy, Society, Science and Technology (Boulding, 1971).

Under the impact of such ethical policy actions as cause, the total social order of the grassroots world-view delivers a common good that is internalised for the well-being of the grassroots as broadly comprehended. The delivery of the common good as a grand ecologically ethicised service now generates responses to the grassroots organisations. These socio-economic responses form the effects of policy directions as cause.

Responses thus carry preferences adapted and emerging after interactions of their own with the ethical policy directions of the grassroots organisations. In this way, a global field of interactive preferences is generated. Every circular completion of an interaction enters the post-evaluation box and provides learning inputs for the grassroots organisation from the global interactive process of change that has now proceeded. An interaction in this sense is equivalent to knowledge formation in this systemic order of grassroots organisation interacting with the total social order. A complementarity of the processes is generated by the interactive preferences emerging from the totality of the subsystems of the social order. Only when this Principle of Universal Complementarity exists will there be evolution of the total system as shown by the expanding subsystems (dotted). Interactions, followed by learning and emerging knowledge induction (Θ), establish the circular causation and continuity interrelationships of the total social order with the grassroots world-view.

In the neo-classical model of marginalist substitution hypothesis, discontinuity of processes is found to exist globally – since Economy, Society, Science and Technology subsystems exist in competition with each other in groups among themselves. The only other way to achive integration is by dominance of one over the others, therefore, we can define cause only in a one-directional flow of arrows, as shown. This means that preferences of polity acting upon markets is distortionary to the case of markets' preferences acting upon polity. This is likewise true for society as a constitutional form (Buchanan, 1975). Hence, there are individuations all across the neo-classical marginalist order. Discontinuity occurs because of the non-integration of preferences, their interaction benignity and dissociation between cause and effect are like two independent actions. Only a dominant model can enforce unilateral preferences in the neo-classical order, as is evidenced by the existence of a dominant nation state over the grassroots, a global order over nation states, an economy over the nature of technological change and its consequential influence on scientific thinking, and so on.

Conflict is shown to occur in the neo-classical model in various ways. Only two cases are shown in Figure 12.1. First, when economic matters affecting markets emanate from the market to polity, this points to competition and a non-interventionist approach. On the other hand, the same process from the side of polity to markets distorts the pure market-led action. Prices, efficiency, productivity, distribution and growth are different in these two cases. Hence, we have two disjointed causes or actions in these two cases.

Double and multiple conflicts occur when the above market-polity conflict is compounded by a greater degree of dissociation of the processes into economic and social ones. These can be further disaggregated into science and technology processes and further micro examples. Thus there is a sequence of independent actions as cause and effect within these individuated processes in the neo-classical order. This case is pointed out in Figure 12.1.

Because of such broken up independent processes, the good delivered either by one system or a mix of systems is conflicting, too, in terms of serving all needs, namely, economic, social and scientific. The economic good is shown in the figure to be dissected. The economic–social good is also shown to be dissected into two conflicting parts. An example of such goods and services is social security as a social good that conflicts with the same viewed as an economic good. Public goods in general are not efficient when compared with market goods.

INDEX OF WELL-BEING AT THE GRASSROOTS

We can now develop the index of well-being, *I*, for the grassroots, in terms of the Principle of Universal Complementarity as follows:

$$I(En,Em,D,G,P)[\Theta] = I(\mathbf{x},\mathbf{f},\mathbf{p})[\Theta] = A(\Theta)\Pi_i x_i^{\alpha i}\Pi_j f_j^{\beta j}\Pi_k p_k^{\gamma k}$$

where

En denotes entitlement;
Em denotes empowerment;
D denotes distribution;
G denotes economic growth;
P denotes microenterprise policy variables generated at the level of producer and consumer organisations serving the grassroots enterprises;
Θ denotes knowledge variable that endogenises the relationships among the targets shown. Θ is thus the result of interactions and cooperation enabled by inherent complementarity existing globally. Θ-values are institutionally simulated at the grassroots by means of post-evaluation of the interrelationships between these institutions and the socio-economic order;
x denotes the vector of socio-economic variables arising by cause and effect of *En*, *Em*, *D*, *G*, *P*. **x**, **f**, **p** are qualified by Θ-values because the targets are so qualified, and, as we have explained, there must exist complementarity overall.
f denotes the vector of appropriate financial variables supporting both **x**, **p** and the target variables.
p denotes the vector of policy variables in the organisations of the microenterprise, supporting **x**, **f** and the target variables.

Th.e product nature of the index in the variables, $\mathbf{x} = (x_1,x_2,..,x_n)$; $\mathbf{f} = (f_1 f_2,..f_m)$; $\mathbf{p} = (p_1,p_2,..,p_s)$ and their elasticities with respect to the index *I* of overall well-being, are denoted by α_i for x_i, $i=1,2,..,n$; β_j for f_j, $j = 1,2,..,m$; γ_k for p_k, $k = 1,2,..,s$. Each of the socio-economic variables and target variables must be non-zero and complementary to each other. This is the cause and effect of Θ-values affecting the variables through interactions between these variables. The grassroots organisations are to monitor these relationships closely in cognisance of the market and socio-economic realities.

But the market and socio-economic realities are now transformed by the advance of the grassroots from microenterprises to hierarchies of them in increasing diversity, size and power. Thus Θ-values being cause and effect of the transformation process endogenously ethicises the market order. The grassroots transformation thus presents the unique model of ethical transformation of the rational economic and social type. This feature makes a distinct difference of grassroots transformation in the global order from the neo-classical marginalist order of markets, institutions, governments and the global relations.

Creative sustainability of the grassroots requires effective monitoring of organisation–target–socio-economic interactions reflected in the continuity of this process. This is reflected in the simulation that exists among these variables by means of Θ-values. Sustainability is also the result of maintaining robust values of α_i, β_j, γ_k, $i = 1,2,..,n$; $j = 1,2,..,m$; $k=1,2,..,s$. Hence, $\Sigma_{i=1}{}^{n}\alpha_i + \Sigma_{j=1}{}^{m}\beta_j + \Sigma_{k=1}{}^{s}\gamma_k > 1$. This feature of $I(.)$ makes $A(\Theta)$ an economy-of-scale parameter. That is, apart from the direct contribution of the socio-economic and the target variables contributing jointly to $I(.)$, there is also the enhancing contribution of knowledge and motivation based on understanding and application of the textual laws, managerial efficiency of grassroots organisation, X-efficiency of the ethical market transformation and human development.

CONCLUSION

We have shown in this chapter that grassroots participatory enterprise needs a distinct model of development supported by its own specific financial instruments and organisational charactersistics. These are extensively interactive in nature at all levels of grassroots enterprises and their activities. Interactions form knowledge induction at the grassroots and bring about their sustainability. Thus the unique model of the grassroots is premised in the Principle of Universal Complementarity, which in turn is derived by interactive cause–effect premised on a world-view of the grassroots. These foundations are extended nationally and globally for the emergence, survival and expansion of the grassroots. It is in this way that the financial instruments, socio-economic variables and the supporting policy variables at the grassroots organisations cause knowledge-based transformations of the total social order. Entitlement, empowerment, distribution and economic growth are thus realised simultaneously rather than in a marginalist substituting way.

In the neo-classical model of received socio-economic order and organisational behaviour, nationally and globally, an individuating and alienating model of competition, perpetually marginalises the grassroots. Neither the well-being nor the survival of the grassroots can be attained in such a model in spite of the good intentions that governments may have for the marginalised interest groups.

Because these two models are mutually exclusive ones of structural shifts of the social economy, and the grassroots model is universally and distinctly induced by knowledge in the Principle of Universal Complementarity, the unique well-being of the future economy therefore rests on the grassroots world-view alone. There can be no compromise among these two conflicting models. If developing economies are to rest their socio-economic future on a well-being based on simultaneous attainment of distributive equity, economic growth, entitlement and empowerment, then the only model for them is the grassroots world-view. Yet our study and global reality proves that the grassroots approach to well-being is in complete contradistinction to the prevalent neo-classical order of trade, development and globalisation in which nation states and the global order are presently submerged.

References

Abdallah, J.S. (1993) 'The New World Order – on the Threshold of Postmodernity' (Kuala Lumpur: School of Social Sciences, Science University of Malaysia).

Boulding, K.E. (1971) 'Economics as a Moral Science', in Globe, F.R. (ed.), *Boulding: Collected Papers*, Vol. 2 (Boulder: Association of University Presses).

Buchanan, J.M. (1975) *The Limits of Liberty, Between Anarchy and Leviathan* (Chicago: University of Chicago Press).

Choudhury, M.A. (1981) *Towards a Comprehensive Manpower Plan for the Province of Newfoundland and Labrador in the 1980s* (St John's, Newfoundland: Institute of Educational Research and Development, Memorial University of Newfoundland).

Choudhury, M.A. (1993a) 'Integrating the Grassroots with World Development', *Bangladesh Observer*, 3 January.

Choudhury, M.A. (1993b) 'Social Frictions and Social Dynamics: The Case of Bangladesh', *Thoughts on Economics*, 3 (3–4).

Choudhury, M.A. (1993c), *Comparative Development Studies: In Search of the World view* (London: Macmillan; New York: St Martin's Press).

Choudhury, M.A. (1994) 'The Muslim Republics of the Commonwealth of Independent States: their Political Economy under Capitalism, Socialism and Islam', in O'Brien, J.C. (ed.), *The Evils of Soviet Communism and Other Critical Essays, II*, being Special Volume 21, Nos. 5 and 6 of the *International Journal of Social Economics* (Bradford: MCB University Press).

Dyke, C. (1981) 'Freedom and Market', in Dyke, C. *Philosophy of Economics* (Englewood Cliffs, NJ: Prentice-Hall).

Ellerman, D.P. (1991) 'The Democratic Firm: A Cooperative ESOP Model', in Wisman, J.D. (ed.), *Worker Empowerment, the Struggle for Workplace Democracy* (New York: Bookstrap Press).

Enke, S. (1962) 'Development with Limited and Unlimited Supplies of Labour', *Oxford Economic Papers*, (June).

Gibbons, D.S. and Kasim, S. (1991) *Banking on the Rural Poor* (Penang: Centre for Policy Research, Science University of Malaysia).

Government of Bangladesh, Planning Commission (1990) *The Fourth Five Year Development Plan 1990–95* (????).

Government of Malaysia (1991) *The Second Outline Perspective Plan 1991–2000* (Kuala Lumpur: Government Printer).

Helleiner, G.K. (1983) 'The Rise and Decline of the IMF', in Torrie, J. (ed.) *Banking on Poverty, the Global Impact of the IMF and World Bank* (Toronto: Between the Lines).

Hirschman, A.O. (1989) 'Linkages', in Eatwell, J., Milgate, M. and Newman, P. (eds), *The New Palgrave: Economic Development* (New York: W.W. Norton).

ILO (International Labour Organisation) (1976) *The Basic Needs Approach to Development* (Geneva: ILO).

Keating, M. (1993) *Agenda for Change* (Geneva: Centre for Our Common Future).

Martin, S. (1988) *Industrial Economics, Economic Analysis and Public Policy* (New York: Macmillan) Chapter 5.

Ministry of Finance (1993) *Economic Report 1992/93* (Kuala Lumpur: Government Printer).

Network (1992) 'Earth People's Fund: Alternative Means of Funding', No. 21, (Geneva: Centre for Our Common Future).

Phelps, E. (1989) 'Distributive Justice', in Eatwell, J., Milgate, M. and Newman, P. (eds) *New Palgrave: Social Economics* (New York: W.W. Norton).

Pratt, R.C. (1983) 'The Global Impact of the World Bank', in Torrie, J. (ed.) *Banking on Poverty, the Global Impact of the IMF and the World Bank* (Toronto: Between the Lines).

Sen, A. (1975) *Employment, Technology and Development* (Oxford: Clarendon Press).

Sen, A. (1985) 'The Moral Standing of the Market', in Paul, E.F., Paul, J. and Miller, F.D. Jr (eds) *Ethics and Economics* (Oxford: Basil Blackwell).

Sen, A. (1986) *Poverty and Famines: An Essay on Entitlement and Deprivation* (Oxford: Clarendon Press).

Simon, H. (1960) *The New Science of Management Decision* (New York: Harper & Row).

United Nations (1991) *Global Outlook 2000* (New York: United Nations).

UNDP United Nations Development Fund (several issues) *Human Development Index* (New York: United Nations).

Vanek, J. (1975) 'The Basic Theory of Financing of Participatory Firms', in Vanek, J. (ed.) *Self-Management (Economic Liberation of Man)* (Baltimore: Penguin).

Weitzman, M.L. (1984) *The Share Economy* (Cambridge, Mass.: Harvard University Press).

Williamson, O. (1981) 'The Modern Corporation: Origins, Evolution, Attributes', *Journal of Economic Literature*, XIX(4).

Wisman, J.D. (1991) 'Is There a Significant Future for Workplace Democracy?', in *Worker Empowerment* (New York, NY: The Bookstrap Press).

13 Conclusion: Towards a Caring Society

Masudul A. Choudhury, Uzir Abdul Malik and Mohammad Anuar Adnan

The chapters in this book have traversed a wide area of issues and topics underlying socioeconomic development, with special reference to Malaysia in that country's towards an industrialised economy by the year 2020 – the Vision 2020. These topics and issues have covered both microeconomic and the macroeconomic perspectives. The chapters have tried to present an alternative framework, particularly as the alternative delineates a world-view that is different from and in contrast to the neo-classical, Keynesian, monetarist, Marxist and post-Keynesian paradigms usually found in the study of the socioeconomic universe. The epistemology of ethics, values, well-being, efficiency, stability and growth – in a simultaneous occurrence of these targets – is found to be foreign to the perspective of development in received mainstream doctrines. Consequently, the institutions, policies, programme and visions of socioeconomic development carried out in the received methodological folds are argued to be alienating between the competing ends of economic preferences and distributive preferences. The embedded methodology of neo-classical substitution principle is found not to enable complementarity between these competing ends. This is found to be true both with and without technological change. Hence, in this sense, the design and meaning of technological change, too, remains to be of an alienating nature. Since it does not correct for the embedded substitution among competing ends in such an economic methodology, therefore, technological change construed in the neo-classical fold cannot be treated as an engine for promoting well-being in the sense of complementarity between the ends at point.

This study has thus been to a great extent, first, a discourse across the areas of received socioeconomic doctrines and their practice as perceived in diverse fields underlying development. Second, it undertakes a study of an alternative development paradigm. The sheer positivistic picture manifested in the fold of received doctrines is contrasted by the positive–normative picture of the alternative. Such a study of the contrast between competing paradigms leads us to develop the methodological formalisation of the episteme, that we called here the Principle of Universal Complementarity. It stands in sharp contrast to the notion of Marginal Substitution of neo-classical economic theory. The resulting differences in the theory, practice, polity-ecology interface and issues of human well-being are then also found to be contrasting ones between these two approaches.

At the end of the line we stumble into what Malaysia has captioned as a vision of 2020 premised in a caring society.[1] The precept of human well-being, human development, alleviation of poverty, grassroots development, polity–market interface, international trade, privatisation, political economy, financial systems and management of growth and distribution with a target towards uplifting the underprivileged target groups in society are all inputs of a grand well-being function for the Malaysian society. An example of such a well-being criterion was formalised.

Above all, the interactive preferences needed to transform individuals and society in the midst of the interrelationships that exist between society land markets in an objectively globalising order reflect the most micro-level self-actualisation process of moral and ethical change in the midst of overall socioeconomic development. Such an interactive *process* of change we treated here as the essence of the alternative perspective of Third-World development. In it, preferences, by being interactive in nature, become endogenously generated in the midst of a polity–market (ecology) interface. Such a *process* is also the knowledge-forming experience of society in the midst of the polity–ecology (market) interface.

The construct of the well-being function is essentially the perspective of what is meant by a caring society in terms of the two parts of its realisation. First, there is the epistemology underlying the concept of a caring society and how that concept is derived from some textual premise. Second, there is the methodology and the mechanism for attaining the goals and precepts underlying well-being as they are epistemologically defined. These two parts are in turn cyclically interacted in the knowledge-based world-view of the kind of socio-economic universe that recreates itself and evolves into higher levels of knowing. This is the nature of the Principle of Universal Complementarity.

Caring in this sense of well-being is thus both an input as well as an output emanating from interactive preference formation and evolution in the midst of the polity–ecology interface. While polity initially derives its textual definition of well-being from commonly adhered to moral and ethical values of the Malaysian society at large, such an episteme must be checked, confirmed, revised and furthered by the common weal. Coercion is thus replaced by responsible exchange, tolerance and accommodation of views premised in the commonly held values.

The necessary constraints respecting the multiracial complex of Malaysian society, the prevailing level of knowledge, the institutional limitations, private and social costs, and external obligations, do exist while targeting the level of well-being. But in the knowledge-based world-view of the interaction model of well-being or caring, these constraints are simply temporary and are phased in. They do not remain permanent at any one level of action.

With regards to the future perspective of a caring society for Malaysia we have a number of observations. The Sixth Development Plan states that[2] 'the objective of the New Development Policy (NDP) is to attain a *balanced development* in order to create a more united and just society'. Nine areas of focus are placed to realise this goal.[3] They are: (i) an optimum balance between growth and equity; (ii) a balanced and complementary development of the major economic sector; (iii) the reduction and ultimate elimination of social and economic inequalities; (iv) a national integration by reducing inter-regional and urban–rural disparities; (v) the development of a progressive society with material development and positive social and spiritual values; (vi) a national pride and consciousness; (vii) the promotion of a productive and disciplined industrial manpower; (viii) the building of a modern industrial economy based on science and technology; (ix) the protection of the environment and technology.

The well-being criterion of a caring society thus emerges from the premise of social equity, economic distribution, appropriateness of growth and development menus and the attaining of material advancement. The singular most complex issue in these choices being that of the concept of *balance*, there is at once a distinction between the neo-classical idea of *balance* as a long-run trade-off between these competing goals, and the substantive concept of *balance* as global complementarity in the interactive–integrative world-view.

It is difficult to infer at the present juncture whether the Malaysian Vision 2020 of a caring society is being premised in anything other than the neo-classical model. Thus, the caring society, although so much desired by the Malaysian Rukunegara (National Declaration), yet remains an issue of contention, at least methodologically, in the neo-classical approach of the Malaysian development plan.

Various chapters presented in this book have brought out the key importance of developing sectoral and grassroots communitarian interlinkages in the Malaysian economy and society. In the well-being outlook of a caring society, interlinkages will prove to be the cause and effect of an interactive and integrative approach to development planning. As the *Second Outlook Perspective Plan 1991–2000* rightly points out, serious problems of sectoral delinking presently exist between the narrowly based electronic, textile, export-oriented manufacturing sectors and the rest of the economy.

Contributors to this book have pointed out that such a lack of interlinkages has caused a setback in the realisation of equality and socio-economic distributions to the target groups in the economy, albeit the reduction of absolute levels of poverty in Peninsular Malaysia. As a result, the Bumiputera Commercial and Industrial Community project could not be realised to date, and the shareholding of Bumiputeras still lags substantially behind other groups in the economy.[4]

Thus a growth and developmental approach that must prove to be the cause and effect of a caring Malaysian society must depend upon a new and different approach for its future economic transformation. Within this new approach the question of *balance* between ethical and moral prerogatives and the prospects of economic growth must be simultaneously realised. The idea of *balance* must not be taken up in a marginalist substitution sense, creating conflicts between the goals of growth and distribution.

The focus of this book has been in evolving out of the sheer positivistic perspectives on economic growth and development to a normative–positive picture with a futuristic outlook premised in the interactive and integrative world-view. This outlook is shown to carry with it the simultaneous realisation of human development alongwith capital development, while maintaining global sustainability, as this is erected on grounds of a total concept of well-being.[5] A caring society is thus the result of a knowledge-centred society enabled by the interactive–integrative world-view.

Towards attaining a caring society in the framework of the interactive–integrative work-view, necessary polity–ecology learning processes are to be generated. This question brought us to deal with the interface needed among institutional, policy and programmatic issues. In summary, the following principal perspectives have been reached in this regard.

Policy Recommendations

1. Development planning must be geared away from sheer imitation of mainstream approaches, because of the substitutional and alienating nature of conflicts between alternatives in these models of economic growth and development. Development planning instead, is to be premised in a nationwide interactive and integrative approach with a human presence in these discussions concerning every aspects of society. Thus the interactive–integrative world-view, where polity–ecology interface can be realised, is to be the framework of development planning.

2. In the framework of the interactive–integrative world view of Malaysian socio-economic transformation, the role of government is to be seen as a facilitator and guider of the transformation process. The role of government is to be principally that of a supplier of information to the agents of change from the grassroots to all echelons of society, to manage public finances, to look after national security and foreign affairs.

3. Thus a grassroots focus to development is to be emphasised in the sense of developing the grassroots through a web of hierarchical micro-enterprising interrelationships at all levels and in all matters, including international trade and areas of sectoral and economic diversifications.

4. Recommendation (3) calls for a global system of interlinkages in the Malaysian economy. Such interlinkages would be sectoral, communitarian and polity-wide in essence.

5. The thrust of the Malaysian socio-economic transformation must be based on its reliance on citizenry, markets and the privatisation process, all taken up by the approach of the interactive–integrative world-view, replacing the same things in a competing and alienating framework provided by neoclassical models and their prototypes. Within this alternative approach, grassroots development as defined in terms of hierarchical coordination among enterprises at all levels is to be promoted by means of the instrument of privatisation.

6. There is to be greater self-reliance and independence of Malaysians in the development process, so that reliance on foreign multinationals and foreign direct investments is minimised. The present concentration of foreign direct investments in its electronic goods sector of manufacturing and a declining share of foreign direct investments in the primary and commodities sectors makes forward and backward sectoral interlinkages difficult. One also views with caution the fluctuations in FDIs in Malaysia. This makes dependence on FDIs unsustainable in the long run.[6]

7. International trade and regional economic cooperation and integration should be pursued by an approach that builds upon interconnections across regional growth triangles. This would be a better approach for Malaysia's own security from the vagaries of the trade and monetary policies set in the industrialised economies. Such a regionally interlinked approach to economic integration should prove to be the appropriate globalisation model for Malaysia. Cases in point that were taken up in this book are: the vulnerability of APEC (Asian-Pacific Economic Cooperation) with US domination, the need for accelerating the realisation of AFTA (Asian Free Trade Area), and the establishment of an effective EAEC (East Asian Economic Caucus).

8. Malaysian sustainable future on the socioeconomic front, in the global order and internally, will depend greatly on the nation's own vision of her educational and human resource development perspectives. Science, technology and socioeconomic development must all be based on such an innovative way of thinking out a Malaysian approach to creative sustainability through interdisciplinarity.

9. Human development taken up within the context of a caring society in the midst of the interactive–integrative world-view would prove to be a knowledge-based understanding and enaction of change in Malaysian society.

10. Malaysia should develop appropriate ways and means to direct some of her foreign direct investments and her dealings with foreign multinationals in the direction of the global perspectives afforded by the interactive–integrative perspectives of development planning, and mentioned above.

11. In the area of monetary and fiscal policies, the Malaysian government should refrain from excessive macroeconomic policy interventions. Instead, microeconomic policies should be allowed to perform the efficient and equalitarian function at the enterprise level. This must mean a good deal of deregulation in the banking sector.[7] The Malaysian Government should thus simply act as a guiding overseer, a provider or information, manage public financial management. Its other principal functions are to look after national security maters and foreign affairs. There must, however, exist a good deal of interactions in all matters between the private sector and the government information system.

12. Islamic financial and other institutions, which have become so popular in Malaysia, are to be increasingly promoted, advanced within the modern financial system. They should be developed as both educational as well as resource mobilisation institutions, providing access to target groups of Malays and others. In this way, money as a financial aggregate can be seen to play an ethical role toward promoting overall well-being.

13. Enterprises in Malaysia, particularly those of domestic origin, should be induced to take up active programmes of human resource development in conjunction with educational institutions, to develop the required popularity of their financial instruments, to link up innovatively with science, technology and socio-economic development and to establish feedbacks between themselves and the educational institutions.

14. For achieving the caring society, an active population policy and human resource development policy are to be pursued. The two goals must be complementary to each other, and are to be connected to the nature of global interlinkages in the Malaysian society and economy at large. In this way, the grassroots focus on development with its hierarchical nature of interrelationships across microenterprises, gains momentum. The internal security of the nation is promoted; self-reliance is enhanced.

Finally, it is observed that the resilience of national life, conscious thinking and responsible actions today have made Malaysia a niche for emulation by the developing world. The prospect for a newer, alternative paradigm of socio-economic development is thus made possible in the Malaysian context by virtue of its challenging and ethical viewpoints of socio-economic development. In this book we have proposed the interactive–integrative world-view as a prime alternative, in sharp contrast to the easily accepted models of alienation and competition, substitution and trade-off given by the neo-classical school and its various prototypes. From what we have noted in the study here, it is plausible that Malaysia can direct herself towards such an alternative model of development. The prospects of Vision 2020 and a caring society for Malaysia, provide the opportunity for such a newer perspective of development and change.

Notes and References

1. K.S. Jomo, *U-Turn? Malaysian Economic Development Policies After 1990* (Townsville, Queensland, Australia: Centre for East and Southeast Asian Studies, James Cook University of North Queensland, 1994).
2. *Sixth Malaysian Plan* (Kuala Lumpur, Malaysia: Government of Malaysia, 1991) pp. 4–5.
3. W.M.N.W. Daud, 'Some Basic Issues of Development in Malaysia', in *Malaysian Development Experience* (Kuala Lumpur, Malaysia: INTAN, 1994).
4. *The Second Outline Perspective Plan 1991–2000* (Kuala Lumpur, Malaysia: Government of Malaysia, 1991); Dato' A.K. Ibrahim, 'Bumiputera Equity Participation in the Corporate Sector After 1990', in A. Buang (ed.) *The Malaysian Economy in Transition* (Kuala Lumpur, Malaysia: National Institute of Public Administration, 1990).
5. D. Goulet and C.K. Wilber, 'The Human Dilemma of Development', in C.K. Wilber and K.P. Jameson (eds), *The Political Economy of Development and Under-development* (New York: McGraw-Hill, 1992).
6. Tan Sri Datuk Z.A. Sulong, 'The Past, Present and Future Role of Foreign Direct Investment (FDI) in Malaysia', in Buang (ed.), *The Malaysian Economy in Transition.*
7. J. Ahmad, 'Banking and Monetary Policies: A Framework for Stability of the Malaysian Economy', in Buang (ed.), *The Malaysian Economy in Transition.*

Index

Printed in the United States
51634LVS00001B/81